PSYCHOPATHIC CULTURES AND TOXIC EMPIRES

WILL BLACK

D1427500

This book is dedicated to my
wonder-filled niece and to Gretel.

This edition published 2015
by Frontline Noir, an imprint of Books Noir

Text copyright © 2014 Will Black
Cover illustration copyright © Victor Wilford
All Rights Reserved

Print edition ISBN 978-1-904684-71-8
eBook edition ISBN 978-1-904684-72-5

No part of this book may be reproduced or transmitted in any form
or by any means without written permission from the publisher.

The right of Will Black to be identified as the Author of the Work
has been asserted in accordance with the UK Copyright, Designs
and Patents Act 1988.

A CIP record for this book is available from the British Library

Typeset in Garamond by Park Productions, www.parkreads.co.uk

Contents

Preface

Estimates of the percentage of psychopaths and sociopaths in society range from 1% to 4%. The proportion of those with psychopathic traits is greater in certain professions, including banking, law and the media. This is not surprising as psychopaths are attracted to environments where they can maximise their influence and rewards.

Many people imagine psychopaths to be like serial killers in films. While it is true that some killers are psychopathic, it is also true that many more people in 'respectable' jobs have psychopathic qualities. Indicators include self esteem being derived from personal gain, power and pleasure, lack of concern for feelings, needs and suffering of others and a tendency to exploit, deceive and coerce. They may appear charming but this is superficial and used to manipulate as, ultimately, other people are prey.

There has been greater focus in recent years on psychopaths who avoid being imprisoned or diagnosed and who gain positions of power. These are particularly dangerous because - as well as having a detrimental impact on those around them - they are in a position to shape society and create what I term 'psychopathic cultures'.

Pathological cultures can be found in families and small networks, larger institutions, global corporations and governments. Once a pathological culture has been established, it can expand and infect healthy cultures - whether directly led by psychopaths or not. Long after a psychopath who infected an institution has moved on, the culture may remain toxic - which is harmful to those working within it. Because the need to conform is so strong, decent people can end up emulating psychopathic traits if they find themselves within a pathological culture.

A range of environments are discussed in this book, using the terms psychopathic, pathological and toxic cultures. The mention of individuals linked to particular organisations does not imply that those people are being defined as psychopathic. It is for clinicians and perhaps history to define individuals as psychopaths, but it for society to decide if the systems surrounding us are pathological or not.

Introduction – from the psychiatric hospital to the prison to the TV screen to the boardroom

Professionals working within psychiatric services are quite rightly highly vigilant concerning psychopaths. The individuals, classed with sociopaths under the diagnostic category of antisocial personality disorder, are not merely of concern to clinicians because they are interesting but because they are considered dangerous, manipulative, predatory and generally not responsive to treatment.

The literature on antisocial personality disorders can be confusing as a result of the different ways in which individuals use the terms psychopath and sociopath. Some use one or other of the terms as a blanket description of all people with antisocial personality disorder. Others prefer to distinguish between the two, generally based in the assumption that psychopaths are born with their condition whereas sociopathy develops during the nurturing and socialisation process.

The sociopath may be regarded as more chaotic and less able to control how they respond to the world than the psychopath, whose callous and exploitative approach to life is innate. According to Dr Nigel Blackwood of London's Institute of Psychiatry, sociopaths can be viewed as hot-headed and psychopaths as cold-hearted. The distinction has a bearing on their life trajectories and on the experiences of those around them. The hot-headed sociopath has the potential to learn to be less hot-headed but it questionable that psychopaths become less cold-hearted.

Scans have shown that psychopaths have less grey matter in parts of the brain related to empathy, conscience and remorse. Many clinicians believe that no amount of therapy will repair this significant shortcoming. Fascinating recent research indicates that at least some psychopaths have the ability to switch empathy on at will. This capacity for selective empathy could actually make them better at manipulating people and therefore potentially more dangerous to society.

The innate biological flaw of psychopaths means they may be more likely to get involved with exploitative behaviours at an earlier age than the sociopath damaged by experiences. They will also, therefore, be more proficient at manipulation and better at appearing plausible to others. Given these differences, psychopaths should – in general – be more likely than sociopaths to avoid incarceration and to climb to positions of power.

When a person is being victimised by someone who is cruel, manipulative and deceitful they are probably less interested in what diagnostic category their tormentor falls into than being free of them. However, as my concern is not just the impact of personality disordered people on individuals but also their capacity to manipulate and corrupt culture itself, I am particularly interested in highly-functioning, powerful psychopaths who avoid diagnoses and incarceration.

Films, books and news reports have helped make many people fearful of serial killers. However, in reality more people will be affected by charming and immoral people leading organisations, in political office or influencing the economy than targeted by murderers. It is chilling to consider the possibility that there may be more psychopaths in positions of power within our communities than psychopathic patients on psychiatric wards. Psychopaths and people swept along by their manipulations have the potential to erode our value systems and have a devastating impact on societies.

My background is anthropology, mental health care and journalism, each of which influences my perceptions and approach. In this book I apply the insights of experts in psychiatry, psychology, criminology and business, to examine ways in which pathological – or sick – cultures have come to dominate many important areas of life. In this context the term culture refers to any human system, whether a family, corporation, political party, gang, paedophile ring, institution or regime. In this book it does not refer to ethnicity.

Some organisations and other cultures may have a level of pathology or dysfunction that can be remedied with attention and effort. In other cases there is a level of toxicity which is so deliberate, pervasive and damaging that it is reasonable to describe it as a psychopathic culture. It could be argued that any culture which suppresses the masses and distorts reality in order to bolster the power of a small minority is pathological – or perhaps parasitical.

As well as being influential in traditionally ruthless fields, like politics and banking, psychopaths and the malignant cultures they create also have influence within the mass media, social care, medicine, the criminal justice system and education. Devious, ruthless, narcissistic, superficially charming and manipulative people having influence within these areas – and others – is clearly of great concern.

There have been efforts by regulators and others to improve standards in professions the public is dependent on. However, even in democracies like the USA and the UK, progress has often been painfully slow. Studies by psychologists and business experts have acknowledged high levels of psychopathic traits among corporate leaders but there has not been a focus on the pathology of the cultures they create and shape. This requires a systemic approach, in the same way that family therapists work with the dynamics of families – but on a much larger scale.

Research into psychopaths only really came of age after World War Two. It may well be that people who would now be described as psychopathic were influential during other turbulent and brutal times in history. However, societies of the past lacked the detailed knowledge of how psychopaths think and operate that we have today. Therefore, the ability to curtail their influence was limited.

Over the last century, society has developed a greater insight into psychopathic drives, machinations and behaviours – and today's researchers are supported by neuropsychology and advanced diagnostic imaging techniques.

Much of the research conducted into psychopaths has centred on those in prisons or secure psychiatric facilities. This research is extremely valuable because psychiatrists and other professionals have been able to draw on intense contact with psychopaths to develop insight into how they think and the games they play. However, as there are more psychopaths in our communities than will ever be put in prison or psychiatric units, it is critical to apply the knowledge gained about them to those in positions of power in society.

The impact of psychopaths on their victims and patient groups in institutions is troubling enough, but the encroachment of psychopathic 'values' on society can be devastating – and it could take considerable time to understand and tackle. This requires the expertise of different professions but also the will of society to encourage the endeavour.

When arrested by police or interviewed by mental health professionals, psychopaths routinely attempt to present themselves as plausible and charming, with stories of being hard done by. The complex strategies and manipulations of such individuals often splits teams on psychiatric units – and psychopaths take pleasure in causing tension and conflicts among staff and patients.

Inadequacies within the disordered personality can get played out by a group of professionals and other patients. Observing these dynamics can generate insight into the mind of personality disorder patients, if teams have the time and motivation to examine how they are feeling and reacting. This, regrettably, is often not the case.

While clinicians are assessing the psychopath, the psychopath is assessing everybody else and they will frequently try to exploit vulnerable mentally ill people, whether economically or sexually. For example, it is not uncommon for psychopaths to try to stay on mental health units to sell drugs, as doing so gives them access to a vulnerable, pliable, desperate and frightened market. It is also a role in which they have power and status. This feeds their controlling and narcissistic tendencies.

Imprisoned psychopaths and those in mental health units routinely push personal boundaries to try to get information from staff about their lives. Such information can be used to manipulate staff and it is not uncommon for psychopaths to make subtle or overt threats about the families of workers. I've known a violent patient to take photos of nurses called to restrain him, as a "memento". The need to maintain firm personal boundaries with patients can make psychiatric units seem like extremely suspicious, hostile and emotionally cold places. This is, in part, driven by and a reflection of the mind of the psychopath.

In relation to psychopaths, the goal of many inpatient psychiatric units is to identify them as such and not admit them. If they do manage to get admitted, the goal of mainstream mental health teams generally is to get rid of them as quickly as possible to limit the harm they can do. This is something the media and public often struggle to understand.

Newspapers sometimes run stories about 'psychiatric patients' being refused admission and then going on to commit violent crimes. Some members of the public do not differentiate between people with mental illnesses and psychopaths – and therefore assume that mental hospitals are the right place for psychopaths. On the whole, however, this is not the case.

Some psychiatric wards are designed specifically for people with personality disorders and there are secure forensic psychiatric units for people posing the greatest threat to society. However, the bulk of psychiatric wards are designed for the assessment and treatment of people with true mental illnesses. These include schizophrenia, paranoia and other forms of psychoses, bipolar affective disorder (manic depression) and obsessive compulsive disorder.

As psychopathy affects the entire character – and appears to be connected with brain abnormalities – psychopaths are not generally considered to be treatable with either drugs or psychotherapy. Psychopaths are therefore not generally considered by psychiatric professionals to have a mental illness. However, medication and therapies may be used to help manage behaviour and reduce risk to both themselves and others.

Psychopaths often exhibit symptoms of other mental conditions, such as paranoia or depression. Psychiatric medication may be used to alleviate those symptoms but it does not eradicate the personality disorder.

Sometimes psychopaths will feign symptoms of schizophrenia after being charged with a crime, in order to have a custodial sentence mitigated by a diminished responsibility defence. In such cases the public and the media often struggle to appreciate and convey the distinctions between personality disorders and mental illnesses.

A great deal of energy and expense was put into giving intensive psychotherapy to psychopaths in the 1960s and 1970s, in the US and Canada particularly. The outcome, unfortunately, appears to have been to produce psychopaths who were better at playing the system and manipulating people than they were before. Those psychopaths who therapists felt made good progress in groups were as likely as non-therapised psychopaths to return to aggressive and exploitative behaviour. This is a testament to the skill psychopaths have in manipulating people.

Psychopaths lack, but learn to mimic, normal human emotions. Therefore putting them in therapy groups with people expressing their true feelings can allow them to find new ways to exploit others. When psychopaths find their way onto psychiatric wards caring for people with various mental health problems, they may dominate group sessions. Conversely, they may feign a lack of interest while actually gathering information to help them exploit other patients.

The empathy switch

It does not seem to be the case that psychopaths cannot grasp the concept of empathy. They appear to perceive the quality in other people and may regard it as a weakness to be exploited. The fact that they can switch so easily between charm and callousness is both disturbing and fascinating. The received wisdom for many years was that psychopaths can mimic empathy but cannot truly empathise. A recent study from the Netherlands, however, suggests that they have the ability to switch empathy on at will.

The research, published in the neurology journal *Brain* in 2013, has extraordinary ramifications. It would help explain how psychopaths can adeptly navigate the complex human interactions necessary to get what they want, while also sometimes being absolutely callous and brutal. It could particularly help us understand the highest performing psychopaths, who manage to negotiate complex educational, social and organisational systems and gain powerful positions – while also being predatory, callous and malicious.

The psychopaths in the study, however, were not politicians or bankers but violent criminals. They, along with a control group, were shown film clips while having functional magnetic resonance imaging (fMRI) brain scans. The clips, which involved interactions between people, zoomed in on actors hands during contact that was either painful, loving, rejecting or neutral.

The reason for choosing those clips was that people who have a normal empathic response have a characteristic neurological response when seeing physical contact between others. For example, if most of us see somebody hurt – even in a film – our brain creates an emotional response as though *we* have been hurt. Regions of our brain associated with a particular emotion are similarly activated when we observe that emotion in others. It is thought that this process of empathy is enabled by 'mirror neurons' in our brains.

As expected, the brain scans revealed that the psychopathic subjects did not have the same neurological response the control group did during the interactions on film. However, after the researchers asked the participants to watch the films again – but this time trying to feel what the characters in the film were feeling – there was a change. Following this instruction, the psychopath group had similar neurological responses to the control group. The research suggests that the default position for most of us is for our 'empathy switch' to be 'on' but in psychopaths the default position is 'off'.

This opens us a whole range of questions about how different people respond to different situations. For example, some normal people – when made to fight in a war – may manage to dial down their empathy. This would seem to be an adaptive process to help protect us from physical harm and to reduce mental anguish.

If normal people can turn their empathy off or reduce it in a war situation, we have to consider the possibility that other people who get caught up in pathological cultures may also do so. For example, there are no doubt many people in the corporate world who started out caring and ethically-minded but became callous, devious, insincere and aggressive. In order to thrive in a setting where compassion is seen as a weakness, perhaps some people turn their empathy off or down. Whether or not they manage to switch it back on when with their families is another interesting question – and this has the potential to be studied.

The findings from the Netherlands study also raise the question that if some psychopaths gain more rewards by using and demonstrating empathy than by keeping it switched off, then perhaps they are less likely to be violent criminals and more likely to rise to positions of power. However, it is questionable that high-performing psychopaths who gain positions of power do less harm than the average low-performing criminal. Powerful psychopaths have more scope to do harm to society and more capacity to avoid incarceration.

The prevalence of psychopaths and their power over society

Within specialist psychiatric units housing people with dangerous personality disorders, the focus has tended to be on management rather than the expectation of making therapeutic breakthroughs – let alone turning them into non-psychopaths. Key characteristics, such as reckless disregard for others, deception, impulsivity, aggression and irresponsibility may be curtailed somewhat by being in a locked environment with a clear structure, but there is little evidence that psychopathy is 'treated'. As it is viewed as disorder of the personality, expressions of remorse by violent psychopaths in specialist units are treated with great suspicion.

Conversely, there are many people whose behaviour and perceptions of others places them squarely in the category of antisocial personality disorder but they go their entire life without being assessed in psychiatric units or put in prison. We may live close to them, work with them or see them in the media. Many of us will have a strong sense that their character is flawed, their actions are damaging or their attitude to other people makes them dangerous. However, for a variety of reasons, we may suppress our intuitions. One reason for doing so is, if we were to dwell on these perceptions, it could shatter our sense of security and comfort.

It may also be the case that when we intuitively know people have dangerous or malicious potentials – perhaps by a cold shiver when we are in their company or by something false in their tone, we change our behaviour. Many people will instinctively avoid potential confrontations with psychopaths by limiting contact or by appeasing them. Limiting contact with them is probably a better choice, if possible, as appeasing psychopaths increases their power over us.

Despite what television dramas and films suggest, most psychopaths do not kill. Sudden violence may well be part of their repertoire to get what they want – or to be used when backed into a corner – but there is much more to them than that. Some ultimately are exposed as rapists and paedophiles but many express their condition by simply being cold, calculating, ruthless and vindictive in their home and work life, business operations or political machinations.

When we live in societies where ruthlessness in business and politics is rewarded and prized, the problem of identifying and curtailing genuine psychopaths becomes more challenging. As our search for the psychopath strays from prisons and psychiatric units to banks, trading floors, media companies and political parties, we become aware that society's ability to challenge and control them has been limited.

In fact, we may tolerate psychopathic qualities in politicians, television and film stars, sportsmen and captains of industry more readily than we do in our neighbours. Glib charm and callousness can, unfortunately, appear attractive qualities in celebrities, politicians and tycoons. It may be amusing to watch them on the television, but it should be remembered that those people are real when they are off the screen and have real impacts on real people.

As has been stated, even highly qualified psychiatric teams may be split over people thought to have antisocial personality disorders. The individual in question may treat different members of the team in different ways and will be expert at playing people off against one another. When people are discharged from wards quickly, there may not be enough evidence for psychiatrists to categorically class them as psychopaths. This means any other agency dealing with them in the future may experience uncertainly, divisions among staff and danger.

If specialist psychiatric teams sometimes lack the ability to quickly diagnose and respond effectively to psychopaths, it is not surprising that other institutions and society itself struggles to identify them and respond to them adequately. After something terrible comes to light, members of communities often find it hard to accept that someone they liked could have committed such an atrocity. Others will say they had suspicions all along.

The above was illustrated by the case of the disc jockey and serial child abuser Jimmy Savile, who used his larger-than-life character to gain entry into the BBC. Savile was already a paedophile before joining the BBC but, once secure within the institution, he was able to amass so much influence over people that he abused children with little challenge. There is even the compelling and sickening suggestion that he managed to avoid incarceration because he procured children for members of the British Establishment.

When Savile joined the BBC in the 1960s, the organisation was aware that it was regarded by many as stuffy and old fashioned. With his Yorkshire accent and brash eccentric character, BBC bosses regarded Savile as a breath of fresh air and he quickly became a popular figure on both radio and television. His distinctive personality and numerous highly-publicised charitable endeavours secured him a knighthood and decades of lucrative BBC work, often giving him access to children and disabled people.

Although many members of the public intuitively regarded Savile as creepy – and despite rumours of him being sexually inappropriate with children circulating for decades – Savile managed to live to the age of 84 without being prosecuted. He was well aware that some members of the public thought he was a paedophile and of specific allegations against him. However, he evaded charges throughout his life and his wealth allowed him to use libel actions and injunctions to kill off news stories and intimidate the press.

After hundreds of accusations of sexual abuse of children and hospital patients came to light in 2012, a year after his death, some people attempted to defend Savile's reputation. Even at the start of 2013 there were still people on social media defending his 'honour' and saying that because he could not contest the accusations in court the matter should be dropped. Fortunately, however, we live in an era of transparency, where society and the media are happy to slay degraded 'heroes' – and where victims of abuse can find a stronger voice than they had previously.

The Savile case and the resultant splitting of views across society is a vivid illustration of how devious psychopaths operate and how they manage to shield themselves by creating tension between other people. It also serves as a useful illustration of how the personality of the psychopath may be revealed more by their impact on others than what they say.

A forensic examination of the life of a psychopath can be like examining the damage caused by a cluster bomb. In the case of child abusers, the primary harm is secretly done to vulnerable individuals – some of whom may have little ability at the time to articulate what happened. Other abusers are drawn in and become part of the paedophile's web, while some victims may subsequently and tragically become abusers themselves.

The Savile case also helps us examine one of the key concerns of this book, whether the world we live in has become more psychopathic – more ruthless, cold, exploitative and antisocially individualistic. If so, we have to consider what processes and institutions are allowing and encouraging this to happen – and how we may all be allowing it to happen. The case illustrates how various organisational cultures and society itself can be infected and corrupted by the psychopathy of an individual, or small number of individuals.

Within hours of the Savile sex abuse story breaking there was fevered speculation on social media about Sir Jimmy's relationship with the Conservative Party. He was known to be a close friend of former prime minister Ted Heath and claimed to have spent 11 Christmases with Margaret Thatcher when 'the iron lady' was in power. Heath is known to have hung around public toilets at night looking for sex – and this has driven speculation that Savile procured young men for him, as he is accused of for other public figures.

For those concerned with sinister conspiracies, the fact that Savile was not prosecuted when alive, coupled with his friendship with members of the Establishment, has fuelled beliefs that serious crimes were covered up. It also raised the horrific spectre of an elite paedophile ring known about and participated in by politicians.

As rumours about Savile's sexual conduct towards children were circulating while Margaret Thatcher was in power, it is understandable that some believe his activities were covered up not only by the BBC but also by senior government figures. Proof that the police covered up their negligence within the 1989 Hillsborough football disaster (emerging just before the Savile story broke in 2012) gave credence to the view that Savile was protected by friends in high places.

It should, however, be noted that by 2012 Margaret Thatcher was a sick old lady and shadow of her former self. She certainly would not have been expected to give evidence and there is nothing to suggest she prevented him from being arrested when she was prime minister. It appears that, for much of the UK in the 1980s, Savile was just regarded as a rather strange, cigar smoking, Marathon running broadcaster.

It seems quite possible that Savile used charity work as a way of insulating or immunising himself against accusations of paedophilia. Perhaps a shared understanding that accusations against him could harm the income and credibility of charitable organisations gave him power over some of those who felt dependent on his 'support'. If this is the case, Savile made probably well-meaning people complicit in his activities.

Speaking on BBC News in June 2014, lawyer Liz Dux, who represents more than 170 people who have made allegations against Savile, suggested that some people in organisations Savile 'worked' with were aware of his abuse but "reports were simply brushed under the carpet". She said: "It had been reported to those in authority and they simply put the reputation of their organisation or his fund-raising or his so-called philanthropic work above the safety of children. That is a disgrace."

More will be said about Savile later in this book but this brief introduction offers a powerful illustration of what can happen when a predatory psychopath gains influence – and the devastating impact they can have if unrestrained.

Some might say that as Savile was not diagnosed as a psychopath he should not be described as one. However, by definition 'successful psychopaths' are people who avoid being identified as such. A murderer or a rapist does not only become a murderer or rapist when they are convicted – and a psychopath does not only become a psychopath when formerly diagnosed. Pathology precedes diagnosis. The prominent psychologist Oliver James commented in 2014 that Savile had a 'dark triad' of personality characteristics, comprising of psychopathy, narcissism and Machiavellianism.

When we come into contact with people with psychopathic qualities we are often overcome by a sense of confusion, deep mistrust and also worry about being led astray by fantasies infecting our minds. We may suspect we are being drawn into danger but we may not be sure. Questions like "Did they *really* do that?", "Am I being conned?", "Am I just imagining this?" and "Can they really be *that* bad?" and "Maybe I am just being paranoid?" tend to flood our minds.

These questions are difficult and divisive enough for experienced psychiatric teams to contend with, let alone family members who need to believe that a person cares about them, colleagues or children in need of approval and safety. It is testament to the persuasiveness of psychopaths and the smokescreens they create that the vast majority of the British public were taken in by a patently creepy man who surrounded himself with vulnerable children.

Whether or not Savile consciously did charity work as a way to shield himself from accusations, the status and work certainly gave him unrestricted access to children. It is well known that paedophiles seek out positions where they have access to vulnerable children, and it becoming clearer that non-paedophile psychopaths similarly seek power. Unfortunately, while psychopaths are imagined as the knife-wielding killers of Hollywood, not enough attention is given to the possibility that many more psychopaths quietly secure positions within society where they can exert maximum control.

Studies of prisoners have helped us understand the minds of psychopaths but they do not reveal the predominance of psychopathic traits within the wider population. Psychiatrists cannot simply turn up to banks, parliaments and media companies and demand that people undergo mental health assessments and brain scans. Nevertheless, in recent years good evidence has been emerging that psychopathic qualities are far from the exclusive domain of prisoners and patients in secure psychiatric units. Those qualities are also found among well paid people in positions of power and within key occupations that society depends upon.

A survey conducted by the British research psychologist Kevin Dutton for Channel 4's 2013 programme *Psychopath Night* produced findings that might surprise those who associate psychopathy with violent crime. The survey, which has been completed by around 2.5 million people, asked a series of questions to find out about psychopathic tendencies of respondents. Participants were also asked their occupation and which source of news they favoured.

Financial Times readers had the highest level of psychopathic attributes, followed by readers of the *Daily Star* and then *The Sun*. Readers of *The Guardian*, the Channel 4 news website and the BBC website were found to have below average psychopathic traits. The show listed the top five 'psychopathic professions', which – from the top – were banker, lawyer, media personnel, salesperson and surgeon. Some might be surprised that politicians were not near the top, but Professor Dutton commented later on Twitter that no politicians had completed the survey.

The following chapters consider how psychopaths operate within key social institutions and the impact their characteristics have on society in general. Only by understanding how psychopaths operate within various areas of society can we understand how they help to create and maintain what I term psychopathic cultures. Once we recognise that psychopathic cultures are as much of a reality as psychopathic individuals, we will have considerably more chance of tackling them.

Chapter 1 – Challenges defining and identifying psychopaths

The challenge of identifying psychopaths is in part related to their deceitful nature and partly to the problem of defining them. Just as teams of psychiatrists, psychologists, psychiatric nurses and social workers can be split by one individual on a mental health ward, professionals with an interest in psychopaths are often divided about the threat they pose to society and about the meaning of the term.

Some people have made distinctions between psychopaths and sociopaths based on how organised or chaotic they are but many experts now class them together, favouring one word or the other to describe people with antisocial personality disorders.

The development of psychiatry has been and continues to be a strange journey and it is probably influenced by the views of and changes within society more than any other medical specialism. Some theorists, as well as clinicians, have gone as far as to argue that because developments within psychiatry have been related to trends within wider society – meaning psychiatry is socially constructed – it is not a rational and scientific discipline.

This line of reasoning can cause the discipline to be cast as something amorphous and subject to the whims of an age, a reflection of paternalistic control within society or even the sinister machinery of oppressive regimes. There is, unfortunately, enough evidence in the history of psychiatry to encourage the critic to maintain their stance and to convince others that their negative perceptions are warranted.

The philosopher Michel Foucault is one of the key figures who placed the development of psychiatry within a social and historical context to argue that it is not a rational distillation of amassed medical knowledge but one of many devices of social control gaining prominence in recent centuries. However, for Foucault society is not simply controlled by elite groups like doctors and politicians, but we all play our part in shaping reality by our perceptions, expressions and actions. Most people do not physically build or run mental hospitals or prisons, but widely-held attitudes help construct the apparatus of social control and enables others to actually carry out society's wishes.

This sort of analysis, fuelled by the challenges of pinning down the experiences, beliefs and activities of people with personality disorders and mental illnesses, has led some to conclude that mental illness itself is a myth and personality disorders are merely socially constructed categories in which to pigeon-hole those who do not conform to social norms. This notion can be attractive to thoughtful, well-meaning liberal people but it ignores the reality of the experiences of those with serious conditions and those in intensive contact with them.

Like many enthusiastic young idealists holding a general belief in people and knowledge of social sciences and philosophy, I was sceptical about many aspects of psychiatry prior to working in the area. I remained concerned about power within psychiatry and wary of the dogmatism of psychiatric professionals even after several years of working intensely with a variety of patient groups.

However, while I have maintained a sense of justice and belief that all patients should be treated with dignity and respect, I am quite clear that psychopaths and people with other personality disorders *do* exist. I also have worked closely enough with people who have multiple voices shouting in their heads and those experiencing mania to conclude that schizophrenia and bipolar affective disorder are also real.

Nevertheless, none of these diagnoses are without problems and this is evidenced by the fact that many patients' psychiatric notes span multiple folders and contain tentative and aborted attempts to fit them into a particular diagnostic categories.

Having followed patients through from child psychiatry to adolescent psychiatry to acute psychiatry to secure wards, I have seen many instances where people have had several working diagnoses before finally being placed by psychiatrists – often reluctantly – in a personality disorder category. The reluctance to diagnose a patient with a personality disorder and to instead first explore a range of treatments for symptoms is based on an empathetic, careful and considerate rationale.

It is not appropriate to diagnose an individual with a personality disorder until they are an adult. Child and adolescent psychiatrists commonly describe and diagnose conduct disorders, attention deficit disorders and behavioural problems. Many of these patients end up being diagnosed with antisocial personality disorder but while under the care of child and adolescent services they are overtly treated with optimism, as though with appropriate support they can transcend their problems. Clinicians working with such individuals may, in reality, have lower expectations than they communicate to families and will be focused on long-term harm-minimisation rather than cure.

There are other reasons why the diagnoses of psychopath may come after a number of tentative diagnoses have been explored, even in adult patients. One example is with patients who come in contact with mental health units after attempting suicide. Depression is an obvious conclusion to draw from a suicide bid but this is often only part of the picture. If they are admitted to mental health units after convincing suicide attempts they will be monitored closely and nurses and doctors will have regular meetings with them to talk about their feelings, thoughts and experiences. The person will be encouraged to participate in groups if the unit has a group therapy programme.

Mental health workers take a great deal of interest in not only what such patients say but also in their tone and speed of speech, eye contact, posture and hand gestures. Staff do not just observe them so closely to protect them from further self-harm but because some people who harm themselves have personality disorders and are likely to become extremely difficult members of the ward community and respond poorly to intervention.

The prevalence of illegal drug use has helped make psychiatry a more complex and challenging field. It is often hard enough to make a firm diagnosis for many patients without the alterations of mood, thought and behaviour brought about by substance use. Many people passing through mental health units have tried or are currently taking illegal drugs. Some of these have personality disorders, the symptoms of which may be either masked or exacerbated by substance use.

Those regularly smoking cannabis may appear to be experiencing symptoms of psychosis when admitted. The hope is to curtail their drug use and work out if the symptoms are caused by cannabis or continue in the absence of the substance. As visitors can come and go from wards and some patients are free to leave and return, it is almost impossible to prevent residents from taking illegal drugs.

Therefore making a distinction between drug psychosis and a genuine psychotic illness, such as paranoid schizophrenia, is often extremely difficult. People with personality disorders taking certain drugs are not immune to symptoms of psychosis and it may not be until some time after their drug use has stopped and psychotic symptoms subside that their psychopathic traits become vividly apparent.

Some patients are well aware that they are not truly psychotic and that their problems are related to their personality. They may consciously use their drug taking as a smokescreen to gain sympathy, lengthen admissions or gain access to prescribed drugs, such as benzodiazepines or methadone, which they can sell. Disclosure of experiences of child abuse – whether true or not – can be another lever used by those with personality disorders to manipulate staff and peers in environments such as psychiatric units, where such experiences will find sympathetic ears.

Sometimes it is not the patient themselves who psychiatric staff identify as having personality disorders but relatives. Within child psychiatry the patient may well be healthier and less difficult than parents or other guardians, but they become a 'symptom carrier' for the family system. An extreme example of this is when children become disturbed as a result of being violently or sexually abused by a family member with a personality disorder. However, many cases are more subtle and psychiatrists cannot formerly diagnose a parent who is not in mental health care themselves.

Teams working with families where they believe a child is being abused may have extremely strong views about a parent, they may firmly believe they are a psychopath, but they will have to tread carefully to engage the family in therapy and keep the child in an inpatient unit. There are cases where psychiatric services go to court to take custody of an at-risk child but, in the main, psychiatric teams have to engage with personality disordered parents in a hospitable and outwardly non-judgemental to help them care for their children more appropriately.

Even in cases where it is categorically proven that parents are abusing children there may be other reasons than a personality disorder. Some abusers fit more easily into the learning disability spectrum than into personality disorder categories but making a firm diagnosis when only seeing parents in meetings about their child is problematic.

From the few examples given above it should be clear that there are many circumstances in which clinicians and other professionals will feel they are dealing with someone with an antisocial personality disorder but they are not in a position to prove it and have limited power to challenge behaviours. However, it should also be acknowledged that professionals working with challenging people sometimes label people as having personality disorders out of frustration and anger.

In psychiatric wards this labelling happens informally in discussions much more often than written in medical notes. It can be a way of expressing exasperation or powerlessness or justifying a lack of progress with a patient. It can also be used to support an argument that a patient should not be admitted or should be discharged.

If teams of psychiatric professionals find it difficult to accurately assess and deal with people with psychopathic qualities, it is not surprising that psychopaths find it easy to con, intimidate, abuse and manipulate members of the wider community.

Most people, when coming into contact with psychopaths, lack the ability to challenge them in a safe therapeutic manner. Some people will intuitively know that something is wrong and try to give them a wide berth. However, for those who get sucked into destructive, exploitative or dangerous relationships with them, the results can be catastrophic. For some people, the psychopaths they encounter will be colleagues, who may make their life unpleasant without ever being diagnosed with a personality disorder.

One reason why many people do not recognise psychopaths for what they are – and sometimes before it is too late – may be related to false impressions given by the television and film industries. Most are not serial killers – in fact psychopaths are more likely to find their way into politics, boardrooms or media organisations than be jailed for murder. While some psychopaths manage to get into senior positions in powerful organisations, others live pitiable lives of petty crime, bullying and manipulation of the unfortunate people around them.

It is interesting to note that Norman Bates, the disturbed killer in Alfred Hitchcock's *Psycho*, does not fit the criteria of psychopath. He more closely resembles a very different personality disorder called dissociative identity disorder (more commonly known as multiple personality disorder). Therefore those people who are expecting psychopaths to be like Norman Bates may be oblivious to psychopaths in their streets, workplaces and families.

Classifying psychopaths

Given that psychopaths can be found anywhere, including high status positions, and have the potential to have a catastrophic impact on society, it is important to outline their characteristics, from the perspective of psychiatry. If society can improve its ability to spot psychopathic behaviour it will be in a stronger position to tackle psychopathic culture wherever it is found.

The seminal work about psychopaths, which laid the foundations for how contemporary psychiatrists and psychologists view them and deal with them, was published in 1941. *The Mask of Sanity* was written by the American psychiatrist Hervey Cleckley and based on his interactions with incarcerated psychopaths. As the title suggests, Cleckley's view was that, in contrast to patients with true mental illnesses like schizophrenia, the disturbed minds of psychopaths are masked by a veneer of superficial charm and studied mimicry of normal emotions.

Despite the fact that Cleckley's research was based on detained psychopaths, he was extremely clear that those with the disorder often have clean criminal records and live within the mainstream community rather than institutions. *The Mask of Sanity* documents examples of high-achieving, non-incarcerated psychopaths, including doctors, business executives and scientists.

Despite success in their careers and often having high social status, psychopaths are notable for being manipulative, deceitful and lacking genuine emotion, according to Cleckley. Tragically, those characteristics help people in certain careers – particularly ones that are rewarded for either disregarding or exploiting the feelings and views of other people.

Although not regarded as mental illnesses, personality disorders are defined by a publication called the *Diagnostic and Statistical Manual of Mental Disorders*. The manual, which is published by the American Psychiatric Association (APA) was first produced in 1952 and has been revised periodically over the decades. Prior to DSM-V being produced in 2013 the last major update (DSM-IV) was published in 1994. The manual is used not only in the USA but also, in varying degrees, by clinicians around the world.

It would not be much of an exaggeration to describe DSM as the Bible of many psychiatrists as it codifies the amassed beliefs of the profession while also guiding clinical decision-making. Though psychiatry tends to be regarded as a conservative profession, the production of a manual defining mental illnesses, personality disorders and 'intellectual disabilities' is a controversial act.

To set the standards on what is deemed to be outside the range of 'normal' behaviour and feeling is an exercise in power, and it ultimately impinges on the freedom of those who are seen to fall into one of the diagnostic categories. It is also problematic in terms of culture. To have an elite American organisation defining how human beings from diverse ethnic and cultural backgrounds should and should not respond to the challenges life throws at them can seem more arbitrary and judgemental than caring.

The fact that the manual is periodically revised reflects the reality that mental illness and personality disorder classifications are influenced by changes within society and the changing perceptions of those who set the standards. This can be illustrated by taking a look at psychiatry books from the 1950s and 60s in which homosexuality and recreational drug use are treated as serious psychiatric symptoms.

However, rather than use the above evidence to dismiss the value of the DSM out of hand, it does actually illustrate that psychiatrists are perpetually refining their own perceptions and clinical judgements as a consequence of experience and new information.

Given the recent completion of DSM-V, there are many good discussions in journals and on websites about the validity or otherwise of creating and recreating diagnostic categories in which to place people. This book is concerned more with the development of a psychopathic cultures and pathological cultures in various powerful sectors than with debates about whether this individual or that can be clinically defined as a psychopath. Therefore, whilst I will be using the DSM to illustrate what psychiatrists regard as antisocial personality disorder indicators, I shall also attempt to apply these to organisational, political and financial systems.

Antisocial personality disorder according to the DSM

From the publication of DSM-IV to the drafting of DSM-V there have been changes in the criteria used to define antisocial personality disorder. These changes will be examined in more detail after each of them has been laid out in full. The changes are extremely interesting and it is therefore worth considering each DSM edition in detail. I have retained the American spelling.

DSM-IV defined people with antisocial personality disorders as follows:

A. There is a pervasive pattern of disregard for and violation of the rights of others occurring since age 15 years, as indicated by three (or more) of the following:

(1) failure to conform to social norms with respect to lawful behaviors as indicated by repeatedly performing acts that are grounds for arrest

(2) deceitfulness, as indicated by repeated lying, use of aliases, or conning others for personal profit or pleasure

(3) impulsivity or failure to plan ahead

(4) irritability and aggressiveness, as indicated by repeated physical fights or assaults
(5) reckless disregard for safety of self or others
(6) consistent irresponsibility, as indicated by repeated failure to sustain consistent work behavior or honor financial obligations
(7) lack of remorse, as indicated by being indifferent to or rationalizing having hurt, mistreated, or stolen from another

B. The individual is at least age 18 years.
C. There is evidence of Conduct Disorder with onset before age 15 years.
D. The occurrence of antisocial behavior is not exclusively during the course of schizophrenia or a manic episode.

If readers take the trouble to play a 'spot the difference' game by comparing the above with the below they will notice many changes between DSM-IV and the revision. The verbatim text above from DSM-IV amounts to 175 words. The text below from DSM-V amounts to 440 words. This is an excellent illustration of how defining psychopaths and sociopaths, let alone responding effectively to the damage they do in society, is incredibly difficult.

DSM-V states:

The essential features of a personality disorder are impairments in personality (self and interpersonal) functioning and the presence of pathological personality traits. To diagnose antisocial personality disorder, the following criteria must be met:

A. Significant impairments in personality functioning manifest by:
1. Impairments in self functioning (a or b):
a. Identity: Ego-centrism; self-esteem derived from personal gain, power, or pleasure.
b. Self-direction: Goal-setting based on personal gratification; absence of prosocial internal standards associated with failure to conform to lawful or culturally normative ethical behavior.

AND

2. Impairments in interpersonal functioning (a or b):
a. Empathy: Lack of concern for feelings, needs, or suffering of others; lack of remorse after hurting or mistreating another.
b. Intimacy: Incapacity for mutually intimate relationships, as exploitation is a primary means of relating to others, including

by deceit and coercion; use of dominance or intimidation to control others.

B. Pathological personality traits in the following domains:

1. Antagonism, characterized by:

a. Manipulativeness: Frequent use of subterfuge to influence or control others; use of seduction, charm, glibness, or ingratiation to achieve one's ends.

b. Deceitfulness: Dishonesty and fraudulence; misrepresentation of self; embellishment or fabrication when relating events.

c. Callousness: Lack of concern for feelings or problems of others; lack of guilt or remorse about the negative or harmful effects of one's actions on others; aggression; sadism.

d. Hostility: Persistent or frequent angry feelings; anger or irritability in response to minor slights and insults; mean, nasty, or vengeful behavior.

2. Disinhibition, characterized by:

a. Irresponsibility: Disregard for – and failure to honor – financial and other obligations or commitments; lack of respect for – and lack of follow through on – agreements and promises.

b. Impulsivity: Acting on the spur of the moment in response to immediate stimuli; acting on a momentary basis without a plan or consideration of outcomes; difficulty establishing and following plans.

c. Risk taking: Engagement in dangerous, risky, and potentially self-damaging activities, unnecessarily and without regard for consequences; boredom proneness and thoughtless initiation of activities to counter boredom; lack of concern for one's limitations and denial of the reality of personal danger.

C. The impairments in personality functioning and the individual's personality trait expression are relatively stable across time and consistent across situations.

D. The impairments in personality functioning and the individual's personality trait expression are not better understood as normative for the individual's developmental stage or socio-cultural environment.

E. The impairments in personality functioning and the individual's personality trait expression are not solely due to the direct physiological effects of a substance (e.g., a drug of abuse, medication) or a general medical condition (e.g., severe head trauma).

F. The individual is at least age 18 years.

Prior to DSM-4 being replaced, a supporting document outlining the reasons for changes to the classification stated: "Overall, the magnitude of the proposed changes is 'substantial'. Significant changes are being proposed in a diagnostic area of DSM-IV that has significant limitations in validity and clinical utility." This seems rather damning about previous efforts to define conditions and vividly illustrates that psychiatry is far from being an exact science.

Getting the classification wrong does not just impact on those who are wrongly categorised as having an antisocial personality disorder and those who would wish greater control to be exerted on real psychopaths. The criteria offered in previous DSMs has been used to define 'subjects' used in research studies – and these research studies shape how psychiatry and other institutions respond to people deemed to have a disorder. The significance of this problem is acknowledged in the 'Rationale for the Proposed Changes to the Personality Disorder Classification in DSM-5' document, which states:

> The entire PD literature is built upon shifting sands: had each of the thousands of PD studies been conducted with a different PD assessment, the study participants would have been a largely different set of individuals, thus yielding study results that would be different to an unknown degree. (DSM-5 website)

One of the things that jumps out at me from the changes made is the greater focus on the qualities of the individual rather than the things they have been found to have done in the past. This seems to be sensible progress as we know that many people who are found to be murderers, serial rapists, paedophiles and fraudsters have no recorded history of behaviours that might have marked them out as psychopathic when younger. It is interesting that the requirement in DSM-4 that "there is evidence of Conduct Disorder with onset before age 15 years" no longer exists in DSM-5.

One of the key criteria in both DSM-4 and 5 is deceitfulness. Given that this is a fundamental characteristic of the psychopath's way of going through life, it does now seem strange that so many of the other requirements outlined in DSM-4, and to a lesser degree DSM-5, are dependent on being discovered to have done certain things or acted in certain ways. The point is society itself might not discover that an individual has the qualities of a psychopath unless he or she is convicted of a crime – and many psychopaths manage to go through life without being arrested let alone convicted.

Two notable but very different examples of people who appear to have had antisocial personality disorders and exerted great power over others are that of the mass murderer Harold Shipman and the prolific paedophile Jimmy Savile. In 2000, at the age of 54, Shipman was convicted of murdering 15 of his patients and a subsequent inquiry concluded he was probably responsible for 215 murders.

Reports suggest Savile was abusing children as early as the 1940s, when he worked in nightclubs – prior to becoming a radio DJ and then a television presenter. He was investigated by the police for sexual offences in 1958 but charges were not brought. Although it is fair to say that many members of the public found Savile somewhat strange over the decades of his broadcast career, allegations by children were largely ignored or mocked until after he died. Within months of him dying, however, hundreds of allegations of sexual assaults had been made. Fresh allegations are still being reported.

The cases of Savile and Shipman are grotesque examples of people with antisocial personality disorder symptoms whose status and power enabled their prolific offending. Both also displayed a shocking amount of arrogance in their offending, as though believing themselves to be untouchable.

For those being victimised by psychopaths, whether famous or not, the ignorance of other people in relation to the true nature of their aggressors is extremely distressing. Psychopaths get through life with superficial charm and are able to con, control and intimidate people without guilt. The peculiar qualities of ruthlessness, sadism, charm, deceit, manipulativeness and a need for control makes it possible for psychopaths to treat victims appallingly while maintaining the trust, support and respect of others.

Even those hurt most by them may not acknowledge that their tormentor is a psychopath, preferring to put their behaviours down to external circumstances impinging upon the aggressor. Psychopaths are often excellent at making others believe they are being hard-done-by and are themselves victims of others. They exploit feelings in others which they lack themselves.

The many difficulties inherent in identifying and challenging psychopaths should not put society off attempting to do so. Whether the psychopath is a parent, spouse, neighbour, boss, policeman, doctor, banker, politician, social worker, celebrity or media executive, the impact they can have on individuals and society is catastrophic. The greater power a psychopath has, the greater their influence on institutions, and other human cultures. Societies and the medical establishment have been enthusiastic and effective at tackling contagious diseases but have been less successful at tackling toxic psychopathic cultures.

Society is gradually realising that psychopaths are not all sinister looking knife-wielding killers and are more likely to be people who seek out 'respectful' positions of power. However, more can be done to ensure everyone has a clearer idea about how psychopaths operate so we can identify and respond more effectively to psychopathic behaviour and cultures.

Identifying how psychopaths operate in society and how they contaminate groups will help society to tackle organisational psychopathy and the encroachment of the psychopath's 'values' (or lack of them) into institutions that are essential to maintain fair and peaceful societies.

Chapter 2 – Psychopathic economics

It may be difficult for some readers to imagine a world where an amoral and antisocial business ethos does not dominate. Growing up immersed in an individualistic, materialistic and money-obsessed culture can make a calculating, grasping and amoral approach to life seem not only acceptable but inevitable.

However, the reality is that the political, economic and cultural world we live within is far from inevitable. It is the product of a turbulent history and complex power struggles going back through time. As the speed of life increases and economic turbulence increases, societies become more ruthless and this is the ideal habitat for the psychopath to flourish and exert influence on culture.

It is extremely regrettable when people, particularly young people, take the view that life is "just how it is" and feel they have no power to shift the balance of power and make things fairer. When people claim to have little power they play into the hands of those with too much – the small percentage of ruthless people who thrive on control and feed on vulnerability. Some of these people have been described by experts as psychopaths, and they – with the help of all who fail to challenge them – create pathological cultures which can seem overwhelming and inevitable.

Since the 1970s, in the UK and other nations, there have been brutal attacks on unions and industries that employ 'working class' people. This sustained attack, which started in Britain under Conservative prime minister Margaret Thatcher, has resulted in the country having very little mining, steel-working or heavy industry left. The deliberate culling of unions and skilled physical jobs has not only devastated once-vibrant communities but it has also created the unsustainable and dangerous situation where the dominant industry in the UK is finance. So not only have communities been sold out by a political class that promised them greater freedom and prosperity, but bankers, financiers, hedge fund managers and brokers have gained excessive power.

The Conservative government of the 70s and 80s refused to support mining communities by increasing wages but the Tories of this decade are more than happy to make taxpayers fund huge salaries and bonuses of inept and sometimes corrupt bankers. Modern investment banking, share dealing, currency speculation and hedge fund management are amoral and often antisocial practices with many consequences on billions of people. It is not far-fetched to say that bankers and financiers have substantial control over politicians in webs of power extending all around the world.

As well as taking money from hard-pressed taxpayers, who cover the gambling losses of financial industries, countries producing the commodities traded by indifferent brokers are devastatingly affected. There is a connection between the greed of the commodity broker sitting in London or New York and the brutality facing miners in poorer countries. However, the broker does not run the risk of being shot if he dares to ask for more pay, as happened to dozens of platinum miners in 2012 at a mine in South Africa owned by British and American investors.

During Margaret Thatcher's relentless attack on the unions, the police were used as paid thugs – agents of oppression to bludgeon striking and protesting miners. This battle between the people who profit from and seek to control industry has not gone away but the lines of the battle have now shifted and span networks of companies in numerous countries. Wealthy investors are far removed from the front line as miners and other industrial workers in oppressive conditions struggle to get enough money to feed their families.

The shift to outsource the manufacturing, mining and other hard physical work to poorer countries means it is easier for consumers to disregard where their products have come from and ignore the blood shed to get them so cheaply. It also means unionised industries can be driven from Western countries, thus moving the politics of those countries steadily to the right to produce an ethos that is so greedy, individualistic, immoral and callous that it can reasonably be described as psychopathic.

Snakes in suits

The public are not stupid and most of us are nowadays well aware when politicians, the media, pushy salesmen or other insincere people are trying to deceive us. Doffing caps to the 'great and good' is thankfully a dying practice and few of us now would assume that those with more money than us are our 'betters'. However, for a variety of reasons, clinicians and others have been reticent about using the term psychopath to describe senior people in organisations or prominent people in public life.

One reason for this reticence is the lack of clarity that has existed about what the term psychopath means and who it applies to. Another reason is that many people did not realise quite how atrocious the behaviour of some politicians, bankers, celebrities and business leaders was until quite recently.

The symbiotic links between the Establishment and media has often been so strong that stories about appalling actions by powerful figures and elite organisations were often suppressed. In recent years this has begun to unravel and we are finding out about activities showing 'the great and the good' in a very bad light indeed – even if we often find out when it is too late to remove them from power and prosecute them.

Another key reason for even the most critical commentator's reluctance to use the term psychopath to describe powerful people is the risk of being sued for libel or slander. Defamation laws favour the rich and powerful. Vengeful rich people clogging up English courts with defamations cases made the country the libel tourism capital of the world.

A person accusing a rich person of something they cannot easily prove in court is at real risk of losing everything they have and their reputation during a trial. To prove, for example, a lying politician has had sex with a prostitute has been shown to be difficult enough when – as in the case of Jeffrey Archer – a judge accepts testimony of members of the Establishment over a sex worker.

To prove in court that an elite figure is a psychopath, which is a nebulous description, is even more difficult than proving wrongdoing. If the accuser cannot prove it they could be ruined by the richer party. The wealthy person accused of being a psychopath merely needs to pay for an 'expert witness' who will offer the view that they are not.

Despite all of the above, experts on psychopathy are increasingly sticking their necks out to assert that senior people within organisations are more likely to be psychopaths than the average person. For example, in 2006 a pair of psychologists published a fascinating and provocative book drawing on decades of time working with dangerous psychopaths, and claiming that people with the same qualities are in senior positions in every walk of life. The book *Snakes in Suits: When Psychopaths go to Work* was authored by Paul Babiak and Robert Hare.

Outlining the many challenges posed by psychopaths gaining entry into the workplace and alluding to the fact that psychiatric professionals had often previously assumed such people would struggle to climb the corporate ladder, Babiak and Hare state:

In addition to the problems their abusive behaviours cause to spouses, friends, and family members, individuals with a heavy dose of psychopathic traits are potentially harmful to professional relationships.

For example, their grandiosity, sense of entitlement, and lack of personal insight lead to conflict and rivalry with bosses and co-workers, and their impulsivity and "live in the moment" philosophy lead them to keep repeating these and other dysfunctional, antisocial behaviours, despite performance appraisals and training programs. Many experts believed that these traits alone make it difficult for psychopaths to have successful long-term careers in industry. At least that was the conventional wisdom until we did our research.

One might think that conning or bullying traits in a job applicant would be so obvious to employers that such candidates would not be hired for important jobs, especially those where the ability to get along with others is critical. One might also think that abusive, deceitful behaviour toward co-workers would eventually lead to disciplinary action and termination. But, based on the cases we have reviewed, this often is not the case.

The authors worryingly suggest that psychopaths get hired into senior positions because the symptoms of their personality disorder actually mirror those that recruiters consider to be good leadership qualities:

Some companies quite innocently recruit individuals with psychopathic tendencies because some hiring managers may mistakenly attribute "leadership" labels to what are, in actuality, psychopathic behaviours. For example, taking charge, making decisions, and getting others to do what you want are classic features of leadership and management, yet they can also be well-packaged forms of coercion, domination, and manipulation.

Despite the clear view of the authors that organisations of all types employ psychopaths, they warn against workers making accusations that another person within the organisation is a psychopath. Offering advice to those who feel they are working with a psychopath, Babiak and Hare state:

Avoid labelling a co-worker a "psychopath." It will get you nowhere and may lead to those in authority wondering about you.

Psychopathy itself is not illegal, despite the problems it causes for those around individuals with these traits. Behaviour, however, can be illegal, unethical, hurtful, and so forth. It is paramount that you focus on the actual behaviour of the individual whom you believe to be a psychopath. Observe it, document it, and if you are intimidated or feel that you are in danger, bring it to the attention of those in authority or, at least, someone you trust.

Following the work of Babiak, Hare and others, psychologists at the University of Pennsylvania Yu Gao and Adrian Raine have focused on psychopaths living and working in the community as well as violent incarcerated psychopaths. Their 2010 article 'Successful and Unsuccessful Psychopaths: A Neurobiological Model', published in *Behavioral Sciences and the Law*, focuses on psychopaths within five populations. These were defined as: community sources, individuals from temporary employment agencies, undergraduate students, industrial psychopaths (who display psychopathic qualities in the workplace) and serial killers.

The pair put forward a neurobiological model to try to explain why some psychopaths manage to use their peculiar qualities to achieve success in mainstream life and avoid incarceration while others resort to violence and find themselves detained in institutions.

The term 'successful psychopath' for Gao and Raine refers to individuals with psychopathic characteristics who somehow successfully avoid being convicted for their crimes or diagnosed as such. As serial killers by definition avoid being caught until they have committed multiple murders, if at all, Gao and Raine define them as 'semi-successful psychopaths'.

Explaining their focus, Gao and Raine write:

> It is hypothesized that successful psychopaths have intact or enhanced neurobiological functioning that underlies their normal or even superior cognitive functioning, which in turn helps them to achieve their goals using more covert and non-violent methods. In contrast, in unsuccessful, caught psychopaths, brain structural and functional impairments together with autonomic nervous system dysfunction are hypothesized to underlie cognitive and emotional deficits and more overt violent offending.

Suggesting that there are different sorts of psychopaths, some with brains more suited to achieving in the world of work and others with brain abnormalities likely to lead them to incarceration, the pair state:

We postulate that intact or enhanced neurobiological processes, including better executive functioning, increased autonomic reactivity, normative volumes of prefrontal gray and amygdala, and normal frontal functioning, may serve as factors that protect successful psychopaths from conviction and allow them to attain their life goals, using more covert and non-violent approaches. In contrast, brain structural and functional deficits, alongside with reduced autonomic reactivity, impaired executive functioning, and risky decision making, predispose the unsuccessful psychopaths to more extreme forms of antisocial behaviour utilizing more overt and aggressive methods of manipulation.

This is an extremely interesting thing to say as it suggests that particularly chaotically violent and particularly well-functioning psychopaths could be distinguished by brain scans. Whether job applicants would be willing to be scanned in case they happen to have the potential to be a killer – rather than a chief executive – is another matter.

Clearly psychopaths who have been found guilty of serious crimes or held in a psychiatric hospital would be far more likely than senior executives or politicians to be scanned to prove differences or similarities. Therefore, without more evidence about the brain functioning of high-achieving people with psychopathic qualities, there could be a perhaps danger of creating a false distinction between different 'types' of psychopaths.

Due to their influence on a larger number of people, a psychopath in a position of power, whatever sector of life they work within, can cause more damage than a low-achieving chaotic thug. A violent psychopath might threaten or harm one person before being incarcerated, whereas a psychopathic media magnate or politician can have a damaging impact on the minds and lives of hundreds of millions of people. Gao and Raine acknowledge this point, stating that non-incarcerated, high-achieving psychopaths "may in the long run be more dangerous and destructive to society" than low-achieving violent psychopaths.

In distinguishing between successful and less successful psychopaths Gao and Raine's model unfortunately fails to address the impact of social and economic background on the psychopath. If somebody with psychopathic tendencies is brought up with opportunities, support and access to a good education they are more likely to be able to play the longer game to get what they want than those with few resources at their disposal but violence and intimidation.

Better educated people with larger vocabularies are more likely to be able to get people to do what they want without resorting to violence, as are people who have acting abilities. Wealthier people are also more likely to be able to afford good lawyers to get them out of trouble. Furthermore, better-looking psychopaths have an advantage over their less-attractive counterparts. Therefore, while the model put forward by Gao and Raine is interesting and valuable, it may not entirely explain why different psychopaths act in such different ways within society.

Given that corporate psychopaths would appear to reflect the values of companies – to ruthlessly and calculatingly gain as much as possible while charming the external world – one might assume that recruiting them is a good idea. They are driven, they get things done, they exert effective control on underlings and their charisma may help promote the company. However, these snakes in suits are also unpredictable, malicious and ultimately self-interested and so can be highly damaging to organisations – particularly in this age of whistle-blowers and rapid dissemination of information via social media.

Clive Boddy, a professor of leadership and organisation behaviour with extensive experience working within and researching various industries, has suggested that corporate psychopaths have a damaging effect on the organisations they work for. In a paper published in 2010, Boddy makes the point that while psychopaths may work within large commercial corporations and governments to meet their own ends, their lack of ethical standards and indifference towards corporate responsibility makes them a threat to the organisations that employ them. He states:

> Corporate psychopaths are motivated by a desire to win, a desire for power and a desire to gain wealth and prestige. It makes sense therefore that corporate psychopaths would be attracted to join such organizations and would try to attain such senior management positions to gain the wealth, prestige and power that they crave.
>
> Corporate psychopaths are only interested in self-gratification and not in the success of other people or even of the organization in which they work. They are interested in running corporations for the power, money and prestige that they crave and they are self-interested to the exclusion of others and are indifferent to the fate of the organizations they work for or of their fellow employees

Alluding to psychopaths' disregard and disdain for corporate social responsibility, Professor Boddy also states:

> The government and financial sectors, with the highest rates of corporate psychopaths in them, are the least likely to be seen as doing business in a socially desirable manner. The Government and financial sectors are also the least likely to be seen as doing business in a way that shows commitment to employees.
>
> Further, the financial sector was the least likely to be seen as doing business in an environmentally friendly manner and the second least likely to be seen as doing business in a way that benefits the local community.

Linking this observation to the global financial meltdown, he goes on to say:

> The presence of corporate psychopaths in greater numbers in some organizations, such as public services and financial services organizations should therefore be of considerable interest to those organizations and their stakeholders.
>
> This may have particular relevance to the current global financial crisis, which, it may be hypothesized was caused by corporate psychopaths in senior positions in financial services companies.

In another 2010 article, by Boddy, Richard Ladyshewsky and Peter Galvin, it is suggested that even if psychopaths account for only a small percentage of people within corporations, the size and power of those corporations means that such people can have a considerable impact on the world:

> It is important to study corporate psychopaths because of the large scale nature of the financial, environmental and human resources that many modern international corporations have at their disposal. Many corporations are bigger in financial terms than nation states are, and for example of the 100 largest economies in 2002, 50% were corporations (Assadourian, 2005). Senior corporate managers thus have the financial power and resources to have a major influence on society on a global basis.

Psychopaths are callous, manipulative, calculating and ruthless. They are good at rationalising their actions and at appearing attractive and plausible to those around them. In many ways they reflect perfectly the character of big businesses, which operate to maximise profits by exploiting the world around them, including customers, staff, politicians and the environment.

In this business and political climate, a company might be regarded as inept for *not* holding down staff pay and not exploiting every opportunity to beat competitors or avoid tax. Companies that deceive and exploit everyone often do rather well and they smooth over criticism with public relations – the glib, charming and white-toothed face the rapacious company presents to the world.

It may seem strange to think of a company as psychopathic but it is worth remembering that organisations are made up of people. Whatever is done by a company and within an organisation is done by people to other people. Antisocial behaviour, interpersonal abuse, deceit and destruction of the environment are not lessened simply because they are done by a group of people within an organisation wearing nice suits. However, it is indicative of how a right-wing ethos has been imprinted on societies that psychopathic behaviour by companies is often valorised as good business acumen and rewarded.

Unfortunately this psychopathic ethos in business has slithered, snake-like, into the public sector and essential services the public depends upon. State-funded schools and universities are played off against one another by governments seeking to push down costs and push political agendas.

Similarly the UK's National Health Service, which is funded by taxpayers, has become dominated by non-clinician business managers. Some of these appear to have the same sort of ruthless mindset that dominates the corporate world. This is unsurprising as most have come from the corporate world with the express goal of cutting costs and taking control from clinicians.

While the right-wing agenda to privatise the NHS talks often of the need to cut 'dead wood' from hospital trusts, the fact is that introducing the profit motive into essential state health services jeopardises patient care and threatens life. For private companies to make a profit from NHS services, money must be syphoned from the organisation and from patient care budgets.

As the organisation was established to treat and care for sick people, any money taken from it as profit is undermining the very thing it was set up to do. Corporate managers and shareholders taking large salaries and dividends from NHS services and their privatisation may be responsible for many more deaths than Harold Shipman. Yet they are treated as saviours by right-wing politicians who have sought to dismantle the NHS for decades. The same thing has happened already to the prison service in the UK, often with disastrous consequences.

While politicians and investors push societies to the right and make the profit motive dominate even the most vital public services, pathological cultures will flourish. It is not that 'lunatics have taken over the asylum' but that the mind-set of the most callous people in society permeates every area of life. Snakes in suits have slithered into the most delicate and precious organisations and have the potential to do a great deal of long-term damage to individuals and societies.

Imposing a corporate culture on vital services, such as healthcare and education, opens the door to corporate psychopaths and the toxic cultures they bring and thrive within. This is incredibly concerning in itself but ever more troubling when you consider that this spread of psychopathic culture has been enabled and encouraged by politicians employed to represent society.

Some may scoff at the notion of psychopathic or pathological cultures within organisations. They might, for example, take the view that businesses are not *meant* to be nice and that ethics and conscience are expensive and unnecessary indulgences for commercial organisations. Some might suggest that businesses are *meant* to be ruthless, exploitative, devious and even malicious. However, this would fail to understand businesses in context and recognise the impact corporations have on various people and groups. It would also fail to recognise that businesses can only survive and thrive in the long-term with the support of wider communities.

Businesses have a variety of stakeholders. These include investors, employees, customers, suppliers, local and national governments, creditors and trade unions. The community at large is also a stakeholder, as the action of businesses have many impacts. For example, companies can have an impact on the environment, pay rates, working conditions in other firms, the local and national economy and politics.

Therefore, a pathological culture within a corporation can be oppressive and damaging for people working within it but a lack of social responsibility of companies can also have damaging and long-term impacts on many others. Long after irresponsible companies have been dissolved there are other people cleaning up the social, ecological, economic, legal and political mess.

Organisations that provide a public service – whether they are commercial enterprises, charities, religions or state-funded bodies – often have more stakeholder groups and these may be vulnerable people. For example, a hospital that is private may well take money from the state, has a responsibility to care for members of the public, takes referrals from other health providers, helps create the medical culture of a society and it has an obligation to share clinical and scientific innovations it develops. Its staff and student trainees are also stakeholders, as are investors, people living nearby and companies supplying it with equipment, pharmaceuticals and food.

To suggest that the culture within such an organisation is nothing to do with anyone except managers and investors is quite wrong. There may well be people within organisations who are preoccupied with costs and profit but it should be remembered that profits are the result of the interaction between the organisation and the wider culture and environment. A symbiotic relationship should exist between organisations and society rather than a parasitical one. Societies are increasingly critical of corporations that feed off the community and environment but give little back.

As has been suggested above, organisations set standards that help shape how other bodies work. This inspiration may be positive or it can be damaging to other organisations and to stakeholders. Economic turbulence and politician-imposed austerity can encourage an ethos of ruthlessness, deviousness and poor practice, weak ethics and lack of social responsibility to spread from cut-throat commercial organisations to public services. Recent examples of this are an excellent illustration of how pathological cultures not only get cultivated in powerful corporations but they can spread like a contagious disease through organisations of all types and sizes.

Chapter 3 – Psychopathic cultures

The relationship between the psychopathy and society is complex, unsettling and murky. In some ways it reflects the sort of disturbing and bewildering relationships that exist between psychopaths and their prey. A psychopath can attack, exploit and con people or abuse children and never see them again, but will have left their mark on the mind of each 'victim'. The very fact that they might be defined as themselves or others as a victim is one indicator of how identity can be distorted by contact with psychopaths.

People who are victimised do not necessarily become bullies, abusers or manipulators themselves – although it happens too frequently to be disregarded. As well as physical injuries a victim may receive from a psychopath, their contact often leaves them with mental scars that impact on relationships and affects the rest of their life.

The callousness and vindictiveness of the psychopath can destroy the optimistic world-view of their prey, which has a pernicious effect on friendships, family life, work, demeanour, beliefs and actions. The experience casts a dark, haunting shadow over their entire world.

The psychopathic snake sinks its teeth into its victims and then slithers off, but the poison stays within those targeted and can spread to other people and actually corrupt the world around them. The psychopathic individual may be long gone but the human culture they nested in is left poisoned, unless an antidote is found. This process not only happens within small communities but it happens on a larger scale within corporations, institutions and entire societies.

We do not know exactly how many psychopaths are in powerful roles within society but we know that they are there by their impact and imprint. The poison of the psychopath can drip through governments, banks, media groups, the entertainment industry, schools and even hospitals, as well as companies of all sorts. The immoral, vindictive, selfish mentality of the psychopath is also reflected in callous economic models and political discourses.

The poison of the psychopath seems to be most concentrated in areas where people make big decisions affecting millions of people in a supposedly rational and detached way. It is easier to justify callousness when you rarely have to come into contact with those you harm and when an elitist education has given you the prejudice and confidence to justify even the most vindictive of policies.

Psychopaths may be few in number but their desire for power and control means that their influence is enormous as their 'values' have in inordinate impact on culture. Children are now born into a world where getting everything you can, presenting yourself in alluring ways and getting the better of other people is considered to be normal. Many of the prominent people who drove this culture in the 1970s and 80s are dead now but the psychopathically individualistic culture they pushed remains strong and dangerous.

Politicians like Margaret Thatcher and Ronald Reagan could be viewed as architects of a selfish psychopathic culture. However, it should be remembered that behind them were hundreds of strategists, advisers and speech writers helping to influence voters, who bought into the discourse of dominance and greed.

This snake pit of psychopathic culture has slithered in every direction and their venom has struck societies all around the world. If the definition of 'successful psychopath' is one who exploits and causes harm to others while avoiding being convicted or diagnosed, those in politics and finance have proven themselves to be the most effective.

Many people are making huge efforts, at great risk to themselves, to expose politicians and other members of the Establishment as cruel, abusive and corrupt and also to prove links between key 'players'. These efforts have been fruitful and should be commended. However, identifying powerful people as psychopaths late in their lives or after they are dead has limited value unless we can learn how they exerted control and what factors encouraged the wider population to trust them and embrace their poison.

Unless we can understand how a small number of psychopaths can exert so much power that they create a psychopathic culture – and make it seem acceptable or even inevitable – identifying individual psychopaths will have limited value. In order to do this it is critical to understand the tendency of the herd to conform and for normal individuals to obey malicious people who claim and wield power.

Power, obedience and cruelty

Psychopathic cultures have not been the focus of psychiatrists, who tend to be concerned with assessing and treating individuals. However, there is a fascinating seam of psychological research concerning power and obedience that sheds light on how psychopathic cultures form, are sustained and impact on individuals. Some of this work was driven by a desire to understand the dynamics that caused seemingly ordinary people to become sadistic killers during and in the lead up to World War Two.

Philip Zimbardo is an extremely interesting and controversial psychologist. He was born in New York six years before the outbreak of World War Two and is particularly known for his Stanford prison experiments, which he led in the early 1970s. In the initial study, 24 subjects deemed to be mentally healthy were assigned the roles of guards or prisoners. The selection of role for each subject was random rather than based on any personal characteristics. The experiment happened at a mock dungeon constructed within Stanford University's department of psychology.

To increase the realism of the experience, the volunteers – who were students – were not told in advance when the study would commence. They were simply woken on the day as though they were being arrested and taken to the dungeon. Those allocated the role of prisoners were then stripped naked, shaved and deloused. To remove their individuality and erode their identity further they were made to wear uniforms and given ID numbers.

The guards were also given uniforms, as well as whistles and truncheons. They were not given any instructions or rules for how to treat the prisoners except that they should maintain order in the jail. Disturbingly, participants quickly fell into extreme roles, with those acting as guards becoming sadistic towards prisoners, some of whom became passive and others oppositional. The study was meant to continue for two weeks but was halted after six days as a result of the distress experienced by participants as well as their actions.

At the start of the experiment some prisoners disregarded the supposed authority of the guards and disobeyed and mocked them. However, once the guards got into their role of oppressors, the prisoners' behaviour changed. Confrontations between prisoners and guards led to guards exerting their authority by making prisoners do physical exercise, such as press-ups.

Prisoners staged a protest on the second day by taking off their uniforms and barricading themselves in their cells with furniture. The guards responded to the rebellion by bringing in off duty colleagues as back-up. They also squirted fire extinguishers at them to force them from cell doors. After gaining entry into the cells, the guards destroyed beds and made prisoners strip naked. Prisoners deemed to be responsible for the rebellion were put in solitary confinement.

In an attempt to maintain order the guards began to use the behavioural technique of rewarding prisoners for good behaviour. More passive prisoners who had not participated in the rebellion were allowed to use their beds and attend to their personal hygiene. Those deemed troublemaking ringleaders were prevented from doing so.

Within two days of the experiment starting one of the students in the prisoner role became distressed, flew into rages and also screamed and sobbed. He was released from the dungeon but replaced by an alternative participant.

Guards became aware of an escape plan on the third day but it was thwarted and those accused of developing the escape plan were punished by being forced to do exercise and clean the lavatories. The guards actions towards the rest of the prisoners also became more oppressive and punitive, with the use of the toilets restricted and some prisoners forced to defecate into buckets in their cells.

Rather than maintain unity in the face of oppression, the camaraderie of prisoners quickly disintegrated and they internalised the oppressive culture. When one prisoner staged a hunger strike, other prisoners chanted that he was a troublemaker. I find this particularly interesting, disturbing and sad. I propose that this example helps explain why people who are not born sadists or psychopaths uphold pathological cultures of all sorts in which they themselves are mistreated. In the Stanford experiment several of the prisoners were traumatised by the time it was halted and some were so distressed they were freed from the study before that.

The oppressive and sometimes sadistic behaviour of the students appointed as guards went beyond that which Zimbardo and his colleagues anticipated. The research team estimated that a third of the guards exhibited sadistic tendencies. This is not a reflection of the research subjects being unusually prone to sadism but rather underlines the impact of a having to function within a pathological culture.

The troubling conclusions of the Stanford experiment, in relation to the ease in which perfectly ordinary people can be made to conform to an oppressive system, echo those of a famous study by Zimbardo's former school friend Stanley Milgram. Born in 1933 – the same year as Zimbardo – Milgram was extremely concerned about power and obedience by the time he became a psychologist. Growing up during the Holocaust drove Milgram's desire to understand why people obey authority figures, even when asked to do things that feel wrong.

The Milgram experiments took place at Yale University in 1961. It could perhaps be suggested that the rarefied setting may have been a significant factor in the obedience participants would ultimately show. However, the experiment has been replicated in various settings and with different demographics of participants with strikingly similar results.

An important context to consider is that it was around the same time as a trial of the Nazi war criminal Adolf Eichmann, which took place in Jerusalem. As one of the architects of the Holocaust, the senior SS figure had organised the mass deportation of Jews to ghettos and death camps. He was given the chillingly mundane sounding title of 'transportation administrator', yet he was committing genocide.

After the war Eichmann managed to escape to Argentina and was not caught until 1960, when he was located by Mossad operatives. He was subsequently drugged and smuggled out of Argentina to Israel. During the trial Eichmann admitted to his part in the Holocaust but maintained that he was 'only following orders' and had little personal power. However, he was hanged in 1962, having been found guilty of war crimes and crimes against humanity.

The Milgram experiments were designed to answer the question "Could it be that Eichmann and his million accomplices in the Holocaust were just following orders? Could we call them all accomplices?"

The methodology was devious as it used actors as mock subjects so that participants could be tricked into believing they were subjecting people to pain at the direction of those leading the experiment. The experimenter was therefore in an authoritative role, the subject was deemed a 'teacher' and the actors played the role of 'learners'. The experimenter encouraged the subject to give electric shocks to the 'learner'. However, there were no actual shocks given as the sounds of distress the subjects heard were faked.

It was made to appear to the real subjects that the actors were their peers and they were randomly given the role of either teacher or learner. In reality it was not random as the volunteers were always played in the teacher role. They were then led to different rooms, from where they could hear but not see one another.

The teacher was then subjected to a real electric shock in order to demonstrate what would supposedly happen to the learner. The teacher was then asked to share with the learner a list of word pairs and subsequently test them to see if they got the pairings correct. When the actors have incorrect responses the teacher was instructed to administer an electric shock. The teacher was also instructed to increase the apparent voltage each time a wrong answer was given.

The distress the teacher heard when shocks were apparently administered were actually pre-recorded sounds played when the teacher used a switch he believed gave shocks. The tension was increased by having the actors bang on the separating wall after the voltage level had increased. In one experiment the anxiety level was deliberately ramped up by the actor mentioning to the volunteers that they suffered from a heart condition.

By the stage the actors were banging on the wall in feigned distress, several research subjects asked to check on the 'learner'. Some participants also asked the experimenters questions about the purpose of the study. However, disturbingly, most carried on administering shocks after being told that they would not be held responsible for their actions. Despite continuing after this reassurance, some participants showed signs of distress on hearing screams from the learners.

The experimenters had a hierarchy of pre-planned verbal prompts prepared which were designed to push the subjects to continue administering shocks. These ranged from "Please continue" and "The experiment requires that you continue" to "It is absolutely essential that you continue" and "You have no other choice, you must go on". The experimenters presented themselves therefore as both calm and authoritarian.

The experimenters were also versed in particular verbal prods to give if the participant said certain things. For example, were the teacher to ask whether the shocks could cause long-term damage to the learner, the experimenter was trained to say: "Although the shocks may be painful, there is no permanent tissue damage, so please go on."

The experiment was only halted if each of the four main verbal prods had been used or the participant had given what they believed to be the maximum shock three times in a row. Research subjects were led to believe that this was 450 volts.

The results of the experiment were surprising to a number of people with an interest in the subject. Prior to the experiment Milgram had asked his faculty colleagues, several postgraduate psychology students and 40 psychiatrists about how far they expected participants to go before insisting on stopping. Each of these groups believed that only a small minority would continue to the maximum voltage, with psychiatrists being slightly more pessimistic than the psychology students and academics.

In reality, 65 percent of the 40 people taking part in the first experiment progressed to the maximum voltage, despite the apparent suffering they were causing. It is reassuring to know that all participants at some point questioned the value of the experiment and they showed distress by trembling, sweating, biting their lips and digging their nails into their flesh. Nevertheless, for the sake of making strangers learn pairs of words, the vast majority obeyed instructions to inflict pain and 'deliver' what could have been fatal shocks.

It would be nice to believe that the people taking part in the first experiment just happened to be particularly obedient. However, the experiment and variations on it have been performed over the decades and in different settings with different sorts of groups, yielding similar results – in excess 60 percent of subjects being willing to administer the highest level of shock.

It can be argued that Milgram's attempt to show in laboratory conditions why people participated in the Holocaust was flawed, as there was more to Nazism than just people following instructions. It was also based on the hate and fear of particular groups and influenced by economics, the media and mysticism. Nevertheless, the number of people willing to act with cruelty just because an authority figure told them to do so is still extremely alarming.

Both the Stanford and Milgram experiments have received much criticism over the decades, not least for putting research volunteers through extreme distress. The findings, however, are also distressing and cannot be ignored. Since people did experience such distress to help produce the findings it seems even more important that we consider the results seriously.

From my perspective the findings have even greater ramifications now than they did when the experiments were first conducted. This is because the political, social and economic world changes faster than ever before, with culture being perpetually contested and pulled in different directions. Therefore, as we have seen with the 'Arab spring' and its aftermath, different people gain authority for a while only to be overthrown by new 'authorities'. This process happens throughout the world and in organisations of all sizes, not just in revolutionary politics.

In tandem with new authority figures rising up, there are sections of societies or organisations willing to follow them. However, there is nothing to guarantee that new powers will ultimately be any more just, ethical, honest or stable than those who came before. Nevertheless, if they gain trust they can get people to obey their instructions, however damaging these may be.

In the context economic crises and political and social instability, large parts of any population will always be hoping for change – or to somehow go back to a different time. This makes us vulnerable to the manipulations of those who promise something new or play on nostalgia. Sadly, it is often the case that society simply wanders blindly from one snake pit to another. We might be injected with a slightly different venom than before but we are still in a snake pit.

Insights from people like Zimbardo and Milgram, however, give us hope that we can learn to spot dangerous leaders and pathological cultures and resist being subsumed and corrupted by them. There may always be people who will be desperate to conform to authority but a growing number instinctively question it. Whilst the experiments demonstrate our vulnerability to conformity, it is important to recognise that mentally well adults are responsible for our own actions, regardless of the manipulations of those around us.

Many readers will have witnessed the sort of oppression demonstrated in Milgram's and Zimbardo's experiments being played out, either in their own lives or in the public sphere. Human beings have long memories and a unique ability to document experiences. Therefore, we must hope that, generally, the systems and cultures we create in the future will be better and less oppressive than those we were subjected to in the past.

Zimbardo and Milgram showed that normal, reasonable people can be made to be oppressive and cruel if put in oppressive cultures – and became mentally disturbed as a result. By the same token we must assume – and we see plenty of evidence in life to support this – that people treat others with dignity, kindness and understanding if they are themselves within a healthy supportive system. Even people who have historically been malicious can be encouraged to conform to a less hostile culture.

Psychopaths shape culture and cultures support psychopaths

Not only can small numbers of psychopaths create psychopathic cultures within organisations or societies, some cultures appear to produce more psychopaths. If a nation can be infected by psychopaths and then increase the population of psychopaths, it is critical that we understand how to decontaminate society of psychopathic 'values'.

Rather than by trying to 'cure' psychopaths, it may turn out that the problem of cultural psychopathy is dealt with by encouraging communities where ethics, honesty, kindness, sharing, humour and compassion are valued more highly than what can be gained by being callous, selfish, abusive and deceitful.

Because the clinical disorder stems from an abnormality of the brain, there may always be some psychopaths in any society. However, if we live in a society where psychopathic qualities are rejected and scorned rather than admired, the power of the psychopath could be limited. By contrast, if we create societies where greed, mendacity, shallowness, cruelty and aggression are rewarded we should not be surprised if our culture becomes more psychopathic and for the population of callous destructive people to increase.

The American clinical psychologist Martha Stout has argued that Western societies produce more people with antisocial personality disorders than societies with less individualistic and materialistic values. In her 2005 book, *The Sociopath Next Door,* Stout explores reasons why the USA produces more people with the disorder than other countries.

Dr Stout favours the term sociopath over psychopath, but essentially she is referring, as other experts quoted in this book do, to people who lack a conscience. Alluding to factors influencing the incidence of the condition, and suggesting that culture may be more important than specific child-rearing practices, she says:

> It is entirely possible that the environmental influences on sociopathy are more reliably linked with broad cultural characteristics than with any particular child-rearing factors. Indeed, relating the occurrence of sociopathy to cultures has so far been more fruitful for researchers than looking for the answer in specific child-rearing variables. Instead of being the product of childhood abuse within the family, or of attachment disorder, maybe sociopathy involves some interaction between the innate neurological wiring of individuals and the larger society in which they end up spending their lives.
>
> This hypothesis is bound to be disappointing to some people, because though altering the conditions of pregnancy, childbirth, and child treatment on a massive scale would be no small project, changing the values and belief systems of an entire culture is an even more gigantic undertaking, with a time horizon that seems distant and discouraging. We might feel a little less daunted if we were to identify a set of child-rearing practices that we could try to correct in our lifetimes. But perhaps society is the true parent of certain things, and we will eventually find that, as William Ralph Inge said in the early twentieth century, "The proper time to influence the character of a child is about 100 years before he is born."

While I share Stout's belief that culture is a key factor influencing the proportion of psychopaths we have in each society, I am more optimistic about the potential for positive changes that could improve matters more quickly than she suggests. In Chapter 1 I used the example of politics in the UK shifting to the right and controllers of public services, like the National Health Service, conforming to a more ruthless and materialistic culture. These examples illustrate that in a short time collectivist societies can become fragmented and distorted by the encroachment of values many would deem psychopathic.

Greed, aggression, exploitation, individualism, selfishness and callousness slithered around British culture and poisoned communities frighteningly quickly from the end of the 1970s. That is not to say that these unpleasant qualities had never been present in the UK but that they had never before been embraced so proudly and sold so aggressively by British politicians.

Although many people get swept along in cultural changes and politicians are good at getting the public to adopt and proselytise values that ultimately harm them, there is always opposition – even if the resistance is trampled underfoot at the time. There are many people who observed the shift to right in the UK, the USA and other nations and were alarmed by the attacks on collectivism and community by people who seemed to be as cold, calculating and vindictive as any psychopath. Angered, outraged and scarred by the experience, many of those who noticed and lamented the shift towards a more callous culture, now have a greater ability to hold instigators to account than citizens have ever had before.

Many who observed the way miners and other unionised workers were treated and other injustices metered out by Establishment figures over the decades have gone onto be lawyers, journalists, activists, politicians, social scientists and teachers. More still have embraced social media and play invaluable roles in disseminating information about cover-ups from the past, atrocious behaviour of Establishment figures and contemporary injustices.

Terrible truths that powerful figures managed to bury from the view of the masses in previous decades have now become apparent for all to see. This is extremely significant because it limits trust in 'authority' figures and makes the public more assertive and critical.

The rapid process of revelation is of course not just happening in the UK, USA and other Western countries. The dissemination of information about the cruelty, deceit and corruption of powerful figures, via the internet and other media, is having an astonishing and cathartic impact all around the world. The social media helped bring about the Arab spring, the aftershocks of which are still being felt as I write.

When newspapers and broadcasters are fearful of litigation by powerful people – or implicated in scandals themselves – brave individuals on Twitter and personal blogs can be counted on to get information about wrongdoing into the public domain. This ability to undermine and challenge traditional power structures is nothing short of revolutionary.

Information is power and the shift in power resulting from mobile phones with cameras, wider web access and social media should not be underestimated. We have never lived in a time when so many people are educated, literate, politically aware and willing and able to share information and perspectives with so many other people.

Psychopaths and psychopathic cultures gain and maintain power by deceit, playing people off against one another, isolating victims and intimidation. As more and more people find it easier to expose deceit, engage with other people to gain a bigger picture and challenge the lies of oppressors, the power of individual psychopaths and psychopathic cultures diminishes.

Technology is often a double-edged sword. The same communications technology that has helped capitalist values take hold around the world and, by doing that, consolidate power in the hands of a ruthless minority, also allows those values and those people to be challenged with an intensity and clarity that would have been unthinkable in previous centuries.

If capitalism itself promotes psychopathy and thrives on the callous, cold, calculating, brutal aggressiveness of psychopaths, it has also produced its own antidote. As well as spawning technology that allows people to find ways of transmitting and receiving uncensored information from around the world, it has made time for people to think and feel. These conditions give the public a better chance than ever before to challenge abuses of power and ultimately tackle psychopathic cultures.

The fact, identified by Martha Stout, that the expression of psychopathy varies greatly in different cultural environments should give us a cause for optimism. This is because it suggests that societies can develop mechanisms that limit the power of psychopaths.

This may seem like a big project and some may be put off by any suggestion of social engineering but it must be acknowledged that psychopaths and psychopathic cultures hinder the well-being and development of society. It is also worth noting – recalling history – that if compassionate, empathic and ethically-minded people do not influence the way in which societies develop then ruthless, brutal, unethical, deceitful people do.

There are of course many barriers to societies developing insight into psychopaths and psychopathic cultures, let alone creating cultures that reject psychopathic mind-sets. If capitalism itself is grounded in and fosters psychopathy then there are likely to be powerful people doing all they can to prevent the public from recognising this.

Attempts to criticise anything about capitalism are often met with accusations that the critics are communists. There has been little development in this simplistic dismissal since the 1950s, as we saw in the 2012 US election. An obvious reason why people criticising psychopathic cultures are attacked, discredited and undermined is that people benefiting most from psychopathic cultures are powerful psychopaths.

One of the most valuable aspects of anthropological fieldwork is that it makes researchers look at their own societies afresh. By stepping outside of your familiar reality and living in communities where people do things differently, think differently and describe life differently, you are encouraged to see the strangeness of your own society.

Therefore, as well as developing insights into the place where they conducted fieldwork, the anthropologist has the potential to reflect on, question and challenge aspects of the familiar world they grew up in. However, the social scientist may well be criticised and attempts have been made to discredit some for questioning assumptions about how their own society should be.

As well as being grounded in psychology, Stout's approach of illuminating issues related to psychopaths in society is anthropological as she makes cross-cultural comparisons and attempts to understand cultural reasons for differences. Rather than just accept the way in which her society functions, Dr Stout has managed to take a step back and look at the USA with perspective by comparing and contrasting it with other countries.

This effort at being neutral and looking at her own country with clear-eyed honesty has helped Stout develop useful insights into factors that may make the USA and other Western capitalist systems particularly prone to psychopathy. In *The Sociopath Next Door* she wrote:

> Though sociopathy seems to be universal and timeless, there is credible evidence that some cultures contain fewer sociopaths than do other cultures. Intriguingly, sociopathy would appear to be relatively rare in certain East Asian countries, notably Japan and China. Studies conducted in both rural and urban areas of Taiwan have found a remarkably low prevalence of antisocial personality disorder, ranging from 0.03 percent to 0.14 percent, which is not none but is impressively less than the Western world's approximate average of four percent.

She also said:

Disturbingly, the prevalence of sociopathy in the United States seems to be increasing. The 1991 Epidemiologic Catchment Area study, sponsored by the National Institute of Mental Health, reported that in the fifteen years preceding the study, the prevalence of antisocial personality disorder had nearly doubled among the young in America, It would be difficult, closing in on impossible, to explain such a dramatically rapid shift in terms of genetics or neurobiology.

Apparently, cultural influences play a very important role in the development (or not) of sociopathy in any given population. Few people would disagree that, from the Wild West of the past to the corporate outlaws of the present, American society seems to allow and even encourage me-first attitudes devoted to the pursuit of domination. Robert Hare writes that he believes "our society is moving in the direction of permitting, reinforcing, and in some instances actually valuing some of the traits listed in the Psychopathy Checklist – traits such as impulsivity, irresponsibility, lack of remorse."

In this opinion he is joined by theorists who propose that North American culture, which holds individualism as a central value, tends to foster the development of antisocial behavior, and also to disguise it. In other words, in America, the guiltless manipulation of other people "blends" with social expectations to a much greater degree than it would in China or other more group-centered societies.

Making the extremely valuable suggestion that it is possible to produce cultures which not only produce less psychopaths but also respond more effectively to those who are innately psychopathic, Stout added:

I believe there is a shinier side of this coin, too, one that begs the question of why certain cultures seem to encourage prosocial behaviour. So much against the odds, how is it that some societies have a positive impact on incipient sociopaths, who are born with an inability to process interpersonal emotions in the usual way? I would like to suggest that the overriding belief systems of certain cultures encourage born sociopaths to compensate cognitively for what they are missing emotionally. In contrast with our extreme emphasis on individualism and personal control, certain cultures, many in East Asia, dwell theologically on the interrelatedness of all living things.

The Sociopath Next Door was published before the banking crisis, the credit crunch and the bursting of the debt-fuelled economic bubble – and at a time when numerous powerful wealthy people were spending a great deal of money to promote the view that climate change has nothing to do with human activity. The book had very mixed reviews on release, split sharply between those who accept the premise and those who believe it to be sensationalist and scaremongering.

If it was published now, following exposure of massive fraud in the banking system, the housing market shown to be held up and consequently jeopardised by lies, journalists jailed for phone hacking and powerful paedophiles uncovered, the response might be different. However, given that wealthy, powerful people tend to do disproportionately well in times of economic turbulence and recession, there are no doubt many who would summarily reject any criticism of capitalist values.

Given the way in which terms like psychopath and sociopath change subtlety over time, the subjectivity of observers and the problems of assessing people accurately – particularly for non-captive subjects – we may never have accurate figures on the percentage of psychopaths in any society. However, given what I have said about the distillation and distribution of psychopathic cultures within societies and the devastating effect a small number of toxic individuals can have, the numbers may be less significant than their impact.

It only takes one or two coldly determined politicians to destroy several industries and to successfully push a pernicious culture of selfish individualism. It only takes a handful of powerful figures in a paedophile ring to cast a dark shadow over a nation while trashing the lives of thousands of people. It only takes a small number of self-interested, inept or crooked bankers, hedge fund managers and investors to bring economies to their knees.

An even greater challenge than identifying individual psychopaths and curtailing their activities is understanding how psychopathic cultures form and are unwittingly nurtured. Unless we learn how to identify the encroachment of psychopathic cultures and restrain them, they can become toxic, amorphous, unaccountable and devastating monsters.

Chapter 4 – Power, politics and psychopathy: Kings, priests, cowboys and colonialists

Just as it seems inevitable, natural and acceptable to many people that corporations exploit people, the law and the environment to make as much money and pay as little tax as possible, political corruption is often regarded as an inevitable reality. Some might imagine that it has always been the case that people in prominent roles in societies use their authority to gain wealth and to secure more power for themselves, their families and allies.

One may try to use anthropology superficially to make blunt claims that society's leaders – whether presidents, prime ministers, Kings, priests, tribal chiefs or shamans have always relentlessly deceived societies for their own personal advancement. This, however, is not supported by evidence. The level of social equality or inequality in societies has varied enormously under different systems and there is at least as much economic inequality under capitalism as any system the world has known.

It is certainly true that roles of leadership in hunter and gatherer societies link to the expression of social – and sometimes supernatural – power. However, when people gain authority in small scale societies where people all know one another, that power is granted and maintained because the community knows the chief or shaman well and it recognises their capacity to lead.

In some societies the role of the chief is inherited, but the level of inequality in such societies is still much lower than in modern capitalist states. Having a slightly larger hut or some ceremonial head-wear does not estrange a chief from the realities of his fellow man as much as billions of pounds, owning private planes, fortress-like houses and employing large numbers of lawyers does. A callous chief who disregards the needs of his hunter-gather community might well get an axe in the head. A psychopathic politician or chief executive may get away with crimes thanks to their teams of expensive lawyers and creative accountants.

Hunter and gatherer societies, while they may have an elite level of chiefs, elders and shamans, are and have always been the most egalitarian in the world. Community spirit and a culture of instinctive sharing are vital for a society to survive against the threats and tribulations living within nature brings.

Such societies have interesting and effective levelling mechanisms in place to prevent one or a small number of people from amassing resources at the expense of others. This may take the form of anything from mockery of arrogance, morality tales or gambling games to ensure everyone retains roughly the same level of wealth. If one person gets 'too big for their boots' their neighbours will bring them back to size, drive them from the community – or worse.

To a capitalist mentality this may seem absurd. This is because we have been brought up to believe that deviousness and ruthlessness should be rewarded and communities only progress if the most ambitious people are encouraged to thrive. However, curiously, these inclinations and perceptions are the very reason levelling techniques have evolved. By acting as a safeguard against greed and domination, levelling mechanisms protect society from disintegrating into violent conflicts fuelled by jealousy, anger and resentment.

As different modes of production have developed and waned, from hunter-gatherer societies via feudalism and communistic systems, to the current dominance of globalised capitalism, not only has inequality and conflict increased but the legitimacy of leaders has been lost. There are few societies left in the world where the community can observe the qualities of their neighbour and bestow power on them with confidence that they will exercise it justly and not abuse it for personal gain.

Kevin Dutton, a research psychologist at the University of Oxford, has posited the controversial suggestion that it is useful for societies to have a certain proportion of psychopaths. In his 2012 book, *The Wisdom of Psychopaths: What Saints, Spies, and Serial Killers Can Teach Us About Success,* Dutton argues that psychopaths are essentially positive people and their ambition, fearlessness and ruthlessness makes them natural leaders of communities. He concentrates rather less on their lack of conscience and their lack of insight into normal human feelings.

I have deep reservations about Professor Dutton's thesis, not least because of the anthropological reality – as outlined above – that even hunter-gather societies curtail the qualities we associate with psychopathy. Furthermore, if you consider the role of the shaman in tribal societies, they have exceptional levels of empathy rather than an absence of it. When entering trances, shamans develop a heightened empathy of patients and also for animals and the habitat itself. One might assume that the best hunters in such communities lack empathy, but to track an animal on foot for hours demonstrates an empathy for that species alien to modern shoppers.

Nevertheless, Dutton does have a point when it comes to leadership in contemporary capitalist societies, though it should be appreciated that not all societies are capitalist and it is not inevitable that global capitalism will be our 'end point'. Capitalist values are currently prevalent, however, and it does appear that conscienceless, domineering, grasping, egocentric people who lack empathy have certain advantages in materialistic, highly individualistic societies.

Another way of putting this is large, economically complex, money-orientated societies have a particular vulnerability when it comes to psychopaths. This is partly because they can easily move and find new feeding grounds – thereby avoiding on-going scrutiny from their original community – who may well have noted their pathology. It is also because there are so many positions in our modern societies where cold, calculating qualities and a lack of conscience are rewarded financially and with power and prestige.

Troublingly, it appears that the more complex, unstable and chaotic an economy or organisation becomes, the more opportunities there are for ruthless psychopaths to exploit systems and seize power. A suspicious person might suggest that powerful psychopaths cause instability in society in order to gain more power.

Given that this is exactly how psychopaths operate in small groups – creating tension and playing people off against one another – it is not beyond the realms of possibility that powerful politicians, financiers and industrialists do the very same thing on a grand scale. In fact, given their capacity to do these things, they may well believe they would be foolish to do anything but.

Positions of power through history

It has been argued by psychologists and business experts that organisations existing under capitalism are ideal habitats for psychopaths to thrive. However, there have been many other structures existing in history that have also been amenable environments for those with psychopathic qualities.

Unfortunately for most of history, societies have had little ability to legally control non-convicted psychopaths. Although there were undoubtedly observers in religious organisations, armies, workhouses, prisons and orphanages who were concerned by the consciencelessness and vindictiveness of dominant figures, their menace coupled with the absence of medical classification would have meant they were difficult to curtail.

The military is an obvious environment in which an aggressive, ruthless and callous person could capitalise on their qualities – provided that they could tolerate the discipline. Whether a junior soldier joining an army to satisfy a desire to kill or someone who manages to rise to a senior rank as a result of their need to control others, psychopaths may be drawn to military organisations.

One might assume that psychopaths find it easier to dwell and rise within ramshackle military forces that are desperate for conscripts. However, given the many atrocities carried out by well-trained soldiers in American, British and Israeli militaries in recent decades, we have to conclude that this is unlikely to be the case. Furthermore, when we take into account the cruelty inflicted by intelligence officers within MI5, MI6 and the CIA in recent years, we have to consider the possibility that people at all levels on whatever side of any war or campaign may have and express psychopathic qualities.

The reader may be thinking at this stage "but armies and military intelligence services are *meant* to be ruthless". This is true but – as the detainment of prisoners at Guantanamo Bay and 'extraordinary rendition' of terror suspects showed – torturing and dehumanising people is not only gratuitously sadistic but also counterproductive. When representatives of an aggrieved society, hit by terror attacks and claiming to be 'civilised' and rational, detains without trial and then tortures suspects, any claim to a moral high ground is lost. Furthermore, the brutal and insensitive process, once publicised, creates more angry young 'radicals'.

If the impulsivity and short-termism of the psychopathic mindset is allowed to impinge upon what should be careful, diplomatically insightful and forward-thinking military decisions, a whole nation can appear to be callous, racist, brutal and corrupt. This clearly does not help efforts to tackle terrorism and instead plays into the hands of psychopaths on the 'other side' who gain power by presenting western powers as 'evil'.

For those who suffer as a consequence of callous military, intelligence agency and political decisions, it may well seem that powerful states are psychopathic. Those of us who live in these states therefore have a responsibility to challenge psychopathic inclinations of our 'leaders' and communicate to aggrieved people in other countries that we do not share their views.

Religions are another habitat in which psychopaths often have been able to hide and gain power over others. The subject of power within religion is clearly a controversial area and judging by some peoples' response to my last book, about apocalyptic religions and cults, one that can cause a lot of anger. My intention here is not to attack and invalidate the beliefs of others but to illustrate how religious organisations of all sizes can enable people with psychopathic traits to exert control over others and exploit them in a multitude of ways.

If we consider the establishment of religions, as they form as cults or sects around charismatic people regarded as prophets – as well as the complex hierarchical power structures of well-established religious organisations – we can identify psychopathy in action. That is not to say all prophets are psychopaths.

Some cult leaders have no doubt had personality disorders but it is often the case that founders of religions are well-meaning people and it is others who subsequently become powerful within the religions who express psychopathic tendencies. This sometimes happens when a religion becomes wealthy or large enough to become hierarchical. It is also more likely when a religious organisation develops substantial power over vulnerable members of the community, such as children.

The history of religion is to a large extent the history of power battles and social and organisational fracture. It is rarely the case that a new religious movement has no links with more established faiths. In some cases new movements are inspired by antagonism towards an established religion. In other cases a schism within one religious organisation leads to a new sect, Church or cult being established.

One example of this is the Branch Davidians, a Seventh-day Adventist splinter group formed in 1955 in anticipation of the return of Christ. The Seventh-day Church itself, which was formed in 1930, grew out of the Millerite moment, which was itself founded in 1833 on a belief that Christ would return a decade later.

As well as illustrating how religious history is littered with power struggles comparable in intensity to those happening within politics, industry and gangs, the Branch Davidians case is also linked to the violent and sadistic abuses of power. In 1993 dozens of sect members were killed by bullets and fire in a Federal Bureau of Investigation raid that followed a 51 day siege.

Some – including myself in my last book *Beyond the End of the World* (2010) – have emphasised the role of the US government and the media in contributing to the tragedy by encouraging the doomed raid. However, it should be noted that sect leader David Koresh had been accused by several people of sexual and violent abuse of children. Furthermore, the extreme level of control Koresh exerted over sect members, including enforced celibacy of other men and limiting the food of individuals, has led to some experts to characterise him as a psychopath.

As the Branch Davidians example shows, when religions or cults are led by people exhibiting psychopathic qualities who are good at finding and articulating 'evidence' that the external world itself is dangerous and corrupt, a split between 'us' and 'them' becomes easily exaggerated and exploited.

This is something that also happens frequently in mental hospitals, as the psychopath manipulates others into acting as pawns in his or her battle with staff. It is quite common for perfectly rational people to be led to believe that psychiatrists, politicians, security services and police are merely agents of oppression. Therefore the potential for vulnerable people in cults or on psychiatric wards to be manipulated by psychopaths is great.

We do not have detailed enough knowledge of the early interpersonal dynamics within established religions to know how particular individuals came to exert the greatest power. Therefore we can only speculate about psychopathic traits of those who shaped dominant religions. However, by looking at the actions of religions through time, we have to acknowledge the manipulative, brutal and sometimes sadistic aspects of religious authority.

Examples of what many would now regard as psychopathy in religions and smaller cults are, tragically, many. The Crusades, 'witch' burnings, child abuse, cult leaders encouraging murder and suicide, ritual sacrifice and ethnic-cleansing based on religious differences are vivid examples of religiously sanctioned violence.

There are also more subtle examples of psychopath-like exploitation in operation within religions. In Christianity, the former rule against remarrying after a husband's death would now seem to many people like an obvious scam to take wealth from widows. Childless widows were prevented from remarrying and therefore ultimately gave or bequeathed their wealth to the Church.

The fact that the Church often offered solace, kindness and companion to such women does not make its ultimate exploitation of them any less cruel or less manipulative. In fact, the superficial kindness the Church offered to the vulnerable widows it preyed upon to amass wealth, demonstrates an exploitative, calculating culture no different from any gang.

When accounting for some of the more brutal eras of powerful religions it is important to acknowledge that those perpetuating violence would have often been zealous 'true believers' rather than predatory psychopaths using religious dogma as an excuse for sadism. This does not make it any better, it merely shows that, under certain conditions, a formerly gentle person can turned into a torturer or killer.

It is impossible for us to look back through time at things like the crusades and witch-trials and burnings with enough accuracy to know how many of those involved participated through genuine beliefs, blind obedience or inherent sadism. However, from modern accounts of child abuse by the clergy it is quite clear that many of those involved acted in such a callous, deliberate and sadistic manner that psychopathy must be a strong consideration.

To commit such violent and cruel acts to children and conspire with others to do so, it seems extremely likely that many child-abusing priests did not believe key aspects of the religion they were employed to sell. Jesus, as presented by the biblical accounts, comes across as gentle, kind and compassionate and places great value on children. However, as the Bible is made up of many myths with a myriad of different interpretations, it is tragically possible to strongly believe in certain key biblical themes while also abusing children. For example, the belief that all human beings are born into sin can be twisted into an excuse to beat children and abuse and exploit them in other ways.

Ironically, it is the psychopath – rather than children generally – who is born with an innate tendency towards maliciousness and selfishness. Therefore it is both interesting and disturbing that psychopathic priests have used the concepts of innate sinfulness and 'evil' as an excuse to brutalise and mistreat women accused of witchcraft and children. It is the same dogma about sin that has given missionaries an excuse to travel around the world and impose new beliefs on certain cultural and ethnic groups.

While it would be wrong to suggest that everyone who imposes beliefs on others is psychopathic, the fact is that the missionary endeavour has often been the silk glove on the iron fist of colonialism. While the missionary was – perhaps in a well-meaning and zealous manner – attempting to eradicate local beliefs, other colonialists were plundering the resources of nations, stealing land, playing tribes off against one another and gaining regional and international military advantage. These actions and this desire to exploit and dominate have a distinctly psychopathic flavour.

As well as ruthless, strategically-minded agents of colonising states, such as Cecil Rhodes, at the heart of plunders of other countries, there were many less privileged people taking advantage of new frontiers. The 'Wild West' is probably the most vivid example of a setting in which a psychopathic mindset (aided by the gun) ruled.

The extermination of native Americans, general lawlessness and violent efforts to shore out the newly plundered land and resources were not the actions of empathic and conscientious people. Many of those who left Britain and other European countries to exploit the 'new world' were people who were fleeing crimes or scandals.

Given the context, in which it was deemed acceptable for human beings – and the buffalo they needed for survival – to be gunned down, and the shady backgrounds of many of those who left Europe for America, it is not surprising that a psychopathic mindset was rewarded and therefore dominated.

The history of film is full of portrayals of gun-slinging psychopaths in the Wild West. Most of us have grown up watching colourful psychopaths shooting each other, blowing open safes, cheating at cards, killing 'Injuns', drinking heavily and living chaotically violent lives. As older films failed to show heads graphically being blown off and bodies being mutilated – as some do now – it is a certainty that the Westerns many of us grew up watching made the era look less brutal than it actually was.

In addition to the caricature of the wild-eyed, volatile and murderous outlaw, a more controlled and prosperous psychopath has frequently been portrayed in Westerns and subsequent genres. The archetype of the exploitative, callous, land-grabbing, domineering and sly psychopath, supported by brutal henchmen, continues to feature in films – whether about mining on Mars, investment banks, corrupt police and lawyers or virtual reality.

The seminal 1953 western *Shane* is about a former gun-slinger drawn into helping a community contend with a ruthless and vindictive cattle baron who is attempting to drive struggling homesteaders from their land. It is a classic movie and its echoes can be seen throughout movie history, from *Star Wars* to tales about gangsters, political corruption and environmental battles. The backdrop has changed over time but the figure of the cruel, powerful, antisocial and morally bankrupt psychopath victimising the vulnerable has always been in the shadows pulling strings.

It could be argued that the popularity of the theme of the small guy taking on the oppressive, ruthless exploiter of land and people is indicative of the healthiness of individualism within American culture. In the movies decent people always rise up against those who have unfairly amassed power and wealth. However, the pervasiveness of the ruthless psychopathic land owner, politician and corporate head in television and film should be of great concern.

This is in part because the archetype clearly rings true for viewers but also because, in the real world, such people are brought down to size less often. Access to expensive lawyers (the hired gun-slinger of our age), the ears of politicians and the mouths of PR gurus gives the successful psychopath many advantages over the contemporary Shanes of political activism, environmentalism and non-traditional media.

Despite the risks of rising up against, criticising, and ridiculing the powerful, the public have become increasingly brave and effective at challenging politicians, corporations, religions, bankers and other 'VIPs' perceived to act against the needs of society or outside the realms of decency.

The social media has been a critical weapon in the battle against the undeservedly powerful. The shifting sands of technology are not only changing the format of the media and how it is accessed but it is also altering the power balance within society – much to the distress of those who are accustomed to owning and wielding that power. This highly significant development will be discussed in some detail within Chapter 8.

Whose politicians are they anyway?

Even in purportedly democratic countries, like the UK and the US, the accepted reality seems to be that a key role of politicians is to promote businesses, while supposedly representing ordinary voters. There are glaring contradictions in this. Business wealth does not necessarily trickle down to ordinary people, and bolstering some industries can be detrimental to communities. An obvious example of this is the armaments industry but there are many other industries that have questionable benefits for citizens and are damaging to health, communities and the environment.

British prime ministers and other world leaders seem to see nothing wrong in going to arms fairs and acting as cheerleaders for companies wishing to sell weapons to undemocratic, oppressive regimes. When the apparatus of war is a major export for some technologically advanced countries, it would appear that politicians feel able to ignore any morality and social responsibility they may have previously claimed to have when electioneering.

More importantly, by brokering arms deals they are likely to be disregarding the ethics and views of the citizens who pay their wages and who voted them in. Once politicians are in power there is often little the public can do to stop them using their position to broker weapons deals. "National interests" is the glib and questionable response given when the public questions the wisdom of arming dictatorships.

Supporting the armaments industry to sell weapons to oppressive regimes clearly is a problematic area for politicians. It makes them look two-faced and exploitative at best and malicious and war-mongering to many. On the one hand, political leaders must be seen to promote business interests of their country. On the other hand, they will have strategic allegiances with other countries – even if those states are despotic and led by cruel, vengeful, immoral tyrants.

Strategic alliances with tyrannical regimes may go back decades but strategic links to key areas may go back much further, forged in wars and colonial periods. Voters in Western states are aware of the need for strategic alliances and may consequently turn a blind eye to weapons sales in the hope that politicians are working in the interests of society. In reality, brokering weapons sales may merely boost the under-taxed profits of callous transnational corporations while ensuring decades of overseas wars.

Western politicians' involvement with the arms industry also helps fuel resentment and terrorism against countries like Britain and America who broker deals and produce and sell weapons. Furthermore, even after peace breaks out – often against the will of ruthless military leaders – countries are often left littered with land mines that kill and maim indiscriminately.

Weapons producers are extremely powerful and have strong links with spy agencies but there are other industries where global influence is as important as money in influencing politicians' relationship with the businesses. Some of these industries may have as damaging impacts on human societies as wars do. For example, the newspaper and broadcast news industry is not as overtly destructive as war but its insidious impact on public consciousness is colossal.

In 2012 it was found that the then UK culture minister Jeremy Hunt had secretly supported Rupert Murdoch's efforts to gain a greater share of the British media. The politician was not punished but ultimately promoted and given responsibility for the NHS – some might say the task of dismantling and privatising the health service.

The fact that a minister was covertly working on behalf of a controversial media giant – already under investigation for phone hacking – shocked many members of the public. Even experienced politicians were surprised when Hunt was rewarded for his actions by being given one of the most prized government positions.

The support for Murdoch's media land grab became public knowledge when a series of text messages and emails between Hunt, his aide, the Murdoch family and their News Corporation staff were submitted to the Leveson Inquiry into media standards. Another minister, Vince Cable, had been sacked from overseeing the News Corp's bid to take control of British Sky Broadcasting (BSkyB), as he was found to be partial – though not on the side of the press baron.

When Hunt was also found to be partial – but in the Murdoch camp – his aide Adam Smith was used as Hunt's "whipping boy", according to the seasoned Labour Party politician Dennis Skinner. The "whipping boy" Smith then apparently resigned. Some MPs were not convinced that Smith had resigned out of choice, not least Dennis Skinner who quipped in Parliament: "When posh boys get in trouble, they sack the servants".

A bloodthirsty business

The above example is not designed to suggest that anyone concerned is a psychopath, but to illustrate the Machiavellian nature of politics and reflect on the relative allegiance of politicians to voters and big business.

There are of course many less subtle examples of exploitative cultures at work. The term psychopathy was not used then – let alone psychopathic culture – but the example of Cecil Rhodes exploiting Africa on behalf of the British Empire, playing tribes off against one another to plunder resources and maintaining the veneer of 'respectability' as communities are destroyed in the name of 'progress' is chilling.

It is also chilling because Rhodes was extremely 'sophisticated' and supported by the British Establishment while brutally preying on a continent. It is further chilling because the Imperialist agenda of Rhodes ranked people in terms of race and deemed black people to be unevolved and requiring external control by a white master race. He would have made an exceptional Nazi.

Some people, even today, use the fact that there have been many civil wars in former British colonies to push a racist agenda. With a disregard for history and anthropology, racists pushing such an agenda are fond of claiming that 'natives' were inherently savage and therefore will invariably fight unless controlled by white masters.

Such assertions fail to recognise the impact of history generally and, specifically, how exerting control on people then subsequently retreating leaves trauma, poverty and a power vacuum. The power vacuum is frequently filled with the most brutal people – who often mirror the ruthlessness of the former colonial oppressor – battling for supremacy.

This has not only happened in African states but also in South America, Middle Eastern countries and India. A comparable process also happens within organised crime when leaders are jailed or killed. Sudden power vacuums in tense environments containing valuable resources is a tried and tested recipe for great bloodshed.

The example of Cecil Rhodes is important to our exploration of psychopathic cultures and toxic empires for a number of reasons. It is the story of a sickly English teenager who was encouraged to go to Africa in 1871 to alleviate his asthma. After a cotton plantation venture failed the ruthless young man, having turned his attention to diamond mining, went on to control the worldwide market of diamonds and become a politician.

The company he formed, De Beers, still controls the global market of diamonds. However, Rhodes' desire was not simply to make money and be a powerful politician but to expand the British Empire around the world and create a global Anglo Saxon master race. Having fortunately fallen short of this mission during his life, but having plundered a continent, furthered his supremacist agenda and caused wars, he wrote the following in his will:

> I contend that we [the British] are the finest race in the world and that the more of the world we inhabit the better it is for the human race. Just fancy those parts that are at present inhabited by the most despicable specimens of human beings what an alteration there would be if they were brought under Anglo-Saxon influence.

The example of Rhodes is further unsettling because many at the time shared his views. He was not just some greedy, callous lone wolf but part of massive systematic colonising project. The agenda of the vast Imperialist machine Rhodes was prominent within was not so different from that of the Nazis. Rhodes happened to have success in diamond mining – which bought him political and military might – but his racist, white supremacist views unfortunately were far from unusual at the time.

A further tragedy is that, despite most people now being far less overtly racist, the process of colonisation and exploitation continues. Colonialism has become more subtle, with Imperialism being largely replaced with the neo-colonialism of faceless, amoral corporations. Large white-owned corporations have control of key global resources, including diamonds, gold, pharmaceuticals, oil and gas. Furthermore, transnational corporations often use contractors in the developing world to get work done cheaply, with working practices that would be illegal in Europe or the US.

Troublingly, due to the nature of globalisation, most of us are agents in this process. While we might criticise Rhodes' exploitative, destructive agenda, the technology I am using to write this book and many will be using to read it is related to neo-colonialism. While most of us do not have the ruthless, exploitative focus Rhodes had or share his supremacist agenda, the demand for cheaply-assembled computers, smart phones, iPads and e-readers means we are all routinely participating in exploitation.

Chapter 5 – Politicians and psychopathic characteristics

Politicians make ruthless decisions that impact upon entire populations and on the future of the planet. For every controversial decision made, there are likely to be people hurt or aggrieved. Although they are expected to listen to and represent individual constituents, politicians are often driven by personal ambitions and more influenced by powerful lobbyists than by the average voter.

Though it is often commented that politicians share many characteristics with psychopaths, they might argue that such criteria do not apply to them as they are *meant* to coolly take decisions in which people are sometimes harmed. The public is well aware of this responsibility but we are unforgiving when politicians are found to have abused their power and to be primarily driven by self-interest. Historically we rarely found out about such betrayals of voters but in recent decades the press and public have been braver at calling politicians to account.

Unfortunately there seems to be an expectation now that politicians will be arrogant, ruthless, narcissistic and insincere. Therefore when specific politicians surpass their peers in those respects, while also appearing to lack morality, alarm bells ring.

It is extremely interesting to consider certain politicians against clinical criteria used to categorise psychopaths. There are several living politicians who I have heard psychiatrists informally describe as psychopaths. I will not name any of these for obvious reasons. Defamation legislation does, however, permit me to discuss deceased politicians in relation to psychopathic characteristics.

Some readers will no doubt find, in the examples below, parallels with living people. Given the commonalities between those who seek and abuse power, such parallels are inevitable. However, the examples below have been chosen for the scope of characteristics and behaviours they collectively span and not to infer specific living politicians are psychopaths.

With each example it is valuable to consider the cultural context in which individuals emerged, amassed power and the factors which sustained their position of dominance. Although there are individuals with antisocial personality disorders in positions of great power in all kinds of settings, they are more likely to thrive if the surrounding culture tolerates and rewards psychopathic tendencies.

Idi Amin

Idi Amin was a barely-literate assistant cook in the British Colonial Army who, with support from Britain, Israel and other states, managed to become one of the most tyrannical politicians in the history of the world. Rather than a 'successful psychopath' it might be more accurate to describe him a chaotic sociopath who was in the right place at the right time. Or, for the millions of lives he destroyed, the wrong place at the right time.

Amin had a catastrophic effect on his native post-colonial Uganda, brutally killing those he felt threatened by. He forced Asians from the country and confiscated their businesses, homes and money. Many Asians fleeing Uganda in 1972 were ultimately victimised more than once because those coming to Britain were subjected to racism and mistrust after arriving. This racism continues, with far-right activists often asserting that they should be 'sent back where they came from' – seemingly oblivious to the fact that Asian Ugandans were violently expelled from a now-vanished British colony.

While Britain maintained a colony and business interests in Uganda and other African countries, the brutality and corruptibility of men like Idi Amin was of value to members of the Establishment. He achieved the rank of warrant officer, which was the highest rank possible for a black African in the colonial British army. It would appear that his rise through the ranks was more the result of his ruthlessness and brutality than his diplomacy, strategic insight or coherence.

A large and aggressive man, Amin excelled at boxing and rugby in the army. Alluding to his qualities, one officer said he was "virtually bone from the neck up, and needs things explained in words of one letter". Nevertheless – or perhaps because of this shortcoming – the British Establishment helped Amin become president of Uganda in a military coup taking place after the country gained independence. The former coloniser sought to exert influence after it had formerly withdrawn and Amin was, at that point, very much a man of the British.

Such was the unpredictability of Idi Amin's character that supporting his rise to power proved disastrous for the British Establishment. Rather than act as a puppet dictator, he turned on Britain and cut ties with British businesses after having his supply of weapons halted. Britain stopped supplying him with weapons because he was using them to wage war on his own people and creating instability in the region. Nevertheless, human rights abuses continued and Amin was responsible for approximately half a million violent deaths during his eight year presidency.

After Israel also stopped supplying Amin with weapons, in 1972, he turned to fellow dictator Muammar Gaddafi, of Libya and the Soviet Union to give him the fire-power required to continue his attack on dissenters and imagined plotters. As well as being brutal, ruthless and paranoid, Amin was also something of a buffoon but his clown-like aspects only added to his menace and unpredictability.

A good indication of both his sense of mischief or his narcissism is the ludicrously grand title he gave himself during his presidency: 'His Excellency, president for life, field marshal Al Hadji Doctor Idi Amin Dada, VC, DSO, MC, Lord of all the beasts of the earth and fishes of the seas and conqueror of the British Empire in Africa in general and Uganda in particular'. His military honours were invented by himself and he used his position to award himself a doctorate in law.

Despite all these apparent qualifications, by the time Amin was deposed, in 1979, his country was in ruin. His nationalistic 'economic war', which took business from Asians and other non-Africans and gave them to his supporters, ultimately caused industries and essential services to be lost. He was initially exiled to Libya and then moved to Saudi Arabia, where he was supported by the Saudi royal family. He died in 2003.

Footage of Idi Amin reveals a ludicrous figure, clowning about and wearing medals he had invented for himself on a garish military uniform, like a terrifying overgrown child in fancy dress. This presentation of himself as a bumbling joker may have proved an effective way of drawing attention away from his cold, ruthless, predatory nature.

As well as his own callous personality, it is important to also acknowledge the significance of Amin's military and economic ties with the UK, Israel, the USA, Libya and the Soviet Union. While it seems fair to call him a monster, Amin was very much a monster put in place and sustained by powerful, wealthy, exploitative people who sought to benefit by his presence and character. That he ultimately fell out with allies does not detract from the fact that Amin was designed to be an agent of Imperialist exploitation.

It may very well be that Idi Amin had an antisocial personality disorder but he was also the product of and part of a larger pathological culture. He was nurtured by an exploitative British colonial system and later expressions of his callousness were related to a reaction against the former colonisers. It would be convenient for us to believe that the terror he imposed on African politics stems purely from a mental aberration but it is quite clear now that the pathology was also in the systems around him.

Richard Nixon

The lives and political careers of Richard Nixon and Idi Amin overlapped but they were extremely different people who worked in very different ways to gain and attempt to sustain power. On the surface this could appear to suggest that both could not possibly have antisocial personality disorders. However, when we consider the extreme differences between the societies they lived within, we can appreciate that different psychopathic and sociopath traits are effective in different contexts.

This insight adds complexity to our attempt to understand what psychopathic cultures are and how they allow certain people to have power. To suggest that Nixon was sustained by a psychopathic culture is not the same as saying that America overall is a psychopathic society – but that certain systems operating within societies encourage and reward psychopathic behaviour.

Richard Nixon was born in 1913 and died in 1994. He was the 37th president of the USA and served from 1969 to 1974. He was a Republican, with a similar background to many American politicians but he is notable for being the only president thus far to resign from office.

He is also notable for bringing American politics into disrepute more than any other president in history, as a result of the Watergate scandal which revealed him to be criminally dishonest. More recently it has been revealed that he sabotaged efforts to end the Vietnam War so that he would win an election. This treason ultimately killed tens of thousands of young Americans and Vietnamese and Cambodian citizens.

Nixon studied and practiced law before working for the federal government in Washington prior to World War Two. During the war he served in the US Navy and afterwards was elected to the House of Representatives.

Nixon was the running mate of Dwight D. Eisenhower, the Republican Party presidential nominee in the 1952 election, and then served for eight years as vice-president. In 1960 he ran for president but lost to

John F. Kennedy. In 1962 he also failed to get elected as Governor of California but in 1968 ran for the presidency again and won with the slimmest of majorities.

In his inaugural address, Nixon spoke of the importance of being a peacemaker and the need to move away from partisan politics into a new era of unity. Despite his outward claim to being a peacemaker, Nixon escalated the conflict into Laos and Cambodia, which helped fuel internal conflict within the US. This was amplified by his administration initiating a war on drugs, which criminalised many young people and increased political radicalism within the country. Nixon ultimately ended American involvement in Vietnam, in 1973.

Nixon was re-elected in November 1972 but the subsequent Watergate investigation revealed that the election was far from a clean, democratic process. We now know that people working for Nixon burgled and bugged the Democratic National Committee headquarters at the Watergate building in Washington in May and June 1972, during the most intense period of election campaigning.

It has also been proved that Nixon's team, under his command, went to great lengths to try to cover-up its involvement in the crimes. A total of 43 people were convicted and imprisoned after the crimes came to light, including several of Nixon's top aides. Nixon himself managed to escape conviction.

Although the five burglars were arrested at the scene during a break-in on June 17 1972, Nixon's political reputation was initially unaffected by the crimes. It was only later, when links were made to senior aides and Nixon's role in covering-up the burglaries, that his reputation was eroded. In the meantime he had been re-elected by a landslide.

If the investigation had been quicker and the public were made aware of the mounting evidence against the Nixon team it would seem unlikely that this would be the case. Because Nixon was re-elected before evidence came to light he was followed by Republican vice-president Gerald Ford rather than the Democrat, George McGovern, whom he had gained unfair advantage over.

After the five burglars were arrested, Federal Bureau of Investigation agents were able to link money found in their possession to a fund used by Nixon's Committee for the re-election of the president. Further evidence linking Nixon's team to the crimes was given by former staff members. Investigators also found that Nixon had a covert recording system in his offices, allowing phone and other conversations to be taped.

Ironically, considering his team's bugging of the Democrat offices, these tapes ultimately indicated that Nixon took an active role in covering-up the burglaries. He resisted handing the tapes over to investigators for as long as he could but the Supreme Court eventually forced him to do so. When Gerald Ford took over as president he issued a pardon to Nixon, which prevented him from being convicted. No such pardon was issued for Nixon's aides, who were jailed.

Considering the qualities of a psychopath, as set out in Chapter 1, in relation to Nixon, is interesting as many characteristics the public became aware of after the Watergate scandal seem to fit. These include: self-esteem derived from personal gain, power, or pleasure; failure to conform to lawful or culturally normative ethical behaviour, lack of concern for feelings, needs, or suffering of others; lack of remorse after hurting or mistreating another, exploitation is a primary means of relating to others, deceit, the use of dominance or intimidation to control others as well as misrepresentation of the self.

Despite Nixon being primarily associated with Watergate scandal in the public consciousness, he has, in my view, been responsible for a more abhorrent crime by covertly sabotaging Vietnam peace talks. Nixon's manipulations only became public in 2013 when tapes of his Democrat predecessor, Lyndon Johnson, were released. The tapes reveal that Johnson was well-aware of Nixon's actions but because he himself gained the information through FBI interceptions he did use the information against his opponent.

In the summer and autumn of 1968 there was a breakthrough in Paris peace talks but because Nixon's campaign was strengthened by the war, any progress in negotiations was a threat to his political ambitions. To sabotage a settlement he established his own negotiations with Vietnamese diplomats using Anna Chennault, his campaign advisor.

Nixon had Chennault communicate the message that the South Vietnamese government should withdraw from the Paris talks and suggest that if Nixon was elected they would get a better deal than they would from Johnson. Concessions previously offered by South Vietnam, that would have enabled Johnson to stop bombing the country, were withdrawn and the Vietnamese ceased negotiations the day before the president was to order a stop to the bombing.

Nixon's lack of conscience was apparent from his willingness to prolong a war to further his personal ambitions. Despite him sacrificing tens of thousands of lives to gain power and breaking the law to maintain it, some might argue that the traits seen in Nixon are qualities shared by politicians the world over. Their sense of entitlement may be so great that their self-interest and group interests exceed their desire to improve society.

Two of the characteristics especially jump out as qualities common to politicians and many other elite groups. These are 'self-esteem derived from personal gain, power, or pleasure' and 'failure to conform to lawful or culturally normative ethical behaviour'. Obviously politicians have to present themselves as working on behalf of the people and therefore few are likely to admit that they are motivated by self-interest and will ignore morality to get what they want.

Cynical people may take it for granted that politicians are selfish and deceitful but to this I would argue that we therefore must choose our politicians more carefully. They are, after all, *meant* to represent society rather than their own interests. However, in a nation like America where there is no control on expenditure on election campaigns, there is always a danger that wealthy people, who tend to speak primarily for elite groups, will have distinct advantages in the 'democratic' process.

Nixon's case shows the lengths politicians will go to seize and retain power. Many voters are now mindful of this reality, however plausible and superficially charming any politician appears to be. As well as gaining and maintaining power by corrupt means, Nixon has helped corrupt politics globally. It is very hard for any politician to claim integrity when members of the public assume they are up to no good and inherently selfish, greedy, deceitful, Machiavellian and morally bankrupt.

Joseph Stalin

Stalin perhaps fits traditional perceptions of what a psychopath is like more than Richard Nixon, with his bungling team of burglars, does. He was a charismatic man, who ultimately was responsible for many millions of deaths. He is quite possibly responsible for more deaths than any other individual in the history of the world. His destructive impact on the world is still being felt.

The cold, calculating ruthlessness of Stalin has been observed in recent years in former KGB officers who have established lucrative Mafia-style gangs with tentacles around the world. These violent gangs are very much an echo of Stalin's brutality and callousness. Rather than secret police upholding a totalitarian government we have state trained killers running lucrative but corrupt companies. It is both fascinating and distressing that, despite communism being traded for capitalism, pathological systems of power and oppression remain.

The young Stalin, like many successful psychopaths, was good looking and appeared confident. He began to train as a priest but his rebellious nature got him expelled from his seminary. Like Idi Amin, an unpromising start was made up for by adapting to and exploiting the chaos of his age and taking control of a nation.

Also like Idi Amin, Stalin adopted flattering, narcissistic titles. These included 'Father of Nations', 'Brilliant Genius of Humanity', 'Great Architect of Communism' and – ludicrously when you consider the misery he caused – 'Gardener of Human Happiness'. The only way I can see that this last title could ever be true is if his example encourages us to stop following such people and to weed out other Stalins before they take hold.

It is estimated that 20 million Soviets were killed directly in World War 2 but Stalin can be held responsible for a further 30 million deaths. These can be attributed to his attacks on his own citizens, in the form of purges and planned famines. In the 1930s Stalin's 'Great Terror' resulted in the deaths of thousands of those deemed enemies of the people and the forced exile of millions to Gulags where they were forced to work in brutal conditions.

Despite Stalin's Red Army being diminished by his purges, Hitler's army was defeated in its attack of the Soviet Union. Stalin therefore was instrumental in defeating Nazism. He survived until 1953, by which time the Soviet Union ruled Eastern Europe.

The paranoia of Stalin helped feed the spectre of nuclear war, which threatened the world long after he died. There are people today who fear nuclear war but this has greatly reduced since the time of Stalin. One could argue that nuclear missiles proved a great deterrent to land wars and one can credit Stalin with thwarting Hitler's ambitions but this does not detract from his psychopathic tendencies.

The example of Stalin and Idi Amin shed light on the mentalities of some of the other dictators who have existed more recently or who are still active. While it is not necessarily the case that all dictators are clinical psychopaths, the cultures they create and perpetuate – where citizens are played against one another and formerly benign citizens are encouraged to torture and kill neighbours – can be regarded as psychopathic.

Conversely, cruel psychopaths can manage to thrive in seemingly civilised and sophisticated political and social environments, with their true character remaining hidden from the masses throughout their lives. However, the public is becoming more critical, less fearful of powerful people and more intolerant of disturbing qualities that would have remained unchallenged previously. Even when such politicians manage to avoid being unmasked during their lives, unsavoury truths often comes out soon after death.

Cyril Smith

The British Member of Parliament Cyril Smith was a larger than life figure. With a booming voice, large frame and vast waistline he was often a figure of ridicule in politics and the media. But to the numerous boys who he sexually abused and physically assaulted, he must have been a terrifying monster. At 6ft 2 inches tall and weighing almost 30 stone, Smith was many times larger than his victims and he was adept at using his political power and the forcefulness of his character to avoid prosecution during his lifetime.

Smith was a Liberal Democrat MP for Rochdale in Greater Manchester for 20 years, from 1972 to 1992. With extensive previous experience in local government and strong contacts within the police and other key agencies, he managed to shake off accusations of beating and sexually assaulting boys, despite them appearing in print from 1979.

Allegations that he spanked and molested boys were first printed by the *Rochdale Alternative Press*, an underground magazine. Local police investigated the allegations but he was not prosecuted. The national satirical magazine *Private Eye* ran an article repeating the allegations soon after the *Rochdale Alternative Press* coverage but no further action was taken by the police.

The allegations were that the abuse took place in a hostel that Smith himself had established. The case has echoes of that of his close friend Jimmy Savile, in that his apparent efforts to help boys by providing a hostel may have been little more than a cover for abuse.

It is interesting to note that Smith did not take action against the publications that ran stories about his abusing boys and throughout his life did not publicly deny the accusations. He died in 2010, at the age of 82, and it was only after this – and after allegations about Savile started to flood the media – that politics, the police and the Crown Prosecution Service spun into action.

Speaking in the House of Commons in November 2012, Labour MP for Rochdale Simon Danczuk called for an inquiry into the allegations. Soon afterwards Greater Manchester Police said it would investigate allegations dating from the mid-70s and Lancashire Police would investigate claims of abuse from before 1974.

A few days after this, the Crown Prosecution Service issued a statement saying that Smith should have been charged with child abuse incidents dating back as far as the 1960s and the police also issued a statement acknowledging that the boys had been physically and sexually abused.

It has more recently emerged that police files concerning Smith, Savile and other prominent figures were held at Scotland Yard and local police forces – as well as many police at the yard, were not able to access them. It has been claimed that this was to prevent officers from leaking information to the media. However, given that both Savile and Smith had strong relationships with the police – Savile even welcomed groups of policemen to his home for coffee mornings – this restriction seems extremely suspicious.

Restrictions on files pertaining to powerful people certainly hindered forces around the UK from properly investigating the sort of allegations of abuse that have been coming to light in recent years. It is astonishing to note that, prior to 2003, there was no national police database in the UK allowing different forces to easily share intelligence.

Child abuse was not the only controversy linked to Cyril Smith. He was also accused of having improper links to a company producing asbestos and of using his political position to try to cover-up the fact that the substance is a serious threat to public health.

Having made a speech in Parliament claiming that asbestos was not a danger to the public, it later emerged that Smith had shares in a company in his constituency that happened to be one of the world's largest producers of the cheap yet carcinogenic building material. His response to the BBC when it was suggested that he had helped cover up the dangers of asbestos was that the claim was "absolute rubbish".

It would be nice to believe that the police, prosecutors and press would be more robust today in their response to the sort of abuses of power we have seen in people like Cyril Smith. However, given other cases described in this book, where police and other agencies shied away from allegations until after perpetrators were dead, this might be optimistic. In fact, if anything, the McAlpine case, discussed below, may make the press less likely to report on allegations about the most powerful people until charges have been brought. In many cases of systematic child abuse this never happens.

Alan Clark

A minister of state under Thatcher administration and a prominent Conservative Member of Parliament for many years Alan Clark was regarded as an outspoken, arrogant and abrasive character even by his own colleagues. Having received the typical education of a Conservative Minister, at Eton and Oxford (where he performed poorly), Clark had a go at journalism and law before focusing his writing on military history and entering politics.

During his decades in politics Clark found many opportunities to demonstrate his elitism, racism and dishonesty. Having once in a meeting referred to Africa as "Bongo Bongo land" he then attempted to dismiss the suggestion of being racist by explaining it to the then prime minister John Major as a reference to Omar Bongo, the then president of Gabon.

As trade minister Clark encouraged the sale of weapons to despotic regimes, including Iraq when it was under the control of Saddam Hussein. The UK had an embargo about selling weapons to Iraq but Clark was secretly encouraging the company Matrix Churchill to go ahead regardless. When the weapons – which were disguised as machine parts – were intercepted by customs officers, Matrix Churchill executives said Clark had encouraged the sale.

When questioned by the police Clark denied any involvement, which led to the Matrix Churchill executives being prosecuted. They were only saved from lengthy jail sentences because Clark was forced to attend court and admit that he had lied to the police when he claimed he did not encourage the sale. The trial collapsed.

If more members of public had taken an interest in Clark's military writing they might have been extremely alarmed. In relation to Iraq he took the view that: "The interests of the West were well served by Iran and Iraq fighting each other, the longer the better" and, even more worryingly he was a fan of Hitler and regarded Nazism as "the ideal system". In diaries published in 1981, Clark said of Nazism: "It was a disaster for the Anglo-Saxon races and for the world that it was extinguished." He even considered leaving the Conservative Party to join the overtly racist and violent National Front.

Clark's private life appears to have been characterised by cruelty, deceit, betrayal and manipulation. Clark married 16-year-old Jane Beuttler in 1958, when he was 30. But rather than share with her the fruits of his own expensive education and seek to enhance her life, he instead regarded her as a victim to be dominated. A diary entry written by Clark when Jane was just 14 and he was 28 reads: "This is very exciting. She is the perfect victim, but whether or not it will be possible to succeed I can't tell at present." Clark did succeed in victimising Jane and cheated on her with numerous women.

In recent years video footage of public relations consultant Max Clifford came to light, which had been taken in 2000. Within it Clifford boasts about knowing secrets of many famous people. In the footage Clifford makes reference to Clark "interfering with" two girls while he was having an affair their mother Valerie Harkess.

In the film Clifford talks frankly to journalist Dominic Carman about creating a false image for prominent people, to prevent them being destroyed by unwelcome truths becoming public knowledge. Carman manages to get the subject onto Clark, which prompts Clifford to talk about Valerie Harkess and how Clark abused her daughters. Clark himself acknowledged, when confronted by the allegations in 1994, that he deserved to be horsewhipped. He also said: "I do not want to cause the Harkess girls any distress. I wish that they would take the money Max Clifford is raising for them and push off." Those two sentences manage to include pseudo-empathy, a veiled threat and ultimately his callousness.

In the Carman footage, commenting on Alan Clark's affair with Mrs Harkess being publicised, Clifford claimed: "Alan Clark loved the whole thing. The only thing about it, you had…they made a lot of money out of it. He'd used them, so they wanted to make money out of it, they had a moan, so they did. He enjoyed it – he sold even more books. The only slightly serious side about it was he'd actually interfered with those girls from the age of fourteen."

Max Clifford himself was charged, in 2013, with 11 indecent assaults on teenagers and he was convicted of eight of those charges in 2014. He had previously described the post-Savile Operation Yewtree arrests of prominent people accused of historical sexual assaults as a "witch-hunt" and had described his own accusers as "fantasists and opportunists". More will be said of Clifford in Chapter 10.

From the available evidence, it seems that Alan Clark fitted many of the diagnostic criteria to be defined as having an antisocial personality disorder under the DSM, as outlined in Chapter 1. His self-esteem – like many politicians – appears to have been derived from personal gain, power and pleasure. His goal-setting was based on personal gratification with the absence of internal standards. He lacked concern for feelings, needs or suffering of others. Exploitation, deceit, and coercion and intimidation appear to have been his primary means of relating to others. It was always clear that Clark used superficial charm to achieve his ambitions, but we now also know that he was deceitful, immoral and sadistic.

Perhaps as worrying as the above, Clark thrived within the British political system and successfully used the legal system to attack those who challenged him. In that regard, it appears to me that a psychopathic politician was supported by an elitist psychopathic culture, where those with power were free to abuse those 'beneath' them and sue and intimidate anyone who said anything that might tarnish the hollow image they displayed.

As well as being supported by the elitist culture of politics, Clark helped strengthen the psychopathic culture of his age. An era where dictators were armed by democracies, voters were deceived, workers and communities undermined, industries destroyed, union members brutalised by police on behalf of a government and child abuse scandal after child abuse scandal covered up.

Uses, abuses and shortcomings of psychopathy in politics

There are unfortunately many people in politics who have psychopathic qualities. Some may appear chillingly psychopathic to observers while they are in power and other manage to hide their true nature throughout their career. The above selection offers a range of politicians who have shown a wide spectrum of psychopathic tendencies in extremely different circumstances.

The abundance of politicians and dictators who express psychopathic qualities may lead some readers to feel that the term should not be applied to them. Some might think, for example, that different rules and morals somehow apply to political leaders – or that qualities which are regarded as psychopathic in the general population are essential for political success.

The most obvious circumstance where this argument could be made is where politicians have also assumed military function, as in the cases of Idi Amin, Colonel Gaddafi, General Pinochet, Saddam Hussein and General Mladić. Overlooking for a moment the unpredictable minds of those individuals and their lack of conscience, it is important to recognise that effective military leadership is not the same thing as megalomania, sadism, or genocide. In fact, some political leaders have exaggerated or entirely fabricated their military credentials, which may have helped legitimise their brutality.

Good political and military leadership requires wisdom, insight into culture, diplomacy, patience and the ability to put the needs of societies above personal views and ambitions. These are not qualities that psychopaths have.

Whether or not they are led by psychopaths, societies where there is no separation between political and military powers tend to be despotic, paternalistic, misogynistic and cruel. In those cases the military often becomes a weapon to intimidate and destroy any opposition, carry out the personal ambitions of despots and protect their ill-gotten gains. These are short-term and medium-term strategies that help the tyrant and perhaps their sons. They are not intelligent and far-reaching strategies for well-functioning societies.

The argument that political leaders need to have psychopathic qualities falls down when we consider global politics systemically and in the long-term. It is the case that a psychopath in power in one country tends to encourage a more ruthless approach to their state from other nations. This does not mean that senior politicians in those other countries *should* be psychopaths in order to respond effectively to the state led by a psychopath. As psychiatric professionals demonstrate on a daily basis, it is possible to understand and respond effectively to psychopaths without being one.

History has shown that nations led by cruel tyrants tend to become isolated, paranoid, belligerent but also ultimately weak. This insight should give us hope that states that do well in the 21st Century and beyond will be democratic and led by diplomatic, compassionate, flexibility-minded leaders.

The world is of finite size and modern transport and communications technologies bring countries ever closer together. Economic co-dependencies and global marketplaces also mean that effective political leaders need to have a global awareness and a sensitivity to culture and change.

This is not to say that some states are not led by and will not in the future be led by psychopaths. However, when this does happen they are now less likely to be held in place – as Gaddafi and Saddam Hussein were – by Western politicians, than in previous decades. Furthermore, both mainstream global media and social media have so much power now that it is much easier for despots to be shown for what they are, leading to populations rising up against them.

Chapter 6 – Rotten pillars of the community

Many readers will remember an aggressive, spiteful or bullying school teacher who they felt should not be working with children. Unfortunately many people will also have encountered priests, social workers, police officers, probation officers or others working within the criminal justice system who abused their power and mistreated vulnerable people in devious and sadistic ways.

If children from supportive backgrounds find it hard to report cruel teachers, we get a sense of how difficult it must be for vulnerable, abused, criminalised and negatively-labelled children to take effective action against respected 'pillars of the community' who may actually be sadistic and calculating psychopaths.

The early part of this book focused on psychopaths working within the business world – 'successful' corporate psychopaths – who not only victimise and deceive other people but also help create a culture of psychopathy. This poisonous culture has a toxic effect on politics, economics and even supportive social institutions such as healthcare and education. This is clearly something the public, as customers and funders of public services, should monitor and challenge. However, a healthy, well-functioning society also needs to be able to identify and deal with toxic individuals who hide behind the façade of respectability in the educational and caring sectors as well as the police force and politics.

In previous centuries the priest was one of the individuals most likely to have the greatest power over people of all generations. Their religious authority, supported by educational, political and economic structures, allowed them access to all areas of our lives. From christenings, to schools, to marital relationships, to orphanages, to death beds to funerals – priests were always in a position of influence. They had access to the most vulnerable people in society and the respectability to sometimes remain above the law.

In Chapter 4 I offered examples of where priests abused their power, such as in religiously-sanctioned torture and executions and instances of child abuse. The reason I raise these issues again at this point is because the example of the sadistic or exploitative priest, supported by the church, can shed light on the broader contemporary issue of 'do-gooders' who use the cloak of 'respectability' to access vulnerable people, victimise individuals, exploit people and cover-up crimes.

Just as cut-throat corporations are a good habitat for ruthless, competitive and materialistic psychopaths, schools, hospitals, churches, social work departments, prisons, police forces and nurseries are places where plausible psychopaths and glib sadists can operate.

Harold Shipman

Shipman is the most 'successful' convicted killer in British history, having murdered more than 200 patients. This, fortunately, is an extremely dramatic example of a 'pillar of the community' abusing his position to kill and also exploit his patients.

As well as being convicted of murder, Shipman was found guilty of forging a will of one victim in order to inherit £386,000. It is perhaps indicative of how arrogant Shipman was and how he assumed he would be above suspicion, that the poorly forged will was produced on his own typewriter. The unique nature of each typewriter's characters made it possible to demonstrate that he typed the document himself. Another possibility is that the poor forgery was a deliberate or unconscious attempt to be caught and end his murder marathon.

One might be tempted to define Shipman as a 'successful' highly-functioning psychopath, due to the years it took for him to get caught and his status in life. However, the reality is that he struggled to get into medical school and his career was far from impressive. Furthermore, that he was not prosecuted earlier for murder had less to do with his intelligence than the failure of agencies to work together to adequately investigate his prescribing activity, drug abuse and his patient death rates. Despite a high-status role – which enabled his murder spree – it could be argued that Shipman's profile was closer to that of a badly-functioning sociopath than a successful psychopath.

Shipman was born into a working class family in Nottingham. His father was a lorry driver and the young Harold was closer to his mother Vera. He was one of four children and his parents appear to have been devout Methodists. One key event in Shipman's life that may have unsettled him psychologically, encouraged his medical career and inspired his murder method was the death of his mother. She died of lung cancer when Harold was 17 and, in the period leading up to her death, was given morphine at home by the family doctor.

The administration of opiates to alleviate Vera's pain was perfectly normal prescribing practice for lung cancer at that time – and it still is. However, the impact of the young Shipman witnessing the pain, the effect of opiates and ultimately the death of the person closest to him, is impossible to estimate. One immediate symptom of his psychological distress was to run (in an era before jogging was popular in the UK), long distances. Such exercise would have caused the release of endorphins (endogenous morphine), numbing not only physical pain but also mental and emotional anguish. Shipman does not appear to have sought or received psychotherapeutic support for his loss and running may have been a method of disassociating himself from trauma.

Shipman attended Leeds University Medical School from 1965 and, after graduating in 1970, worked at Pontefract General Infirmary. In 1974 he moved into general practice, first becoming assistant general practitioner and then a GP at Todmorden Group Practice in Lancashire. The following year, pharmacy staff discovered that large quantities of addictive controlled drugs were apparently being prescribed by Shipman. It was assumed at that point that Shipman was using opiates and consequently he underwent treatment for addiction at a psychiatric service in York.

Shipman's rehabilitation was ineffective, as months later he was convicted at Halifax Magistrates Court of dishonestly obtaining drugs, prescription forgery and unlawful possession of the opiate pethidine. He received a £600 fine and was allowed to work prior to and after being convicted. It is interesting and troubling to me that the case was not committed to a higher court, which could have given him a stronger sentence, as pethidine (known as Demerol in the US) is a highly-addictive relative of heroin.

When this case came to light, the General Medical Council (GMC), which regulates doctors in the UK, investigated Shipman but made no attempt to strike him off. This inaction and the court's leniency allowed him, in 1977, to join Donneybrook House Group Practice in Hyde, Cheshire. He stayed there until 1992, when he established himself as a single-handed GP in Hyde.

In March 1998, another local doctor, Linda Reynolds, became concerned about the number of deaths of Shipman's patients and reported her concerns to the coroner. Dr Reynolds had become troubled by the number of elderly former patients of Shipman that had been cremated rather than buried. An initial police investigation found no evidence of wrongdoing and the case was dropped. Tragically, Shipman managed to murder three more patients before he was charged, in September 1998. His final victim, Kathleen Grundy, was killed in June 1998. This case ultimately proved his undoing.

It was not the death of Mrs Grundy itself that led police to recommence the investigation but the fact that a will – forged by Shipman – left money to him rather than to her children – including lawyer Angela Woodruff. The investigation led to Kathleen Grundy's body being exhumed and traces of diamorphine (heroin) were found in a post-mortem.

The police then investigated 14 other specimen cases where suspicion pointed to Shipman because he had signed the death certificates. The cases, all deaths occurring between 1995 and 1998, revealed a pattern of him making false entries in medical records to suggest that patients were in poor health and giving them lethal overdoses of diamorphine.

In January 2000, a jury at Preston Crown Court returned guilty verdicts against Shipman on 15 counts of murder and one of forgery of a will. Shipman was not struck off by the GMC until 10 days after being found guilty.

The following month Alan Milburn, then health minister, announced an independent inquiry into the Shipman case. In March 2000, relatives of the victims were angered when it was announced that the inquiry would sit in private. Consequently a group of relatives and friends of Shipman's victims, along with several media organisations, applied to the High Court for judicial review of the decision for the inquiry to sit in private. The group won and, in September 2000, the health minister announced that the inquiry would be public.

Given the fact that concerns about Shipman should have been shared among agencies and taken more seriously, it seems shocking now that there was an attempt to make the inquiry private. However, a different way of looking at this is, given the failure of public bodies to deal adequately with Shipman, it is unsurprising that there was an attempt to have the inquiry in private.

Given that one of these organisations, the GMC, was at the time composed almost entirely of doctors – who should understand personality disorders and drug addiction – it is a major embarrassment to the body that it failed the public so badly.

Despite the inquiry, which estimated the number of murder victims to be at least 215, relatives have never got clear answers about why Shipman murdered their loved ones. Prior to conviction and afterwards Shipman insisted he was innocent of all charges.

When, in 2001, police visited Shipman in prison to interview him about the murders he refused to engage and turned his chair away from the detectives. Officers attempted to show Shipman photos of his victims but he reportedly closed his eyes tightly. He hanged himself in Wakefield Prison in 2004 after losing some privileges as a result of not participating in the prison programme. Though he never verbally gave an explanation for his actions, his responses to prison life underlines the importance of power for Shipman. This appears to be a key driver of his criminality and perhaps also his choice of career.

Liam Donaldson, the then Chief Medical Officer for England, published a report in 2006 entitled *Good Doctors, Safer Patients*. In the report Sir Liam criticised the GMC and said complaints against doctors had been dealt with in a haphazard way. He also characterised the GMC as being "secretive, tolerant of sub-standard practice and dominated by the professional interest, rather than that of the patient".

Since Shipman's conviction there have been significant changes in how the GMC operates. The organisation has become more transparent and now has an equal split between lay members and doctors. It has previously been composed primarily of members of the medical profession. This shift towards a greater number of lay people has been followed by other regulatory bodies in the UK. As such bodies are meant to protect the public from inadequate or malicious members of a profession it seems critical to allow 'outsiders' into councils.

Paedophile rings and positions of power

The case of Harold Shipman is extremely dramatic, both in terms of the number of victims and failure of the system around him to respond to what, with hindsight, seem like strong indicators of a dangerous mind. Paedophile rings should be of equal concern and any suspicions should be met with considerable attention by the authorities. Although – as far as we know – the number of people killed directly by paedophile rings is smaller than those murdered by serial killers, the ultimate number of people whose lives are damaged by child abuse is considerable.

There are many reasons why the true level of harm caused by child sexual abuse and other forms of child abuse is impossible to measure. One key reason is many people never disclose what has happened to them or how mistreatment has affected them. From studies following the lives of people who do disclose, we know that child abuse victims experience higher levels of anxiety, depression, alcohol and drug abuse, self harm, incarceration and suicide.

Therefore it is highly likely that there are many people who have not reported being victimised but who experienced some of the problems listed above. In fact, given the value of support and therapy, it is highly likely that many of the victims who do not disclose abuse actually experience worse problems than those that do.

There may be significant numbers of people who have committed suicide, leaving those around them bewildered, who were contending with painful private thoughts, feeling and memories as a result of child abuse. There are also many ways for a life to be destroyed without the victim actually committing suicide.

Those who have been victimised may spend their lives feeling as though society sees them as worthless people, when actually society failed to protect them from some of the most malicious people around. Those who become addicted to drugs may find themselves seen first and foremost as an addict rather than a person with feelings, thoughts and a burdensome history.

The abuse of young people in children's homes, approved schools and prisons has often been swept under the carpet and victims frequently ignored or discredited. There is a tendency for society to wash its hands of troubled, abused children and disregard them even if they manage to become well-functioning adults. This reality is extremely dangerous as it has helped calculating, sadistic people to prey on vulnerable children and to establish paedophile rings – while reducing the chances of perpetrators facing justice.

Not surprisingly, relationships have been found between paedophilia and psychopathy (Nurcombe 2000, Plotnikoff & Woolfson 2000). It should be stressed, however, that there are many sex offenders who are not psychopaths. Some sexual abusers fall more easily into other personality disorder categories than psychopathy, while others have learning disabilities.

Nevertheless, psychopathic paedophiles are an important group to consider as they are more likely to be violently sadistic to victims while maintaining the veneer of charm to others, avoid prosecution and intimidate and undermine victims. Furthermore, psychopaths are more likely than those other categories of abusers to be able to form, protect and profit from paedophile rings – whether financially or by gaining leverage over other abusers.

In recent decades, paedophile rings have been identified in many countries and many more have been alleged and are under investigation. Others have been alleged and appear to have attracted little interest by the authorities historically, although there is mounting public pressure and political momentum to tackle the problem. In the next chapter I will draw on examples of paedophile rings, alleged cover-ups and ongoing efforts by victims, advocates and the criminal justice system to bring historical cases to light.

Chapter 7 – Paedophiles, procurers, politics and cover-ups

Considering specific cases allows us to gain an appreciation of how paedophiles target victims and position themselves in organisations where they can access and have power over potential victims. By focusing on key examples from recent decades we can also consider how calculating psychopaths create, strengthen and protect paedophile rings.

One British journalist who has focused great attention on powerful paedophile rings in the UK is Nick Davies. He wrote about uncomfortable links between abusers working in key institutions at a time when much of the print media was steering clear of the subject or covering it very superficially.

In a 1998 *Guardian* article entitled 'The sheer scale of child sexual abuse in Britain' Davies pieced together information about individual paedophiles and cases to illustrate troubling links between them:

> Even though most abusers – whatever their age or sex – work alone, there is clear evidence of some conspiracy, of the existence of paedophile rings, sometimes deliberately infiltrating parts of the child protection system, often taking advantage of each other's political or social power to conceal their activities.
>
> Often the links between abusers lie beneath the surface of less horrific conspiracies. Take, for example, the case of Greystone Heath, an approved school for boys in Warrington, which for years enjoyed an unsullied reputation until police finally discovered that it had become a hot spot for paedophiles. This one institution – whose history of abuse is echoed now in scores of others – is a model of everyday paedophile collusion.
>
> It appears to have started in 1965 when a 21-year-old student teacher named Keith Laverack went to work there and embarked on a campaign of buggery and indecent assault. Over the ensuing four years, he raped at least 16 boys, three of whom he shared

with his colleague, Brian Percival, the clerk and storeman at the home. Once these two men had established sexual rights over the boys at Greystone, other abusers joined the staff: Alan Langshaw, who raped at least 24 boys; Dennis Grain who raped at least 18; Roy Shuttleworth who raped at least ten; Jack Bennett who indecently assaulted two; and Steve Norris who assaulted an unknown number.

The Greystone abusers then fanned out. Keith Laverack went to childrens' homes in Cambridgeshire; Alan Langshaw became Principal of St Vincent's Catholic boys' home in Formby; Grain and Shuttleworth were both promoted to other homes in the Warrington area; Steve Norris went to North Wales. At their new homes, all of them continued to rape boys who were in their care and wherever they went, they crossed the paths of other paedophiles.

As Nick Davies states, Keith Laverack was at the centre of a web of men who groomed, manipulated and raped a large number of children. Laverack, who by all accounts was superficially charming, was found guilty of raping and assaulting numerous children. Many of his victims have had extreme difficulties in their lives and some have been completely destroyed. Several became addicted to alcohol and other drugs, some became violent criminals, and others became self-harmers. Some became all of those things and some, tragically, died young.

Although I have not met Laverack directly I have been party to some of the long-term devastation his crimes have caused. Within mental health wards I worked on I met patients who were sexually abused by him when they were children. Decades later, as they tried to make sense of and find direction in their lives, their abuse by Laverack and others was a constant and disabling shadow. Even his conviction had a destabilising impact on some victims and their families, by dredging up terrifying and painful memories.

One survivor, who I will not name, was often extremely aggressive to staff during the time he was on an acute psychiatric ward. This lashing out at authority figures is perhaps not surprising given how he had been treated in institutions as a child. By the time he was admitted onto a mental health unit he was married with children and, although there was no suggestion that he had sexually abused his or anyone else's children, he admitted to being violent towards his wife.

His wife stood by him and often visited the ward but she was clearly extremely scared of his volatility and was concerned about the impact this would have on their children. He had come into the unit as a voluntary patient and expressed a desire to his key workers to improve his behaviour and better control his anger.

The patient was, however, quickly discharged from the unit. This was a result of his aggressive and threatening behaviour, along with being considered to have an antisocial personality disorder. Although it seems highly likely that the man's volatility was strongly influenced by being abused as a child, it was deemed to be such a danger to staff and patients that he lost an opportunity to work through his experiences and learn to manage his anger more effectively.

Although abused little boys sometimes grow into large, angry and aggressive men, it is important to recognise that the stories they have to tell are significant and can help themselves and others. Laverack received an 18 year jail sentence (in 1997) after many victims courageously came forward to give evidence against him. However, there have been many occasions historically when victims have been ignored, silenced and discounted, undermined or threatened. There probably have been even more occasions when victims stayed silent because they felt powerless, assumed people would not take them seriously or feared that disclosing abuse would destabilise the lives they had struggled to build.

It is often extremely difficult for victims of abuse to speak openly about their experiences, particularly to representatives of state institutions. Therefore it is critical that the police, teachers, social workers, mental health professionals, probation workers and representatives of other agencies give victims opportunities to discuss their experiences, however challenging and provocative their behaviour may be.

Even when specific victims of sexual abuse become aggressive, manipulative and impulsive adults, there are problems in defining them as psychopaths. Most would not have been born with those inclinations – they are more likely to be the result of atrocious early experiences combined with a resultant loss of trust in authority figures and social institutions.

Another way of looking at it is that the poison of predators in powerful positions has been allowed to infect vulnerable children, who years later find themselves in conflict with other institutions. Therefore, this is a good example of how one or a small number of psychopaths can create a volatile pathological culture which ripples out in all directions.

Many of the people abused by Laverack have since spent time in prisons, mental hospitals and in conflict with those around them. One victim, Stuart Shorter, was featured in the biography *Stuart: A Life Backwards*

(2005) by Alexander Masters. Shorter was born with a disability and had a chaotic life of abuse, mental instability, addiction and violent criminality – including armed robbery. He came into contact with the author when Masters was working at Cambridge hostel for rough sleepers. The book was dramatised by the BBC in 2007.

Born in 1968, Stuart Shorter suffered from facioscapulohumeral muscular dystrophy, a condition characterised by weakness of the upper body. After being sexually abused by a brother (who went on to kill himself) and a babysitter, he requested to be placed in a children's home. Tragically, being put 'in care' was perhaps a movement from the frying pan to the fire for Shorter as it is there that he came into contact with the predatory Laverack.

Stuart Shorter's life after leaving care was unsettled to say the least. But it was not merely characterised by drug addiction and violent crime. He was the first person to sell *The Big Issue* magazine in Cambridge and he was an ardent activist for homeless people, featuring in a short BBC documentary called *Private Investigations*. In the programme he criticised plans to ban homeless people from Cambridge city centre. Homelessness in the city has long been a notable feature because tourists and well-off students attract beggars and buskers from around the UK.

Stuart Shorter died in 2002, at the age of 33, after being hit by a train. Although an open verdict was returned, there are strong suggestions that he killed himself. He had a history of suicide attempts and he had previously told his sister Zoe that if he were to commit suicide he would make it look like an accident to spare his mother the pain of knowing that both of her sons took their own lives. Although described by Alexander Masters as a psychopath, the desire of Shorter to protect his mother from anguish suggests an empathy that appears lacking in Laverack and other members of his paedophile ring.

In his 1998 *Guardian* article Nick Davies alludes to some more of the links between individuals in the paedophile ring that Laverack was a key part of. The ring appears to have not only spanned children's homes and reform schools but was linked to a key institution that produced social workers and helped shape public policy. This example is an excellent, if terrifying, illustration of how predatory psychopaths can infiltrate key organisations that society depends upon, poison the system, corrupt individuals and spread a psychopathic culture.

While he was Principal of St Vincent's, Alan Langshaw recruited a care worker named Edward Stanton, who joined in Langshaw's orgy. Stanton appears to have got the job through the good offices of Roy Shuttleworth, who was continuing to abuse the boys at Greystone and who is believed to have known Stanton from their time in Birmingham when they took the same course in residential child care.

That course in Birmingham, in turn, is believed to have been lectured by Peter Righton, a notorious paedophile who attempted to legitimise his obsession in a series of academic studies. Righton, for his part, belonged to the Paedophile Information Exchange, along with Jack Bennett who joined in the abuse at Greystone. Righton had earlier worked in the same children's home in Maidstone, Kent as Peter Howarth, who went on to become a legendary abuser in the homes of North Wales where he shared his indulgence with Steve Norris, formerly of Greystone.

Each of these men claims to have abused alone. Even though their paths connected so frequently, even though the Greystone abusers were assaulting boys in buildings within yards of each other, even though several of them were raping the same boys, they claim never to have colluded with each other. No one who has been involved with investigating Greystone believes them.

The evidence suggests that such abusers not only collude to give each other work and access to children, but also to infiltrate the child protection system. Peter Righton lectured not only in Birmingham but in numerous other colleges. Before he was finally taken to court and convicted, he became a highly regarded consultant in child care and, eventually, the Director of Education at the prestigious National Institute of Social Work in London, a position from which he was able to have some influence on government policy.

The Paedophile Information Exchange (PIE) referred to above was not an organisation established to tackle sexual abuse but to legitimise and promote sex with children. It was set up in 1974 in the context where a great deal of work was being done to promote women's rights and gay rights. PIE members manipulatively used discourses about liberation – misappropriated from feminism and gay rights activists – to push for sex with very young children to be legalised. The group also managed to infiltrate gay rights and civil liberties groups.

The age for consent for gay people at that time in England was 21 and, as this inequality was something members of the Gay Liberation

Front sought to change, the PIE aligned itself with this campaign – but to push its pro-paedophilia agenda. In the late 1970s the PIE became a subscriber of the National Council for Civil Liberties (NCCL), which later became Liberty. The NCCL was a well-established campaign group concerned with promoting civil liberties and human rights.

During that period PIE continued to campaign to overturn the age of consent and it also lobbied against a ban on 'child pornography' (which is more correctly referred to as 'images of child abuse' nowadays). The NCCL took the view, in a 1976 submission to the Criminal Law Revision Committee, that: "childhood sexual experiences, willingly engaged in, with an adult result in no identifiable damage". It also pushed the argument that 'child pornography' should only be deemed illegal in cases where it has been it proven that the child had suffered harm.

The NCCL did not exclude PIE until 1983, despite the homes of several PIE committee members being raided by police five years before that. An extensive report was submitted to the Director of Public Prosecutions after the raid. This was followed by the prosecution of some members. The organisation officially disbanded in 1984 but there is evidence that members of the network continued to exchange information about children, as well as indecent images.

One founder member of PIE who continued to exchange information with paedophiles in the years after the organisation was shut down was Peter Righton. It is impossible to estimate the harm he caused to children, both indirectly through his communications with other sex abusers and directly. In 1992 the British Customs and Excise service intercepted two packages containing images of child abuse posted to Righton from the Netherlands. As a result of this the police raided Righton's house, where they found hundreds of letters proving collusion between him and other sex offenders.

The content of the letters indicated that the 'leading expert' on child welfare and residential care had abused and also prostituted many children in a career of offending which started in the 1950s. Among those corresponding with Righton were aristocrats, senior church figures, teachers and at least one person working at the heart of the British government. Even as I write this, decades later, there is not clarity on who that governmental figure is or if there were more than one in contact with Righton.

Despite his letters alluding to the abuse of numerous children and collusion with a paedophile network, Righton was only convicted of importing and possessing illegal 'pornographic material'. For this he received a fine of just £900. The material he imported included indecent photographs of boys under the age of 16. The chairman of the bench, Robert Rowland, reportedly told him: "We are aware that you are of previous good character, but we think these are serious matters and the penalty we impose must reflect that".

In 1994 Righton was featured in the BBC *Inside Story* documentary *The Secret Life of a Paedophile*. The documentary traced his career back to a number of roles where he had close contact with children, including teacher in a boarding school and probation officer. From Righton's diary, which was taken by the police, it is apparent that his grooming and abusing had started before he taught at Red Hill School in Kent. He worked and lived at the school from 1957 to 1962.

Mark Thewlis, one of those abused by Righton at Red Hill, told the documentary: "It was as if he had a magnetic hold over you – you couldn't be anything in the school without the attentions of Peter Righton." Mr Thewlis also said that his abuse started when he was 12 and he knew of six other boys being abused by Righton at the same time. In a diary entry from the period, Righton acknowledges the illegality of his actions, stating: "Legally I haven't a leg to stand on – it's an official crime for a man of 37 to make love to a boy of 15."

Although complaints were made to the police about abuse at the school, an inquiry was dropped due an apparent lack of evidence. Two teachers reported Righton to the headmaster but the predator simply denied the allegations and was allowed to move onto to another job without action being taken.

Asked by *Inside Story* to phone and then meet Righton as the programme was being made, Mark Thewlis covertly recorded his former teacher acknowledging how much "hurt" could be done by "seducing boys". He assured Thewlis that after leaving Red Hill he had no professional contact with young people and stopped having sex with children at that point. In the recording he alludes to the damage done to one particular boy, whose name is bleeped out from the programme. Testimony from victims, backed up by Righton's own handwritten records, shows that the assurance was a blatant lie as the child sexual abuse continued for decades.

In their search of his house, police found a handwritten list by Righton entitled 'Some boys'. The disturbing document lists children he sexually abused during his adult life. Righton's list traces his paedophilia back to his student days at the University of Oxford and through the decades after leaving Red Hill. It contains more than 100 names and the age of each child, some of whom were pre-teen. Disturbingly, many of the names have a tick next to them – perhaps to indicate penetration – and some are graded a, b or c, as though he marked them against one another.

After leaving Red Hill, Righton went to Keele University where he produced research that would inform the work of social workers. At that point he attempted to resume a relationship with someone he had abused when they were a child. At Keele he met powerful contacts in the world of child welfare, paving the way for him to gain an influential position at National Institute of Social Work in 1965 and become a government advisor.

The BBC documentary includes an interview with retired social worker Anne Goldie, who said that Righton had admitted to her that he 'had sex' with numerous children when he was worked in the residential sector and maintained contact with some for many years afterwards. With obvious regret, Ms Goldie says in the broadcast: "He knew me to be a lesbian and he assumed a group loyalty and that he could trust me with this information. That assumption at that time was an accurate one for him to make. I did nothing." Goldie did, however, in later life support whistle-blowers who had concerns about abuse within institutions.

As well as abusing children himself in the decades after leaving Red Hill, including during his key role at the National Institute of Social Work, Righton was in constant contact with other paedophiles. One of these, Charles Napier, was a PIE treasurer and had been banned from teaching in British schools after being convicted of indecently assaulting five pupils. However, in 1978 Napier managed to secure a teaching job in Sweden.

In letters to Righton from Sweden, Napier details his grooming activities: "I always put my address on the board and invite visits. Every school form has one hour swimming each week. I now visit the baths and I'm slowly building up a chart of which forms go when." He also described to Righton sexual activity with young boys.

Rather than report Napier – as any social worker is obliged to - Righton went to Sweden to visit him and get close to the boys Napier had groomed. The *Inside Story* documentary includes footage of Napier getting boys drunk and encouraging them to touch one another. There is also footage of Righton's visit, where the two are seen with boys. In 1980 Napier applied to the UK Department of Education to be allowed once again to teach children in Britain. Righton supported his application with a reference. He wrote: "[Napier] no longer constitutes a sexual risk to children in his charge."

In November 2014 Napier pleaded guilty to 29 further sexual offences against boys in his care. He was remanded in custody, facing a jail sentence.

The indifference Righton had to the damage that sexual abuse causes to children was made apparent in a chapter he wrote in the 1981 book *Perspectives on Paedophilia*, edited by Brian Taylor. That writing should have been a clear clue to Righton's perversions and it is extremely troubling that it did not lead to an investigation at that time. He claimed in the chapter to have "counselled" numerous paedophiles and child abuse victims but he made no reference to his involvement with PIE, which sought to remove the age of consent. Attempting to justify sex with children by distinguishing it from violent sex with children, Righton wrote:

> Any adult who rapes, pesters, or offers sexual violence in any form to a child is a serious social menace, and must be firmly prevented from committing further assaults – by treatment whenever possible, but by imprisonment, prolonged if necessary, should there be no feasible alternative. There is no question that children need to be protected by sexual marauders; what I contest is the assumption that children need protection from (in the sense of denial of) any kind of sexual experience with an adult, however loving, gentle or even educative.

At this period Righton and other paedophiles were attending regular parties involving young boys on a house on the river Thames owned by Charles Napier. Boys who were taken to the parties report being offered money to be abused by men.

One PIE member who attended – and also appears in footage with Napier – was educationalist David Bloomfield. He was chief executive of the Standing Conference on Schools, Science and Technology until 1993, when he was found guilty of possessing images of child abuse. BBC journalists working on *The Secret Life of a Paedophile* attempted to interview Bloomfield about his associations with other sex offenders but he refused to comment.

In 1991 Peter Righton was commissioned to work on a national project called the Charter for Children. The aim of the project was to improve the standards of care of children in social care and other institutions. The contract enabled Righton to visit children's homes and boarding schools across the UK and gain access to vulnerable children. He was still working on the project in 1992 when he was arrested for importing images of child abuse. When his colleagues found out about his arrest he claimed to them that had never abused a child. He was sacked from the job prior to being convicted.

From when he was awaiting trial, Righton and his partner Richard

Alston lived on the estate of the 8th Lord Henniker in Suffolk. It appears that Righton used the alias Cantwell at that time to avoid identification. Rather than keeping him away from temptation, however, living on the estate brought Righton in close contact with vulnerable children. The estate had been used as an educational and recreational centre for children since the mid-1970s and hundreds of young people, many of whom were from residential care, stayed there.

Some of the children sent to the estate at the time Righton was living there were under the care of the London Borough of Islington. Children's homes in Islington were under investigation at that point as a result of *London Evening Standard* reports that children in care in the borough were being exploited by paedophiles, pimps and child pornographers. A paedophile ring appears to have infiltrated Islington's 12 children's homes at that time.

At least one Islington abuse victim is known to have been sent by the council to New Barns School for emotionally disturbed children in Gloucestershire. The school took children aged between seven and 14. Peter Righton was vice-chairman of the board of Governors of New Barns School from 1991 and Richard Alston was headmaster. The institution was shut down in 1992 after allegations of violent and sexual abuse were made by dozens of pupils. One care worker, Alan Stewart, was jailed for four years for sexually assaulting three girls at the school. Other members of staff were charged with child cruelty and false imprisonment but not convicted.

Righton lived until 2007 without being charged of any further crimes. Despite the reach of his influence, the strong evidence linking him to paedophile rings and the many years in which he was an active abuser, few people in the UK were aware of him until relatively recently.

Information about Righton and his network have come to the fore recently because the momentum to tackle paedophilia has grown in recent years. However, it could also be the case that investigations have been dormant because there had been Establishment cover-up related to powerful people associated with Righton's circle. Therefore it could have been inconvenient politically for information about Righton's activities to be made public. If this is the case, it would explain the blasé nature of some of the abuse and correspondence between paedophiles. They may have believed themselves to be protected from on high.

Revelations about Jimmy Savile and public horror were a catalyst that alerted a large number of people to Righton and the paedophile ring he was associated with. On October 24 2012, as the UK was reeling in the horror of the allegations surrounding Jimmy Savile, the Labour MP Tom Watson dropped a bombshell in the weekly prime minister's questions (PMQs) session. The question concerned Peter Righton and also pointed to the possibility of a paedophile ring connected to Margaret Thatcher's government. Addressing David Cameron, Mr Watson said:

> The evidence file – used to convict paedophile Peter Righton – if it still exists, contains clear intelligence of a widespread paedophile ring. One of its members boasts of his links to a senior aide of a former prime minister, who says he could smuggle indecent images of children from abroad. The leads were not followed up, but if the files still exist, I want to ensure that the Metropolitan Police secure the evidence, re-examine it, and investigate clear intelligence suggesting a powerful paedophile network linked to Parliament and Number 10.

To shed more light on this for members of the public and the press, Mr Watson subsequently posted a blog entry entitled 'A little more background on today's PMQ's'. He also posted a link to the blog entry on Twitter, which rapidly disseminated it. I include key extracts of the blog entry here:

> I cannot give much more detail until the police have been given more time to investigate whether evidence still exists from the mid-nineties, but here is what I can say.

Last week I was contacted by a former child protection specialist who for some years had been concerned that a wider investigation regarding the activities of convicted paedophile, Peter Righton, was not fully investigated.

> The central allegation was that a large body of material seized in the raid on Righton's home had not been fully investigated. Though Righton was the subject of a BBC profile in 1994, *The Secret Life of a Paedophile*, little had been done to follow up the leads from the case. A specialist unit in Scotland Yard had the material which supplemented a wider investigation into organised paedophile rings in children's homes.
>
> Over the last few days I have spoken to two other child protection specialists who share the concern of the gentleman who contacted me.

Within the material seized at Righton's home were letters from known and convicted paedophiles. The contact, who has seen the letters, claimed that one paedophile in particular was of great concern. He said that the paedophile, who worked with children, boasted of a key aide to a former PM who could help get hold of indecent images of children.

As I write this we are still waiting to hear of cases related to the Righton files, which detectives have apparently been re-examining since Tom Watson's parliamentary question. The public has also been waiting to hear why allegations of abuse in children's homes were not responded to quickly and effectively and why information from investigations was hidden from public view.

Welsh Children's homes and an alleged paedophilia cover-up

Post-Savile concerns about powerful paedophiles rings led to renewed interest in historical sexual abuse allegations related to children's homes in Wales. Widespread belief in a political cover-up of an Establishment paedophile ring also helped an old story about Lord McAlpine being a child abuser to spread rapidly across social media.

The allegation has been made in the early 1990s in the now defunct *Scallywag* magazine, but McAlpine did not sue the publication or distributors for libel at that time. However, he did take action against the BBC, ITV and many individuals after his name circulated on Twitter.

It was picked up by Twitter on 2nd November 2012 after Iain Overton, then of the Bureau of Investigate Journalism – which had been working with *Newsnight* on a piece about historic abuse – tweeted the following: "If all goes well we've got a *Newsnight* out tonight about a very senior political figure who is a paedophile." The tweet itself did not name McAlpine but Overton had reportedly already disclosed the name to television journalist Michael Crick, who contacted an incensed McAlpine – who denied the allegation.

Newsnight went ahead with the item but did not name McAlpine. The piece included an interview with a man who said he had been raped by a senior Conservative in a Wrexham hotel in the 1980s, not far from the Bryn Estyn children's home. This individual, Steve Messham, subsequently stated that he was wrong about the attacker being Lord McAlpine and said it was a case of mistaken identity.

Nevertheless, allegations about McAlpine continued to circulate on social media. This was in part fuelled by the fact that he had previously owned some 'art' featuring naked prepubescent children, produced by Graham Ovenden – who was later jailed for abusing girls who posed for him. McAlpine died in 2014 and never commented on the images he had owned or on Ovenden's convictions for indecency and indecent assault.

McAlpine is not the only government figure to have been linked to the North Wales abuse scandal. In late October 2012, days before the *Newsnight* interview with Steve Messham, a former Conservative minister made the claim that a senior Tory close to Margaret Thatcher had sexually abused children in Wales. Rod Richards, who was formerly leader of the Welsh Tories, alleged that Sir Peter Morrison was part of a paedophile network responsible for the abuse of hundreds of children in 40 Welsh care homes. Victim accounts suggest that sexual, physical and emotional abuse of children took place in the homes for more than 20 years.

Morrison, who died in 2005, was MP for Chester from 1974 until 1992, a Conservative Party chairman and parliamentary private secretary to Margaret Thatcher. Rod Richards, who had helped set up an investigation into child abuse in North Wales care homes, alleges that Morrison and another leading Conservative figure were named in documents as regular visitors to homes. Two of the homes visited – Bryn Estyn and Bryn Alyn Hall, which are both near Wrexham, are linked to a considerable number of sexual abuse allegations, including some involving Savile.

The allegations against Peter Morrison were not a surprise to everyone. Nick Davies of *The Guardian* had reported in 1998 that Morrison had previously received a caution for having sex with underage boys in public toilets. Morrison's colleague Edwina Currie, a former Conservative health minister, claimed in her 2002 autobiography that he regularly had sex with teenage boys. In the book she described him as "a noted pederast with a liking for young boys".

The judge-led Waterhouse Inquiry was established in 1996 by then Secretary of State for Wales William Hague amid allegations of hundreds of incidents of abuse of children is care, dating from the 1970s to the 90s. Morrison's name did not appear in the final *Waterhouse Report*, which was published in 2000. After Rod Richards made allegations about Morrison in 2012, a spokesman for William Hague said that the minister had never seen information implicating Morrison.

There has been much public criticism over the years about the way in which reports of abuse in Wales were handled and about the depth that various investigations and inquiries went. There are still many people who feel that abuse was covered up to protect powerful people. There were a number of reports of abuse in children's homes in Wales throughout the 1970s and 1980s but very little information was made public. Some allegations were dealt with internally but disciplinary action was rarely taken, let alone charges brought.

Progress started to be made in the mid-1980s when Alison Taylor, a residential care worker and children's home manager, was told by residents about incidents of abuse in a number of homes. Ms Taylor discovered that although reports of several of the incidents described by the children were filed by care staff, no further action was taken.

Ms Taylor subsequently made allegations of abuse to senior council figures but no action appears to have been taken. In 1986 she took the allegations to the police and was then suspended by the council. The reason given for her dismissal was a breakdown in communications between Ms Taylor and other members of staff. The council subsequently offered her a financial termination agreement on the condition that she signed a confidentiality clause. She refused and was dismissed. A 1989 tribunal led to a settlement which did not include a confidentiality clause.

The absence of confidentiality agreement allowed Ms Taylor to go to the press with allegations about child abuse in care homes. Police did look into some allegations in 1990 but were allegedly hindered by a lack of co-operation from the responsible agencies. No prosecutions were made but a document known as the *Cartrefle Report* was submitted to the council.

Alison Taylor continued to investigate cases and pass information to the press. She gained the trust of residents and former residents, who told her about more cases, as did other whistle-blowers. By 1991 she had amassed a dossier of allegations from more than 100 children who said they were sexually and violently abused. She submitted evidence to the police, the council and the Welsh Office. The police conducted an investigation but it led to no charges at that point. For such an investigation to have been successful the police would have needed the cooperation of social workers and care staff. This may have been lacking.

In 1993, after a new Director of Social Services for Clwyd was appointed, North Wales Police undertook a fresh investigation of child abuse. At that point 2,600 witness statements were taken and around 300 cases were sent to the Crown Prosecution Service. Out of those cases just seven people were prosecuted and convicted. Six of these were residential social workers, three of which had previously worked at the Bryn Estyn home. Peter Howarth, the former deputy head of Bryn Estyn, received a 10-year jail sentence in 1994 for sexually abusing boys.

As was mentioned previously, in the article by Nick Davies, Howarth worked with Peter Righton in Kent. He died of a cardiac condition two years into his prison sentence. It is both interesting and troubling that Howarth and Righton were convicted, after so many years of abusing children, around the same time. A positive take on this is that by the early 1990s abuse claims were being taken more seriously and authorities became more responsive and responsible. A less positive possibility is that authorities and powerful individuals aggressively resisted action for decades and buried information. The following information about the *Jillings Report* supports this thesis.

The Jillings Report

I hope very much that by the time this book is read a great many people in Britain and beyond will be familiar with the content of and political wranglings around the *Jillings Report*. However, there is a good chance they will not. The report, which should have shed light on specific cases and paedophile networks five years before the *Waterhouse Report*, has been restricted from public view for decades. In fact, there was an attempt to destroy every copy, which fortunately failed, and some heavily redacted versions have found their way into public hands.

There has been renewed pressure to publish the report since other revelations about child sexual abuse in the UK were disseminated in 2012. Some content from the report has been reported on by newspapers and is available online. However, until the full report is made public there will be speculation about details within it. Such are the beliefs about the involvement of powerful figures in an extensive paedophile ring in Britain that there will be speculation about the involvement of certain individuals and Establishment cover-ups until the unedited report is released.

As with the later *Waterhouse Report*, the cases investigated by the *Jillings Report* authors go back to the 1970s. The process began in 1994 when, in response to numerous allegations of child abuse in North Wales, Clwyd County Council commissioned John Jillings to undertake an investigation. Jillings had previously been director of social services at Derbyshire County Council. The panel of the inquiry also included Professor Jane Tunstall, an expert on social work from Keele University, and child psychologist and psychotherapist Gerrilyn Smith.

The panel experienced immediate opposition to their task. Their request to meet the chief constable was reportedly refused and the team were denied access to a police database of incidents. This meant the panel had to spend considerable time collecting dozens of witness statements from people who had already been interviewed. It also meant victims had to go over traumatic experiences yet again, unnecessarily.

The police also allegedly refused to allow the inquiry access to 130 boxes of material that had been provided by the council. The panel, in the conclusion of the report, admit that such obstacles led them to consider terminating the inquiry. Commenting within the report on the police response to requests for information, the panel wrote: "We were disappointed at the apparent impossibility of obtaining a breakdown of data. We are unable to identify the overall extent of the allegations received by the police in the many witness statements which they took."

The report states that physical and sexual violence was common in the care sector in North Wales. The panel found that children who complained of abuse were often ignored or punished. The panel estimated that up to 200 residents from children's homes in the region were abused.

The report claims that, rather than face criminal charges, some staff linked to abuse were given the opportunity to resign or take early retirement. As well as neglecting to deal with perpetrators, such an approach would have failed to address the likelihood that abusers were part of a broader ring. We know from other cases that changing jobs, moving house or retiring does not stop a paedophile from being a paedophile.

After being produced, the report was held back from publication and most copies were destroyed. This appears to be due to concerns about libel actions and fears that it would lead to more claims by victims. The council's insurers, Municipal Mutual Insurance, reportedly expressed concerns about compensation claims and suggested that the then chair of the council's social services committee, Malcolm King, would be sacked if he went public about the findings. Within the report, a representative of the company is quoted as saying: "Draconian as it may seem, you may have to consider with the elected members whether they wish to remove him from office if he insists on having the freedom to speak."

Many years later Malcolm King spoke out strongly about the suppression of the report. In November 2012, he said: "Because it was suppressed, the lessons of the Jillings report were not learned. It was the exchange of financial safety for the safety of real people. It was one of the most shameful parts of recent history."

The report itself reads: "The most striking fact to emerge is that five men who shared in common their employment as residential care workers at the Bryn Estyn home were convicted of serious offences involving at least 25 young people. Twenty of the victims were boys, five were girls. The age range was 10 to 16. Many of the allegations involving these men consisted of specimen charges; many others were left on the file."

Commenting on a culture of silence, the panel also wrote: "At Bryn Estyn, professional misgivings were discouraged and complaints viewed as disloyal. As a consequence, abusive and dangerous practices escalated out of control and unchecked." They also said: "Our findings show that time and again, the response to indications that children may have been abused has been too little and too late."

In November 2012 the Welsh Labour Party MP Ann Clwyd urged the House of Commons to ensure that the full report is published. She said: "I would ask that the Jillings report be published. I saw it, I wasn't supposed to see it – it was shown to me, I saw it at the time. It was subsequently pulped by the then Clwyd County Council because they were afraid of the attitude of the insurers. I would say please get the Jillings report published because it shows rape, bestiality, violent assaults and torture, and the effects on those young boys at that time cannot be under-estimated."

Mr Jillings has since denied that the report includes descriptions of bestiality. However, he did say: "What we found was horrific and on a significant scale. If the events in children's homes in North Wales were to be translated into a film, Oliver Twist would seem relatively benign. The scale of what happened, and how it was allowed, are a disgrace, and stain on the history of child care in this country."

The Waterhouse Inquiry and Operation Pallial

It is interesting that a Secretary of State should order an inquiry into child abuse in North Wales so soon after the *Jillings Report* had been hidden from public view. Ronald Waterhouse, a retired judge, and his team looked into hundreds of cases of child abuse in care homes in North Wales that were alleged to have taken place between 1974 and 1990. The inquiry interviewed 260 witnesses, many of whom required psychological support after giving their harrowing evidence.

Evidence was given to the inquiry until May 1998 and a 500,000 word report was submitted to the Welsh Secretary in late 1999. The report was published in February 2000, four months after it was submitted to the Secretary of State.

In the report, Waterhouse concluded that: "Widespread sexual abuse of boys occurred in children's residential establishments in Clwyd between 1974 and 1990." The report said there were also incidents of sexual abuse of female residents, although these allegations were less numerous.

In relation to the Bryn Estyn home, the report states: "The evidence before us has disclosed that for many children who were consigned to Bryn Estyn, in the 10 or so years of its existence as a community home, it was a form of purgatory or worse from which they emerged more damaged than when they had entered and for whom the future had become even more bleak."

The report contains 700 allegations of abuse and identifies 28 alleged abusers. Many more names were redacted due to either pending prosecutions or lack of evidence, according to Waterhouse. The report names and criticises numerous people who failed to offer adequate protection to vulnerable children. The report states that the inquiry recognised "the existence of a paedophile ring in the Wrexham and Chester area" but found no evidence proving that there was a "wide-ranging conspiracy involving prominent persons and others with the objective of sexual activity with children in care". This is at odds with accounts of some former residents.

In November 2012, amid a flurry of media interest in historic abuse cases, Children's Commissioner for Wales Keith Towler called for a fresh investigation. The resulting investigation is Operation Pallial. A preliminary report, published in early 2013, refers to 140 allegations of abuse at 18 Welsh children's homes from the period of 1963 to 1992. Of the complainants, 76 had not come forward before. At the time of writing, allegations have been made against 120 individuals by 236 people. Numerous arrests have taken place and legal proceedings are ongoing, which limits what can be included in this edition of this book.

The first person to be charged in relation to Operation Pallial was John Allen, who established the Bryn Alyn Community of residential homes in 1968, a lucrative and toxic empire which included 11 children's homes. Allen had been jailed for six years in 1995 for the abuse of six boys in his homes. In the wake of Waterhouse, Allen was charged with many further offences, stretching from the 1960s to 1980s. However, in 2003 a judge threw the 44 charges against Allen out on the grounds that media focus on him meant he could not get a fair trial, and because of the amount of time that had elapsed since offences were said to have taken place.

Nevertheless, in November 2014 Allen was convicted of dozens of offences against 18 boys and one girl, aged between seven and 15 at the time of the attacks. Victims spoke of a culture of fear at his homes and Allen's tendency to shift from apparently friendly to violent and abusive and back again rapidly, sometimes giving his victims money or gifts after attacks. The prolific predator claimed in court that his accusers fabricated allegations against him in a bid to gain compensation. Aged 73 when convicted, there is a good chance that Allen will die in jail.

As well as offences against children within his homes, it is alleged that Allen abused children elsewhere, which had been trafficked by a paedophile ring. There is more to learn about the relationship between Allen and other paedophiles, and about connections between rings. This should emerge as other Pallial cases come through the courts and other investigations come to fruition.

Learning from paedophile rings

It does not appear to me that, as societies, we have a good understanding of the minds of individual paedophiles, let alone the sinister cultures of paedophile rings. We know from the cases that have come to light that they are variable in terms of social make-up. Some, as described above, have been composed of teachers, social workers and care workers but with apparent links to other individuals – possibly even politicians and civil servants.

Some other rings identified in the UK in recent years have been made up of young Asian men and some have been composed of gang members who had involvement in various other criminal activities. One paedophile ring, that molested and traded indecent images of toddlers, involved women working in nurseries. The way in which gangs groom and exploit underage girls and boys, often with the aid of drugs, has been observed in many countries and has links to prostitution and human trafficking.

What all these types of paedophile rings have in common is the relationship of power over children and the ability to instil fear in victims to prevent them from reporting crimes. In the example of the Welsh cases discussed above, the death of key people, the loss of evidence and the damage done to victims means we may never know the exact make-up and dynamics of the network of abusers. We also may be always left wondering why certain people disregarded evidence and hindered investigations.

However high into the British Establishment the network went, we can be sure of one thing – the abuse was systematic. It was not just lone abusers opportunistically taking advantage of children – it was an organised network of trusted, powerful professionals who were deceitful, manipulative and sadistic. They went to great efforts to position themselves in places where they would have maximum control over vulnerable children. They corrupted children and caused untold psychological and emotional damage to people they were employed to care for and nurture.

Putting premeditated, systematic abuse down to the sexual urges or inclinations of the perpetrators would be a flawed analysis, playing into the manipulations of Righton and other PIE members. Sexual abuse is not about normal sexual pleasure – it is about power, control, cruelty, deceit, corruption, violence and malice. These are characteristics of the psychopath. The characteristics required to establish paedophile rings and for networks to 'flourish' in different locations, smugly operating under the noses of the authorities, are those of devious psychopaths.

Some might say people like Peter Righton, Peter Howarth and Keith Laverack were 'successful psychopaths', as they gained positions of power and took a long time to get caught. I would argue that, whatever their personal pathologies, they created a psychopathic culture – and authorities were poor at recognising it and tackling it. As with other paedophile rings around the world.

Sex abusers create and exploit a culture of fear, shame and silence that prevents victims and witnesses from coming forward and giving evidence. As this culture of fear and shame breaks down, the psychopathic culture of paedophile rings also erodes, as it does in other areas of life when psychopathy has dominated.

Adults have had sex with children in many parts of the world historically. It still happens in many places without it being regarded as a crime. The term paedophilia was not used until the 19th century, and for much of its history was used as a diagnostic category rather than a criminal category. The *Diagnostic and Statistical Manual of Mental Disorders* still regards a sexual interest in children as a medical condition. Links have been made between paedophilia and various mental conditions, including personality disorders.

Clearly research into the mental health of individual paedophiles is extremely valuable. It can help identify risk factors and patterns of behaviour which can help reduce the number of children being abused. It can also help experts support those who are at high risk of offending to resist their drives. However, this is dependent on paedophiles engaging with professionals and being motivated to not offend.

Given what we have learned in recent decades about paedophile rings and the superficial charm, status, deviousness and lucidity of those involved, it is clear that they are skilled at manipulating people, corrupting systems and avoiding justice. The wealthier ones also have the legal system weighted in their favour and they can threaten defamation action at the slightest suggestion they are linked to child abuse. Those paedophiles in gangs have the mystique of their business and drugs to allure young people and the threat of violence to hold them and enforce silence.

Predatory psychopaths are extremely difficult people to deal with, even when in secure psychiatric wards or prisons. However, understanding them and managing their behaviours is not beyond the ability of professional teams. There is probably more that psychiatric professionals could do to support investigatory bodies when there are suspicions about paedophile networks. They can shed light on characteristics as well as group dynamics. A systemic, multidisciplinary approach is required if authorities are to bring rings of paedophiles to justice more effectively and more quickly than has historically been the case.

The archetypal image of the dirty old man in a raincoat flashing children has perhaps blinded us to some of the realities of paedophilia. As we know from some of the paedophiles discussed above, they are often charming, accomplished, articulate people. They often appear as warm, caring, affectionate and kind friends to children, until they transform into sinister molesters or violent monsters. Rather than be armed with a gun or knife, the weapon of such people may be an understanding smile, soothing voice, charm and wit.

Learning all that we can about paedophiles with psychopathic traits can shed light on the communication strategies and other patterns of behaviour of psychopaths more generally. Societies have been slow to tackle paedophile rings and recognise that the apparent characters and roles of those we trust are sometimes masks and shields.

The more we can scrutinise the masks of aggressors, the faster we can identify threats in the future. Sometimes, like in the case of Savile, the sinister character in the mask was staring us in the face – and laughing. In other cases – and in other examples of psychopathy in public life – the masks are much more effective and the abuse more subtle.

Chapter 8 – The media: glittering distractions and power

Having previously worked in the mental health field, when I became a journalist many people commented that "it must be very different" or said things like "Wow, that's quite a change". In reality there are many commonalities. Both involve getting alongside people at challenging times of their lives, interviewing them and those close to them and then documenting the interactions. Although reports in psychiatry are deeper than in journalism – and aimed at supporting health rather than selling newspapers or manipulating public opinion – both disciplines can involve interacting with people who are distressed and aggressive.

As a reporter I covered murders, arson attacks, suicides, fraud, animal abuse and stories related to gang behaviour. I met victims of crime and also people who were responsible for crimes. Many of the aggressors in stories were far from being cunning successful psychopaths. They were generally rather inept or desperate people. My experiences within psychiatry stood me in good stead for dealing calmly with volatile, overwhelmed, aggressive and difficult people – particularly editors and news editors.

There have been quite a few times when I felt that people within news organisations had a good range of personality disorder traits. This perception was not diminished by watching some of Fleet Street's 'finest' arrogantly parade before Lord Leveson's Inquiry into press standards in 2012.

The volatility, aggression and bitterness of editors and others in the news industry can be partially explained by their own rather desperate position. Newspapers have been losing circulation and been under considerable financial pressure for many years. Numerous titles that had been around for a very long time have vanished, become free or become printed less frequently. To drive sales, many papers became increasingly sensationalist, favouring titillating celebrity stories over those about issues that are genuinely in the public interest.

Once sordid celebrity stories became staple fodder, the private lives of stars became territory to be aggressively – and sometimes illegally – invaded. Some papers became increasingly unethical in how they found stories. Journalists resorting to phone hacking ultimately dragged tabloids further into the gutter and tarnished perceptions of the whole profession. This sullying by association was unfair on the vast majority of journalists and newspapers as most good stories are got through building relationships with contacts rather than criminality.

The Leveson Inquiry occurred because journalists employed by Rupert Murdoch's News International – the then British branch of News Corp – had conspired to hack voicemails. In 2007, the *News of the World's* royal editor Clive Goodman and private investigator Glenn Mulcaire – who worked exclusively for News International for years – were jailed for hacking voicemails to generate stories about royals. Prince William had been perplexed to discover that stories had been produced about private aspects of his life and realised that the most likely source of the information was from his voicemail or that of his confidants. Goodman received a four-month sentence and Mulcaire was jailed for six months at that point.

The line emanating from *News of the World* was that Goodman was a "rogue reporter", despite the fact that the court heard that Mulcaire also hacked the voicemails of Max Clifford, model Elle Macpherson, politician Simon Hughes and some figures from the world of football. Scoops from those clearly would have been no help to Goodman, who was under extreme pressure from his editor Andy Coulson to produce sensational royal stories. Coulson resigned from the *News of the World* when Goodman and Mulcaire pleaded guilty, in January 2007.

Despite the strong suggestion from evidence heard in court that phone hacking was happening on a significant scale at the *News of the World*, David Cameron appointed Coulson as the Conservative Party's director of communications a few months after Goodman and Mulcaire were jailed. When the Tories became part of a coalition government, in 2010, Coulson became the government's director of communications. Given how out of touch with certain parts of society the Conservative Party was seen to be, it seems likely that Coulson's tabloid expertise helped get Cameron to Number 10.

If Cameron had ensured Coulson was thoroughly vetted, he would have discovered that he was accused of workplace bullying when at *News of the World*. In 2008, an employment tribunal upheld a claim of unfair dismissal of a sports journalist and referred to a "consistent pattern of bullying behaviour". Coulson's predecessors in the communications director role all were subjected to what is termed 'developed vetting', which is undertaken by MI5. The process goes deeply into the individual's life, relationships and proclivities. It ensures that people with dark secrets, who therefore are vulnerable to blackmail, are not appointed to sensitive roles.

Had Coulson been subjected to developed vetting, questions would have been raised about the extent of phone hacking at *News of the World* and why he resigned if he – as he claimed – had not been complicit. Prior to the royal phone hacking case, there had been a number of allegations made to the police about *News of the World* gathering information by illegal means. However, it is interesting to note that those cases were not pursued until after complaints were made by representatives of the royal family. The Metropolitan Police still has questions to answer about sitting on important information for years – and allowing the 'rogue reporter' line to be maintained despite evidence of wider criminality.

Following the conviction of Mulcaire and Goodman, News International made large payments to prominent individuals who had their privacy invaded by *News of the World*. However, paying off victims through civil processes did not, ultimately, prevent the public from finding out about the industrial-scale phone hacking at the paper. *The Guardian* ran numerous pieces about voicemail hacking and other poor practices at *News of the World*, while politicians also focused considerable attention on ethical shortcomings and suspected criminality at the paper. American investigative agencies also began to scrutinise the activities of Rupert Murdoch's titles and the ethics of the wider News Corp empire.

In London in January 2011, as it launched Operation Weeting, the Metropolitan Police said it had significant new information about activities within *News of the World*. Andy Coulson had resigned from his post of government communications director a few days before, citing "continued coverage of events connected to my old job at the *News of the World*" at his reason for stepping down.

Three journalists from the paper were arrested in April 2011. When Glen Mulcaire had first been arrested in 2006, the police found extensive records of his 'work' hacking phones for *News of the World*. Mulcaire kept meticulous notes of his activities, including the mobile phone numbers and voicemail pin codes of a huge number of people spanning public life. It could be said that police finding this information is what eventually brought *News of the World* down but, ultimately, it was the criminality that destroyed the paper.

In July 2011 the Home Affairs Select Committee was told that Mulcaire had information on almost 4,000 individuals. It later emerged that as well as using the pin codes himself to listen illegally to voicemails, Mulcaire taught *News of the World* journalists how do so. By the summer of 2011, the police had alerted 170 of the people Mulcaire had files on to tell them that they may have been targeted. Of those who had made complaints against *News of the World* by that point, a handful received apologies and compensation from News International. The empire contested many others.

There was growing media coverage of phone hacking during the first half of 2011. But the turning point, in terms of prominence, came when it emerged that a teenage murder victim's voicemail had been hacked after she disappeared. Milly Dowler, a 13-year-old from Surrey, had gone missing in March 2002 and her body was discovered in September the same year. Serial killer Levi Bellfield was convicted of the murder in June 2011.

Within days of the conviction, *The Guardian* reported that police had discovered that *News of the World* had gathered information on the Dowler family after Milly vanished. It was also claimed in the *Guardian* article that Mulcaire hacked the girl's voicemail on behalf of *News of the World* while police investigated her disappearance. *The Guardian* piece claimed that *News of the World* journalists had deleted messages, which gave hope to the Dowler family because if she was listening to and deleting messages she would have been alive.

It has emerged more recently that *News of the World* told Surrey Police about its knowledge of Milly Dowler's voicemails, and an issue of the paper on April 14 2002 alluded to a message from a recruitment agency. It is interesting that the police, at that point, did not seem to investigate why *News of the World* was illegally listening to a child's voicemails.

When it emerged, in July 2011, that the Dowler family had instigated a claim against *News of the World*, Labour Party leader Ed Miliband said the then chief executive of News International Rebekah Brooks should "consider her conscience and consider her position". Mrs Brooks denied knowledge of phone hacking during her editorship but ultimately did step down. The prominence of the Dowler voicemail hacking case influenced politicians to express concerns about News Corp's desired takeover of BSkyB.

The momentum of the case against *News of the World* staff – and public anger – was also driven by allegations emerging in 2011 of voicemails of families of soldiers killed in action, relatives of victims of the 2005 London bombings and campaigner Sara Payne were hacked. The last had particular resonance because *News of the World* had supported Payne's campaign for parents to have access to information about sex offenders in their area, after her seven-year-old daughter Sarah was murdered by a paedophile. Rebekah Brooks issued a statement saying that *News of the World* was not aware of Glen Mulcaire investigating Sara Payne.

On July 7 2011, then chief executive of News Corp James Murdoch announced that *News of the World* would close after publishing its final edition on 10 July. He stated that the paper was "sullied" and said "if recent allegations are true, it was inhuman and has no place in our company." The announcement followed decisions by prominent companies to pull lucrative adverts from the paper. Rebekah Brooks resigned as News International chief executive a week after James Murdoch announced the closure of *News of the World*. A few months later the empire launched a very similar paper to the *News of the World*, called *The Sun on Sunday*.

Since 1999 there have been 104 arrests of News International staff or others working on behalf of or linked to the organisation. More than 90 individuals have been arrested or re-arrested since Operation Weeting began in 2011. Investigations are continuing as I write, but to date 26 people have been charged by the police in the UK. Many of the charges have related to ways in which information was gathered or perverting the course of justice. Some cases have been concluded and others are still active. Other investigations into News Corp are taking place in the USA and have been pursued in Australia.

After a high profile 'hacking trial', which concluded in 2014 and in which Rebekah Brooks was cleared, some media attacked the CPS and police with the deceptive line that, after an expensive police investigation, only Coulson was convicted. In reality, of eight people charged with voicemail hacking around the time Coulson was, six were convicted. Coulson was the only one who pleaded not guilty and was convicted – five others pleaded guilty.

In the 2014 coverage, newspapers also tended to ignore the fact that hacking took place on an industrial scale at *News of the World* – and therefore there were a large number of individual crimes and victims. They also neglected to point out that several other people have been convicted of crimes in relation to News International over recent years. For example, in 2005 two individuals pleaded guilty to breaching the Data Protection Act, two pleaded guilty to conspiracy to commit misconduct in a public office and one was convicted of acquiring private customer information from British Telecom's database.

In 2007, as discussed above, Goodman and Mulcaire pleaded guilty to charges of conspiracy to intercept communications, better known as phone or voicemail hacking. In 2012 Andy Coulson was charged with conspiracy to intercept communications and he was found guilty in June 2014.

In 2013 former *News of the World* chief reporter Neville Thurlbeck, news editors Greg Miskiw and James Weatherup and reporter Dan Evans pleaded guilty to conspiring to intercept communications. Glenn Mulcaire, who had faced fresh charges – including that of hacking Milly Dowler's mobile – also pleaded guilty.

In July 2014 Andy Coulson was jailed for 18 months, while both Miskiw and Thurlbeck received six month custodial sentences. Weatherup was given a four-month suspended sentence and ordered to do 200 hours community service. Mulcaire also escaped a prison term by receiving a six-month suspended sentence and 200 hours community service. Dan Evans, who admitted misconduct in public office and perverting the course of justice as well as phone hacking charges, received a 10-month sentence, suspended for a year and 200 hours community service. The judge said he would have given a custodial sentence but took into account that Evans gave evidence against others, including his former boss Andy Coulson.

When sentencing Coulson, Miskiw, Thurlbeck, Weatherup and Mulcaire, Mr Justice Saunders said: "Over the period there were many thousands of phone hacks and many hundreds of voicemails were accessed illegally. Targets of phone hacking were politicians, celebrities, and royalty. In addition there were people who were targeted simply because they were friends of, worked with, or were related to famous people."

He also said: "Many hours were no doubt spent by Mulcaire and by reporters listening to messages which did not provide any leads for stories. They did however pick up intensely personal messages, some but not all of which were about relationships. Other personal material included messages left by doctors' surgeries and clinics which the recipients were entitled to expect would remain private. As a result of intercepting thousands of messages, the *News of the World* discovered information about famous and powerful people which ended up as front page exclusives and caused serious upset and distress to the subjects and to those close to them. An additional consequence was that, as nobody knew how the *News of the World* had got the stories, an undercurrent of distrust developed between friends and family who suspected each other of selling the information."

The judge went on to say: "All the defendants that I have to sentence, save for Mr Mulcaire, are distinguished journalists who had no need to behave as they did to be successful. They all achieved a great deal without resorting to the unlawful invasion of other peoples' privacy. Those achievements will now count for nothing." Andrew Edis QC, the lead prosecutor in the hacking trial, said the journalists who were convicted "utterly corrupted" the *News of the World*, which became "at the very highest level a criminal enterprise".

The charges Rebekah Brooks was cleared of were conspiracy to intercept communications, conspiracy to commit misconduct in public office and perverting the course of justice. During the trial, the media got excited by information emerging that Brooks and Coulson had an affair spanning six years. This was interesting because it revealed hypocrisy, as while pursuing stories about celebrity affairs they were having one. However, it is more interesting to me that Rebekah Brooks, one of Britain's most notable journalists, failed to notice one of the biggest industrial scandals of our age right under her nose – despite the fact that one of her partners was at the centre of it.

Jurors could not reach a verdict in relation to charges against Coulson and Clive Goodman of conspiring to commit misconduct in public office. The charges relate to allegations of paying police officers for the acquisition of royal phone books. In June 2014 the prosecution said they would pursue a retrial of Coulson and Goodman.

In addition to charges mentioned above, it is possible that Rupert Murdoch's UK company, now known as News UK rather than News International, could be charged as a company. The Metropolitan Police have questioned senior News Corporation and former *News of the World* figures under caution. For such a prosecution to be successful, it would have to be proven that the "controlling minds" of an organisation committed a crime.

Financial pressures upon the paper were no justification for *News of the World* staff to hack phones, as it had an enviable circulation. Sensationalist stories generated illegally were not desperate measures to survive but devious scams to bolster dominance within the market and the careers of individuals. If Coulson had been less successful at getting explosive splashes into the paper he might not have got his role working with David Cameron. The success of *News of the World* also increased the political power of News International and of Rupert Murdoch, who has publicly denied knowledge of illegal practices in his newsrooms.

It was newspapers that were not filled with salacious stories and celebrity tittle tattle – and whose staff did not hack phones – which suffered in the circulation war. It is difficult for more serious newspapers to compete when the public is more interested in stories about footballers and actors having sex than political corruption or economic exploitation. It is also hard for ethical and law-abiding newspapers to compete when some papers employ people who hack phones and use various other 'dark arts' to get stories.

It should be stressed, however, that circulations generally had been declining for some time before the hacking scandal came to light. Circulations had been falling for many years all around the world, primarily because of changes in the way that people consume news.

Threats to journalism and the decline of the traditional press

In recent years it has become common to lament the decline of the newspaper industry. There are very good reasons for this. Diligent and effective press covering all areas, from the most obscure parliamentary committee to the dodgy dealing in some backwater local council, is essential for democracy to be transparent and therefore effective.

Journalists are tasked with holding people to account, particularly those who have power. As papers become more under-resourced and more inclined towards cutting and pasting from press releases ('churnalism') it becomes harder for the public to hold key organisations like councils, corporations, police forces, schools and hospitals to account.

Another reason to lament the economic precariousness of the print media is that it has caused newspapers to change hands so frequently that it is hard to keep up with who owns which titles. Many newspaper titles that existed since the early days of the industry have vanished and overall there has been a consolidation of power into the hands of a small number of people. This loss of press plurality has the potential to undermine democracy.

The power of newspapers to challenge powerful people and organisations has diminished over the decades, in part because papers are so dependent on advertising revenue. This can lead to journalists losing control of what gets into papers while advertisers and media sales staff gain more power. What this means is stories about wrongdoing within big companies and other lucrative advertisers are more likely to be kept out of the press and fluffy PR-driven bits of churnalism fill the pages instead.

Challenging financial circumstances of newspapers has also led to a more risk-averse editorial culture as struggling publications could be dragged under by an expensive libel case. The confidence editors have in running bold, controversial stories is also eroded by the contraction of the market. They are less likely to take the risk of drawing their paper into a libel case if there are few jobs they could go to if they were sacked.

As well as there being reasons to lament the decay of the newspaper industry, there are good reasons to celebrate it. Newspapers are not sacred things but products designed to make money, influence public opinion or both. Very few 'quality' national newspapers make a profit and therefore are being kept going by wealthy people with political agendas. All newspapers, whether broadsheets or red tops, should be recognised as part of the apparatus of propaganda and distraction.

Newspapers and broadcast media are part of what the sociologists and philosophers Max Horkheimer and Theodor Adorno described as "the culture industry" – products which are alluring and comforting distractions from the stark realities of life. Some may believe that whatever news media they consume, they are being made aware of 'reality'. However, what readers and viewers receive is extremely partial, filtered by politics and shaped by the political views of media owners and editors – who are often extremely right-wing control freaks.

There is little control on who edits newspapers or owns media companies. Apart from money, the only limit in the UK is monopolies and mergers regulations preventing one organisation from gaining too much control of the media. However, in many countries this does not happen. On the whole, rich white men dominate the news media and use their power to influence public consciousness and politics, as has been the case in Italy with Silvio Berlusconi.

In democracies, professionals with power over people tend to require that checks are made into their backgrounds. Doctors, nurses, lawyers, teachers and other professionals are vetted to try to ensure that law-abiding and hopefully ethically-minded people are appointed. Conversely, owners of media companies and their editors, despite having considerable power over the global community, do not undergo criminal record checks and are certainly not assessed for personality disorders.

Given the devious, exploitative, bloodthirsty, fickle and callous nature of the news media, psychopathic traits could well be useful in the industry. It is ironic therefore, that something even colder than the most callous media tycoon or bloodthirsty editor has challenged their dominance – the computer.

It is another strange irony that computers – amoral machines developed by large corporations, universities and the military – have quite quickly become a tool allowing the less powerful to challenge the mighty. Gadgets in our pockets can transmit information and photos that can lead to revolutions and bring down governments. This became very apparent in the Arab spring. One does not need to be a trained journalist to break a global news story or to disseminate information that can tip the balance of an election or even a war.

As I write this, in summer 2014, considerably more people are reading Twitter – and for longer – than any newspaper. In fact, despite it being their nemesis, journalists source a great many stories from Twitter. Rather than go out and actually meet people or pick up the phone, many now trawl Twitter for celebrity spats and meltdowns, salacious gossip or ranting politicians. Lead stories in national newspapers are now routinely built around a single foolish tweet or Facebook update.

The hacking trial made history because it was the first trial of that size and complexity to be 'live tweeted' in great detail. The dramatist and author Peter Jukes began to tweet from the start of the trial and his Twitter following increased dramatically. People were so riveted by tweets from the trial that many supported him financially through the trial by 'crowd funding' his activities. As a result, he could afford attend the trial each day for eight months and offer such meticulous reporting that it was nothing short of revolutionary.

The relentless effort and accuracy of Jukes put to shame journalists from mainstream media, who were accustomed to doing sporadic tweets from a trial while gathering information for a few hundred word news piece. By contrast, Peter tweeted around half a million words. However, when the trial was over he suggested that his efforts actually made some papers less inclined to invest in court reporters. Instead they relied on his detailed coverage and that of fellow 'hacking hack' James Doleman. Other, rather bitter journalists – and those with connections to News International – harangued Jukes on Twitter as he shared the trial with the public.

The presence and popularity of the internet is the main reason why newspapers have lost sales and become so dependent on advertisers for revenue. While this has effectively castrated formerly bold publications and turned their journalism into churnalism, the migration of readers to the internet has given ordinary tweeters and bloggers power beyond that of some experienced editors.

In a short space of time we have moved from an era where a member of the public would be lucky to get a letter printed in a newspaper to one where words written by anyone can be read by hundreds of millions of people around the world. In the few years I have used Twitter I have seen numerous incidences where people with a small following had their posts retweeted by thousands of people. This can result in their words reaching millions in a matter of hours and the following of the individual multiplying at a pace that no newspaper could hope to emulate.

Although journalists take stories from social media and use platforms to publicise stories, the truth is that social media is the mortal enemy of the traditional media. The level of outrage expressed by the traditional press in 2012 after Lord McAlpine was tenuously linked to a child abuse ring was huge. Given the frequency in which newspapers smear people, I believe the apparent level of tabloid outrage was not as much about a man being unfairly treated as an opportunistic attempt to rubbish social media. It seemed to me to be a desperate attempt to regain power, authority and ultimately market share.

The efforts by the mainstream media to attack and undermine Twitter after the McAlpine non-story ultimately failed. One reason for this was many news reports were no more than free PR for an unpopular, tax-exiled millionaire who made considerable money exploiting a mistake while actual victims of child abuse were forgotten. McAlpine's apparent grasping nature and his PR overkill made him lose sympathy rapidly. Personal attacks by social media users continued and some tweeters continued to post information about his collection of images of children made by a sex abuser.

Despite the efforts of newspapers to characterise Twitter users as malicious, stupid and ignorant, the McAlpine episode may have drawn more people to Twitter than it sold traditional newspapers. It also showed how out-of-touch the Establishment was in relation to social media. After McAlpine said he would sue all Twitter users who mentioned him, his team told the press that they had access to technology that would tell them 'how many followers each person has'. This was a ridiculous thing to say as the number of followers each Twitter account has is apparent for all to see.

Having initially stated he would sue all Twitter users who in anyway drew attention to him, McAlpine eventually said he would only sue those with a large number of followers. He and his legal team arbitrarily defined this as accounts having more than 500 followers. This added to the perception of McAlpine and his advisers being hopelessly out-of-touch, as a huge number of accounts have more than 500 followers.

He was then frustrated in his efforts to get personal information about account holders, despite requests to the site owners and an attempt to use the Metropolitan Police in his mission. As libel is a civil action in England, McAlpine's attempt to use the police to gain personal data on individuals was highly questionable.

McAlpine and various right-wing newspapers characterised Twitter as a wild west, needing to be tamed – perhaps by an ageing Conservative gun-slinger. A wild shower of bullets fired in the air, however, did very little. There was more caution about retweeting controversial things for a few days but ultimately McAlpine was viewed by many as an exploitative money-grabber who tried to throw his weight around in a world beyond his control.

Lord McAlpine ultimately won a libel case against Sally Bercow – the wife of the House of Commons speaker – as a result of a tweet mentioning that his name was trending. This meant that a large number of people had already tweeted about him by that point. McAlpine also got out-of-court settlements from the BBC and ITV, despite his name not being mentioned by either broadcaster. It is debatable, however, that his reputation was restored and in the process the English judicial system has been criticised by many. The whole affair reinforced the view that defamation action is a vindictive rich man's sport and England is the libel capital of the world.

In some ways Twitter and other social media has a similar ethos to punk in that it is anarchic and if the old order tries to participate it is treated with disdain. When David Cameron joined Twitter in late 2012 he was immediately greeted by a flood of insults and sharp criticisms. The right-wing press wrote off those who attacked him as 'trolls' but this is an extremely simplistic and defensive representation. It was easier for them to disregard the validity of the critics than acknowledge that the situation shows how out-of-touch they had become.

The pattern of use of Twitter and other social media is very interesting and the demographics are significant. Social media gives a stronger voice to angry dissenters and the disenfranchised than they have ever had before. Rather than – like most media – favouring the Establishment, Twitter and other social media tip the balance the other way.

In a recessionary period the unemployed and underemployed will have more time and more inclination than many to voice grievances on Twitter and use it to mock the powerful. Rather than – as in previous downturns – the unemployed and underemployed being isolated and powerless, they now can find comradeship on social media and criticise and satirise those who they feel are responsible for their hardship.

We have moved very quickly from a situation where wealthy, conservative people use print and broadcast media to consolidate their power, to one where swarms of articulate bloggers and Twitter users can attack like bees or piranhas. However, the speed at which unpopular policies and those who announce them can be lambasted may ultimately help politics. If observed carefully, social media can work like large – if anarchic – focus groups.

The anonymity afforded by the internet allows people to act differently than they would normally, but over time the truth tends to come out. Court cases of abusive trolls have revealed pitiful people seeking attention or a feeling of power. Nevertheless, malicious people using the internet as a long-distance weapon can cause real harm, and cases of suicides following online bullying have made headlines in recent years.

On Twitter it can take a while to work out who is persistently accosting people out of malice, as opposed to mischief or a genuine critique of issues they represent. The mainstream media has a tendency to gloss over distinctions and therefore describe people as trolls, whether they are mocking politicians or threatening rape.

Unlike newspapers though, which often spread toxic prejudice that gets regurgitated by members of the public, the nature of social media means vindictive, narrow-minded perspectives are ignored in favour of novel, entertaining and inclusive ideas. This difference is a severe challenge to the power of manipulative media organisations – and the politicians who benefit from the dissemination of malicious discourses.

Twitter particularly is structured in a way that elevates those who say original, inspiring or witty things and quickly turns those who make the most foolish and vindictive comments into figures of scorn. The retweet facility means that people with the most interesting ideas and most lucid ways of putting things gain prominence and influence. Conversely, people who are malicious get challenged quickly by other members and can be mocked, blocked, suspended and even identified and arrested.

Most of us have just been finding our way with social media over recent years but from what has been seen already it is clear that old power structures are weakened as traditional media is challenged. If it is the case that some powerful people in society have gained wealth and status by exploitation, lies, corruption and rigging the system, the failure of the media they control and rise of new, democratic media is highly significant.

The shift in power from those who own the apparatus of publication has been aided by the internet but it is certainly not a new ambition. In any culture there are tensions and often conflicts between those who seek to maintain power and those who would like to take it from them. It has manifested itself in different ways during different phases of technological advancement.

Communication technologies – from cave art to hieroglyphs to parchments, stone bulletins, news sheets, newspapers and the internet – have been pivotal to social transformation. They have been key weapons in battles between those who have and those who seek power. We can appreciate this if we reflect upon the impact of the printing press.

One key development enabled by the printing press was the large-scale reproduction, adaptation and dissemination of sacred writings. Prior to this, spiritual authority was retained by the Catholic Church, who controlled the production and dissemination of sacred texts. The 16th century reformer Martin Luther, along with other revolutionary theologians, used print media to challenge Catholic dominance and promote new interpretations of Christianity.

In 1517 Luther published *Ninety-Five Theses on the Power and Efficacy of Indulgences*, which he nailed to a church door in the German university city of Wittenberg. The writing challenged key aspects of Roman Catholic doctrine and practices. This radical writing transformed the religious, social and economic landscape by encouraging the protestant reformation. The technology ultimately led to the religious and cultural plurality we enjoy today.

The printing press enabled the production of a myriad of radical pamphlets, newspapers, novels and political treatises. Rather than being the preserve of tiny elites, reading and writing became increasingly common and new ideas spread and germinated rapidly. This meant that public discourse was increasingly shaped by revolutionaries and radicals and the power of traditional authorities was gradually eroded. The trend has continued as we have developed other media technologies. The world has been changed forever by the democratisation of the means of publication, and it continues to change rapidly.

New communication technologies threaten the 'natural' social order and encourage political debate and revolution. In the 20th century the television was frequently blamed for the antisocial behaviour and the breakdown of society, although public broadcasters like the BBC saw it as a means of educating the masses. Perceptions of the internet have been similarly divided. Some immediately saw its potential to encourage liberation, equality and free-speech while others worried it would erode social structures and values. In reality both of these things have happened, as they are inextricably linked.

As more and more people have stronger voices, amplified by media technologies, old social structures inevitably break down. It is those who have lost their traditional authority – such as press barons, politicians and the Church – who are most troubled by the change. There may be attempts – as in the case of McAlpine and the right-wing press – to challenge new technologies, but ultimately they have become the property of the masses and cannot easily be taken away in a capitalist society.

The internet has become such an important tool in business that if it ceased to function, corporations and economies would struggle to function. All sorts of markets are now so dependent on the internet – for trading and information used by traders and investors – that nations would be destabilised if the web went down.

This reality means, ironically, that as long as capitalism as we know it operates, the masses will have communication tools at our disposal to challenge aspects of the system. As is often the case, the seeds of revolution are present in the machinery of oppression. Conversely, newspapers – which have been present through the development of global capitalism and helped drive it – are dying as a result of changes in advertising and consumption patterns.

Such has been the power of newspapers and their owners that the loss of their influence shifts power relationships globally in unexpected ways. The next chapter outlines the history of news media and examines how press barons and media moguls became some of the most powerful people the world has ever known. The cultures they created may appear liberating and illuminating or pathological and imprisoning – depending on your point of view. Nevertheless, the troubling reality is they have often had more influence on the public consciousness than elected politicians.

Chapter 9 – Press barons, media moguls and political influence

An abbreviation that pops up a lot on social media is MSM, meaning mainstream media. The term is usually used in a pejorative manner, often within a complaint that some or other important story is not being covered by the corporate press. Behind the term, therefore, are implicit assumptions that misinformation is being peddled by the Establishment through the media and large news corporations distort or neglect the truth. If we consider the history of news media, we can see that there are good reasons for these perceptions.

By the 17th Century newspapers were becoming increasingly common in Europe. Literacy levels were low, so those who could read commonly read papers aloud to those who could not. Early newspapers were often full of stories that state rulers wanted to be known – such as their own successes – mixed liberally with sensationalist dross. The public's appetite for news was such that papers did not need to supplement income through advertising for quite some time.

Newspapers from the very beginning had a strong whiff of tawdriness. Nevertheless, some editors used them as an effective means of exposing corruption and abuses of power. For instance, in 1766 William Bolts produced a newspaper in Calcutta aimed at British readers but which dared to criticise the East India Company and British government. As a result, he was eventually forced to return to England but then published a 500-page book detailing corruption within the company and the exploitation and abuse of Indians.

A similarly bold newspaper, *The Bengal Gazette*, was produced by James Augustus Hickey from 1780. The East India Company took great exception to his publication and he ended up being fined for defamation and then imprisoned. After spending four months in prison he was fined again, which bankrupted him and killed off the paper.

Similar situations, where agitators, critics or satirists use newspapers to challenge those in power – only to be sued or imprisoned – have happened throughout the history of journalism. The British magazine *Private Eye* has been sued for libel numerous times since it was first produced, in 1961. It has managed to survive many legal attacks – in part due to a number of wealthy investors, including the satirist Peter Cook. On the whole, however, powerful figures have warded off perceived radicalism by dominating the newspaper industry and other media.

In the 19th Century, when newspapers were the communication medium with greatest influence, the figure of the press baron came to the fore. By the early part of the 20th Century the press baron had become the media mogul, having expanded their empires and cultural influence into other forms of printed publishing, radio, film, and television.

In the last decades or so they have spread their influence onto the internet but with less success than they might have hoped for. Even the sharpest media magnate, like Rupert Murdoch, can seem out of their depth when plunging into the anarchic and murky world of social media. The former tabloid editor Piers Morgan is mocked persistently on Twitter. Furthermore, traditional publishers have not fared well economically compared to the fortunes of web pioneers and social media innovators. Nevertheless, the press barons did have it their way for a considerable time.

Any attempt to illustrate how culture has become what we experience today requires a focus on the news industry. To represent a sense of the power various media giants have held over the centuries – and articulate some of the tensions this has caused politically – I will focus on a selection of individuals.

This book is about the development of culture and the architecture of power as much as it is about psychopathy and therefore naming individuals does not mean I am suggesting they are psychopaths or their organisations are or were psychopathic cultures. In fact, the tenacity and deviousness of newspaper owners and staff has often helped remove unsavory people from power and bring criminals to justice. Nevertheless, from this collection of examples there will be behaviours that readers find reprehensible, both in themselves and in their long-term impact on the human world.

Alfred Harmsworth

Harmsworth, who became the first Viscount Northcliffe, was a British press baron and publishing magnate who was active in the late 19th and early 20th Century. He had and still has a colossal influence in political and public discourse. As well as printing popular newspapers, his company Amalgamated Press published non-fiction books under the Educational Book Company subsidiary.

Unlike many media company owners of today, Harmsworth was a journalist and this helped him tap into the public's appetite for sensation. As a result, he developed a number of extremely popular tabloid papers and also expanded his empire by buying up and turning around the fortunes of failing newspapers.

In 1896 he created, with his brother Harold, the *Daily Mail*, a British paper which during his lifetime had the highest circulation of any newspaper in the world. He managed to give readers the sense that they were buying a quality newspaper that was both cheaper and easier to read than some of the older and loftier papers. One of the tag lines of the early paper was "the penny newspaper for one halfpenny".

The belief that they are reading a quality paper, a cut above other tabloids, still seems to be held by *Daily Mail* readers. Most journalists I know would take a different view. My perception is that it is a rather tawdry paper full of deliberately half-baked, spiteful, prejudiced narratives, with the layout designed in such a way to give an extremely superficial veneer of respectability.

Viscount Northcliffe was also responsible for founding the *Daily Mirror* and he acquired *The Observer* and *The Times* when they were struggling financially. Owning such a broad spectrum of newspapers, in an era before other forms of mass media, gave him considerable influence across society. He had the power to destroy political careers and even bring down governments.

Northcliffe's titles expressing outrage about a scarcity of artillery shells for troops fighting in World War One brought down the Asquith government and led to a coalition being formed led by David Lloyd George, who actually offered Northcliffe a post in his cabinet. Northcliffe did not take the post but instead became director for propaganda, which probably gave him more power than many government ministers had.

Germans high-command was aware of Northcliffe's power and reportedly attempted to kill him by sending a warship to shell his house on the Kent coast. The shelling, in February 1917, struck a number of houses in the area and killed a woman and child. Northcliffe himself was not injured in the attack. The house still bears scars of the audacious assassination attempt.

Although one can appreciate the efforts Northcliffe made to support troops and bolster the war effort, it has to be said that a newspaper

proprietor being able to remove governments is inherently anti-demo-
cratic. Some have even suggested that Northcliffe helped push Britain
into the First World War. An editorial in *The Star* prior to the war stated:
"Next to the Kaiser, Lord Northcliffe has done more than any living man
to bring about the war."

Alfred Hugenberg

The German anti-Semite Hugenberg was a key figure in the rise of nation-
alism leading to World War Two and he regarded himself as Hitler's puppet master. Born in 1865, Hugenberg had a devastating effect on German
culture and international politics. His toxic impact is still being felt today.

While Hitler was still a small child, Hugenberg was already plotting
genocide. The businessman and media magnate helped Hitler become
the German Chancellor, before he ultimately had his own power stripped
away by the Nazi Party. Both he and Hitler seemed to regard the other
as a necessary evil to achieve their own goals.

In 1891 Hugenberg helped form the General German League, an
ultra-nationalist organisation which was succeeded by the Pan-German
League. By 1899 Hugenberg was calling for the annihilation of the
Polish population.

After a time working for the Ministry of Finance, Hugenberg became
a businessman. He was involved with the steel industry but his power
increased during the Great Depression when he acquired dozens of local
newspapers. His influence was strengthened when he gained control of
various film and media companies.

In the build-up to World War One, Hugenberg had been involved
in a number of nationalist bodies and he succeeded in pulling already
right-wing parties even further to the right. Like many Machiavellian
leaders, he exploited divisions by playing people off against each other.
However, due to his media influence, he not only spread poison through
political bodies but was able to infect a nation with his agenda of genocide and conflict.

Hugenberg was an elitist but saw in Hitler someone who could mobi-
lise support among the working classes. Consequently he aided Hitler and
the Nazi Party, despite the fact that the Nazis were political competitors
of his German National People's Party (DNVP). He financially supported
the party and used his media empire to ensure Hitler got extensive and
positive coverage.

After gaining a stronger profile, Hitler broke links with Hugenberg, who responded by giving him unfavourable press. However, the benefits to each of them of collaborating outweighed the disadvantages and by early 1933 Hugenberg's newspapers were running pro-Hitler articles once again.

If Hugenberg at that time regarded Hitler as a means of gaining political power for himself and the DNVP, the plan failed. In a deal devised by President Paul von Hindenburg, Hugenberg agreed to Hitler becoming Chancellor on the condition that he gained the ministries of economics and agriculture. A series of bad decisions by Hugenberg, however, angered farmers and ministers and he was driven out of the cabinet.

In late 1933 Hugenberg's Telegraph Union news agency was taken over by Hitler's Ministry of Propaganda. He was allowed to keep most of his other media interests until 1943, when the Nazis bought the remainder of his news empire. Although he was stripped of political power before the war, Hugenberg was allowed to remain at the Reichstag as a guest until 1945. He was detained by allied forces at the end of the war but a denazification court ultimately deemed him a 'fellow traveller' rather than a Nazi. This allowed him to keep his remaining wealth. He died in 1951.

William Randolph Hearst

Hearst was born, in 1863 – two years before Hugenberg – and he died the same year as the German manipulator. Given that Hearst lived in America and was not in league with Hitler, one might assume he was a very different person from Hugenberg. However, his ruthless quest for power, his deceitfulness, his desire to stir up trouble and the callous way in which he encouraged war suggests he and Hugenberg had more similarities than differences.

As a result of the epic 1941 film, *Citizen Kane*, which is based quite loosely on his life, Hearst for many represents the archetypical press baron. The Kane character starts out with the intention of using journalism for the public good but becomes corrupt and degenerates into a ruthless and tyrannical figure obsessed by power. Kane is presented as a damaged, narcissistic control freak that ends up in solitude and filled with regret.

The moral of *Citizen Kane* is that wealth and power are ultimately hollow without love and compassion. Like *Shane*, it could be regarded as an anti-psychopath film, and its success perhaps highlights a widespread public concern about callous, powerful manipulators – both at the time of release and in subsequent decades.

Although the director Orson Welles and Hearst's biographer David
Nasaw have denied that Kane is an accurate reflection of Hearst, there
are striking parallels. Some speeches by Kane are almost the same as those
made by Hearst, who was furious about the film and did all he could to
prevent its release. After he failed to do so, he banned mention of the
film in any of his newspapers.

For me the film and controversy surrounding it is reflective of something even more interesting than Hearst himself. It represents the moment
when the film industry – and subsequently television – became more
powerful than newspapers and press barons. That is not to say that those
who came after Hearst have not had extreme power over populations.
However, they have often achieved this by investing heavily in films
and television. What was once a threat to press barons became part of
their weaponry.

For most of Hearst's life, however, newspapers were the most powerful
way of influencing popular opinion and politics. Like Hugenberg, he
was from a wealthy background and like Harmsworth he recognised the
power of producing sensationalist publications for mass consumption.

Despite his prosperous background, Hearst's engagement with elitist
culture was often antagonistic. He attended Harvard for a while but was
expelled for putting on drunken parties in Harvard Square and disrespect-
ful behaviour towards faculty members. This reportedly included sending
chamber pots to his professors with images of their faces illustrated in
the bowls – not unlike tabloid journalism itself.

After leaving Harvard, Hearst used his family's resources to enter the
publishing business. He started by taking over *The San Francisco Examiner*,
which his father already owned and then bought *The New York Journal*.
His efforts to dominate the New York newspaper industry led him to
sink rapidly to sensationalism. The term 'yellow journalism' was applied
to his output, referring to poorly-researched and often fabricated stories,
using dubious sources and massive but misleading headlines.

Despite questions about the integrity of Hearst's output, the public gorged on the sensation and this enabled him to acquire more and
more papers across the US. In addition to dozens of newspapers, Hearst
acquired and developed numerous glossy magazines. *Cosmopolitan, Good
Housekeeping* and *Harper's Bazaar* are some of Hearst's magazines that
are still published. At its peak, Hearst's empire was the largest newspaper
and magazine producer in the world.

His other media interests included the news agencies Universal
News and International News Service, the film company Cosmopolitan

Productions and a radio station. Given the fact that Hearst's family fortune would have allowed him to dominate most industries, his focus on media suggests that power was a stronger motivator than money. In fact, the media aspect of the Hearst's family's empire was relatively unprofitable and was subsidised by the more lucrative businesses of mining, forestry and ranching.

As well as through his media domination, Hearst expressed his desire for power through politics. He was elected to the House of Representatives twice and made unsuccessful attempts to become Mayor of New York, Governor of New York and the Lieutenant Governor of New York. Hearst might not have had quite the same ruthless political ambition that Hugenberg had but power was clearly a major motivator. His control of so many media interests gave him more influence than many politicians.

Just as Northcliffe was accused of war-mongering and Hugenberg helped lay the foundations of the holocaust, Hearst used his newspapers to encourage American military invasions of various countries. These included Spain, the Philippines, Cuba and Puerto Rico. He directed his journalists to employ his techniques of yellow journalism to spread lies about other nations and individuals in order to get the public behind military conflicts. In 1936 the economist and financial journalist Ferdinand Lundberg, in his book *Imperial Hearst*, claimed that Hearst took bribes from powerful people overseas to distort news.

The Great Depression wiped out a considerable proportion of Hearst's fortune, much of which was tied up in land and property. In 1937 a court stripped him of control of his company due to non-payment of debts. He still was able to work within the Hearst Corporation but had limited power. For such a control freak, this must have been an extreme blow and incredibly frustrating.

Hearst's influence over the public waned as his newspapers and other media outlets were progressively sold off or closed down. By the time *Citizen Kane* came out, Hearst was in the process of selling his art collection, rare books and items of furniture. In 1941 alone he reportedly put approximately 20,000 items up for sale.

Silvio Berlusconi

The media tycoon and former Italian prime minister Berlusconi is one of the most powerful figures in Italy since Mussolini. His dominance of the Italian media has aided his political career and his political status has no doubt benefited his businesses and offered him protection from legal problems. Despite an obvious conflict of interests, he refused to sell some of his media holdings while in political office.

Berlusconi started his business career in construction before moving into the field of advertising and then the media. In the 1970s he established the cable television company Telemilano and then acquired further cable channels. He founded the giant Fininvest group in 1978. As well as television and print media, the company owns banking interests and the football team A C Milan. There have been attempts to curtail Berlusconi's dominance of the Italian media and capacity to influence political views through his news platforms. These have largely failed.

The ownership structure of Fininvest has caused great suspicion and the lack of transparency has led authorities to posit links to the Sicilian Mafia. Rather than own it directly, Berlusconi has established 38 separate companies which own Fininvest. These companies are called Holding Italiana 1 through to Holding Italiana 38.

The identity of Berlusconi's business associates, who have invested hundreds of millions of pounds in the firm, are hidden. The holding companies have been investigated for a range of illegal and corrupt practices, including money laundering. In the 1990s the Bureau of Anti-Mafia Investigation commissioned a report on the organisation in an attempt to support accusations that Berlusconi was involved with the Mafia.

Over the decades Berlusconi has been accused of numerous crimes, including abuse of office, extortion, perjury, bribery of police and judges, false accounting, embezzlement and money laundering. He has been party to dozens of criminal proceedings. Some cases against him were dropped as a result of laws passed by his own government, including restrictions on the time prosecutors have to proceed with cases and changes to accounting regulations.

Although Berlusconi was found guilty of providing false testimony in 1990, in relation to involvement in an illegal elite secret society in the early 1980s, he escaped punishment because the trial ended just after an amnesty was passed. He first became prime minister of Italy in 1994 and held the office again from 2001 to 2006 and from 2008 to 2011. In 2012 Berlusconi was sentenced to four years in prison for tax evasion, yet he remains free – though undertaking community service at a care home – despite more recent serious convictions.

In June 2013 Berlusconi was found guilty of paying the Moroccan dancer Karima El Mahroug for sex in 2010, when she was 17. Although having sex with a person of that age in Italy is legal, paying for sex with a minor is a serious offence.

He was also found guilty of abusing his public office to ask police to free El Mahroug from custody when she was accused of theft. It is alleged that he did so to stop her divulging his activities with her. In a phone call to police, Berlusconi falsely claimed she was related to then president of Egypt Hosni Mubarak and suggested that keeping her in custody would lead to diplomatic problems.

As a result of these convictions, Berlusconi was sentenced to seven years in jail and banned from public office for life. However, due to the length of time appeals take in Italy and the fact that he would not be jailed until an appeal has been concluded, it is quite possible he will never be incarcerated.

Rupert Murdoch

The Australian tycoon Rupert Murdoch has things in common with most of those mentioned above. In terms of the span of his influence – both geographically and demographically by his various newspapers alone – he is comparable to Hearst. His dominance of television and other media exceeds the influence of Berlusconi as his reach spans more countries.

Rupert Murdoch is currently 83 years old and his political perspective is rather right-wing. In the UK he has close associations with the Conservative Party but has on occasion backed the Labour Party and has reportedly had talks with Nigel Farage, leader of the right-wing anti-EU United Kingdom Independence Party. In the US, the political commentary in his Fox News Channel is distinctly right-wing.

Although Rupert Murdoch is often seen as being supportive of the Establishment, he has sometimes been extremely antagonistic towards it. He has often shown contempt for the British class system and made efforts to undermine traditional Establishment structures. This might be, in part, due to feeling pushed out from certain elite social networks earlier in life, as a result of being Australian.

Murdoch's appetite for challenging power structures he disapproves of has not diminished with age. His mercurial temperament and personal agenda means that politicians who climb in bed with him can be quickly kicked out if he tires of them or they fail to satisfy his political desires.

By the time Rupert was born, his father Keith had already built a small media empire. The young Murdoch benefited from the opportunities afforded by his father's wealth but also from his interest in the family business. While at school he edited pupil publications and also worked part-time for his father's *Melbourne Herald*. Later, while studying philosophy, politics and economics at Oxford, Murdoch consolidated his experience by working on *The Daily Express* and student papers.

When Rupert Murdoch was 21 his father died and he then returned to Australia to run the family company, which was then called News Limited. He subsequently acquired newspaper titles from across Australia and, like Hearst had done in the US, increased the amount of scandal in the papers and the size of the headlines. He also placed a greater emphasis on sports coverage.

Having built a strong base in Australia, Murdoch started acquiring foreign titles. He entered the British market in 1968 by buying the *News of the World* and acquired *The Sun* the following year. *The Sun* had been struggling but he turned it around by filling pages with bare breasts and celebrity scandal.

By also acquiring *The Times* and *The Sunday Times*, in 1981, Murdoch managed to dominate different ends of the British market – but with both tabloids and broadsheets disseminating right-wing views. His titles were supportive of Margaret Thatcher's government and, after she was deposed, the Murdoch press continued to favour the Tory Party for some time.

After Thatcher's successor John Major narrowly won the 1992 election, the front page of *The Sun* proclaimed "It's The Sun Wot Won It". While indicating alliance for the Tory Party, the headline also can be seen to be undermining Major by suggesting he needed the patronage of a Murdoch tabloid to get elected. It is also interesting because it suggests that at least some in Murdoch's empire by then saw the organisation as a king-maker, with the power to distort the electoral process in an undemocratic way. Recently, however, Rupert Murdoch has claimed to have disapproved of the headline. He told the Leveson Inquiry in 2012 that he gave the then editor Kelvin MacKenzie "a bollocking" for the bold front page claim.

In March 1997, just before the UK general election, *The Sun* ran the front page headline "The Sun Backs Blair", with the later edition including a photo of Labour Party leader Tony Blair holding a copy of the paper. While it is likely that by then Murdoch preferred the Thatcherite and glib Blair to the uninspired John Major, the reality is that Labour were already heading for a landslide victory. News International was therefore akin to a cunningly opportunistic 'rain-maker' performing a rain dance before an inevitable downpour. The front page made it seem as though Murdoch's tabloid had the power to influence the outcome of the election.

Murdoch regularly met Tony Blair during his term in office. He also had frequent contact with Blair's successor Gordon Brown, who became the Labour Party leader and prime minister from 2007. By the time David Cameron became prime minister, in 2010, Murdoch's press was behind the Tory. Cameron has been widely criticised for his close relationships with Murdoch and his former *Sun* and *News of the World* editors Rebekah Brooks and Andy Coulson.

In 2011 the FBI began an investigation into possible voicemail hacking by Murdoch's News Corporation journalists in the US. The investigation has been examining the possibility that News Corp employees accessed voicemails of victims of the September 2011 terror attacks. Since then Murdoch has reconfigured his empire by splitting his film and visual media interests from print media. This may have been to protect lucrative aspects of the company from scandals related to newspapers, and it was certainly designed to appease jittery shareholders.

In May 2012, a report by the House of Commons culture committee stated that Rupert Murdoch is "not a fit person to exercise the stewardship of a major international company." However, no authority exists to prevent a person – however unethical they are perceived to be – to own a media corporation which shapes the views of populations.

Chapter 10 – Celebrity culture, the Establishment and the masks of psychopathy

People with narcissistic personalities are clearly attracted to the celebrity lifestyle and there is no shortage of narcissists in the entertainment industries. People who are narcissistic also often have psychopathic tendencies but performers may be particularly good at hiding these. Due to their ability to turn on their charm when required, and aided by publicists and the aura of television and film, even the most callous and abusive celebrities have managed to hide their pathology from the masses.

This is changing, however, as the public is less star-struck than we were in previous decades. We are also, generally, increasingly suspicious of prominent and powerful people. Britain over the last couple of years has been watching a stream of household names be hauled into police stations and charged with rape and sexual assaults. Some have been found guilty and for others legal proceedings ongoing and so cannot be covered in this edition.

In some cases, the celebrity in question initially denied the charges. Some then used expensive lawyers to block media reports and some have used their publicists to attack the credibility of their accusers. This final approach was weakened significantly when publicist to the stars, Max Clifford, was arrested for a string of sexual assaults on teenagers spanning decades.

From the onset, Clifford's abuse was meticulously planned and he employed all the deviousness in his communications one would expect from Britain's most famous Machiavellian publicist. Even in the early stage of his career, when he had limited prominence and power, Clifford manipulated girls by saying he would make them famous and enable them to meet famous people. He even phoned them, masquerading as notable and powerful people – including Hollywood directors – as part of his manipulation of the girls.

Clifford was the fifth person to be arrested as a result of Operation Yewtree and he not only publicly insisted upon his innocence but characterised his accusers as "fantasists" and "opportunists". When he was first arrested, in December 2012, he was questioned about two allegations dating from 1977. The following April he was charged with 11 indecent assaults on girls and women aged 14–19. The allegations stretched from 1966 to 1985. A statement by Clifford, issued after charges were announced, included the following extracts:

> The allegations in respect of which I have been charged are completely false and I have made this clear to the police during many, many hours of interviews.
>
> Nevertheless a decision has been taken to charge me with 11 offences involving seven women, the most recent of which is 28 years ago and the oldest 47 years ago.
>
> I have never indecently assaulted anyone in my life and this will become clear during the course of the proceedings.
>
> Since last December I have been living a 24/7 nightmare. A black cloud has been placed over me, obliterating the bright blue skies that I have been fortunate to live my life under for the vast majority of the past 70 years.

During the trial, which took place in spring 2014, Clifford's maintained his innocence and, on a daily basis, posed outside court for photographers as though he was a film star on a red carpet for a premier. On one occasion he crept up behind a journalist and mimicked their delivery to camera, which the trial judge later described as "trivialising" proceedings and indicative of a lack of remorse. During the court proceedings he was observed to wink at a witness after she gave evidence. For victims giving evidence, after decades of anguish, to have the narcissistic Clifford attempting to turn the trial into a circus can only have added to their distress.

It emerged during the trial that one of Clifford's victims wrote to him 35 years after being abused, at the age of 15, following counselling. The letter, which was found by the police in Clifford's bedside drawer when he was arrested, contains profound and chilling insights into his predatory personality, manipulations and actions. The author of the letter also shows considerable empathy for Clifford's own daughter in relation to ultimately discovering that her father is a paedophile. The woman resisted going to the police until after her parents had died, in order to spare them distress. The following is extracted from the letter, which was read out in court.

I wondered if you remembered as I do the child sexual abuse you engaged in, befriending my parents, flattering their daughter, talking of an acting/modelling career, offices near Bond Street. They were impressed even though no-one had heard of you... Lots of famous names, places and yet still down to Earth. A local lad done good.

Recommending restaurants, funny stories, little secrets you fed them to gain their trust. The abuse started in your office. You sat behind your desk, eventually persuading me to strip, convincing me that my protesting was ridiculous and very childish. 'Don't you want to be grown up?'

You took pleasure in degrading me, visiting me at home, taking me out to meet fictitious people, abusing me instead and returning me to my home with a story so my parents didn't become suspicious. Names of people we had met, places we had been to, so they would be fooled that their daughter was in safe hands and not those of a paedophile.

The abuse continued. A friend's flat where you wanted me to act out a scene. You raped me. You blackmailed me with lies about photographs that had been taken. Fooled me into believing that you were somehow protecting me by stopping them from being published. Even inventing another person who telephoned and continued with the pretence and demanded that I talked dirty to them.

What was his name? That's right Max, pretending to be Terry. I had no one to turn to. You were very clever. A+ in grooming children. How proud you must be. What chance did I have? You made my life a living hell, up until the point when I even contemplated suicide. You got worried then and backed off.

Too dangerous for you. You might have been found out. You repulsed me then as you do now, wearing the mask of someone who has values, hiding behind charity work, trying to cleanse yourself of the guilt you must feel perhaps and stating that you don't have sympathy for paedophiles.

You pretend to be normal. But you know inside you're not and you will never escape that shame. It must feel horrible to know that the real you is so vile and repulsive. It must be frustrating that you have no one to talk to about that. Perhaps you've even tried to bury the memories, almost fooling yourself that you are a different person now.

Better than that, convinced yourself almost that it didn't happen, or does it continue? Are you still abusing children? I remember driving, pulling up behind you at traffic lights in Raynes Park, you in your yellow Jag, so obvious that it was you. What to do? Wanting to get out of the car, confront you, let you know that I still remember, wanting everyone to know the real disgusting creature that you are.

I wonder what your daughter would think of you if she knew or perhaps she does know and it's a secret that you share. How terrifying for you knowing that you have so much to lose. She was a child when I was a child. Perhaps you abused her too, or did you draw the line there.

Perhaps you've made excuses, fed her a line, and you think she's fooled as well. If she does suspect, maybe she's not ready yet to face the reality, too painful, too horrific, every little girl's worst nightmare. Of course one day she will find out the truth and perhaps you won't be around to beg her forgiveness or to feed her the excuses or blame someone else.

What an awful memory she will be left with. I truly feel huge sympathy for her. I can't imagine how unbearable it would be to find out that your father was a paedophile. It would probably ruin her life and certainly make her doubt everything about your relationship. You may have gotten away with it for years but inside you can't escape from the monster that you are, the repulsive, vile reality, that terrible, festering secret of yours which burdens you.

Your secret, not my secret. The hypocrisy of your life. You say you can't bear hypocrisy and that is what spurs you on, when you yourself are a hypocrite worse than any of those you seek to shame. A paedophile who publicly condemns other paedophiles to divert attention. A double bluff. How many others like me are there out there?

Despite his protestations of innocence and characterisation of Operation Yewtree as a "witch-hunt", the jurors found Clifford guilty of eight counts of indecent assault. The jury failed to reach a verdict on one charge and he was cleared of two. When sentencing Clifford to an eight year jail sentence, Judge Anthony Leonard said that he was sure Clifford had also indecently assaulted a 12-year-old girl in Spain. However, the charge could not be pursued in a British court. After the trial was concluded detectives said that further allegations had been made.

As has been stated, we should not assume that all sex offenders have antisocial personality disorders and we certainly should not assume that everybody accused of rape or child abuse is guilty. However, the deviousness and vindictiveness some prominent people have displayed in trying to shake off allegations and smear victims certainly reveals some unpleasant personalities behind the showbiz masks. It demonstrates that some of the jovial and 'light-hearted' figures we saw on our television screens in years gone by were far from what they seemed.

To abuse victims, who felt people would not believe their word against prominent celebrities, their aggressors must have seemed like terrifying Jekyll and Hyde characters, secretly able to transform into monsters. Watching them on television subsequently, being warm and friendly to audiences, must have been sickening for victims who had observed and experienced their darker aspects.

The average person – who grew up watching and listening to people now revealed to be child abusers and rapists – may justifiably feel betrayed by media organisations and the justice system. A substantial amount of money was paid to grotesque monsters who then used their wealth and status to undermine and smear victims in attempts to evade justice.

When a well-liked person in any community turns out to be a paedophile, rapist or killer, the community goes through various processes. Many people feel angry – at the person and perhaps also at themselves for not managing to spot signs and do something to stop them. Others may be angry at specific people, for example police, the aggressor's family or friends, who they feel should have been able to expose their true nature and bring them to justice. Some people feel denial and, even after most of the community has accepted the awful reality, they will privately believe or publicly insist that the person is innocent.

As a result of the complex range of feelings and thoughts different people have after the shock of discovering that there was a sinister presence living among them, the aggressor can cause community tensions. In some cases communities are split and, as well as recriminations, there can be on-going unrest and feuds.

All these dynamics and more are played out when it emerges that famous people are rapists, child abusers or killers. Some struggle to believe that those they admire have done terrible things and will look for ways of discrediting victims or witnesses. Some will be angry with those who they feel should have been noticing and reporting the attacker's activities. They will, justifiably, scrutinise the culture that supported them and suggest they should have been monitored more closely. Some may wonder if behaviours were ignored by people who would lose financially or in other ways by the aggressor being exposed. Others will look for a widespread conspiracy.

The term I use within this book, psychopathic cultures, is not something that has been historically focused on in academic literature, and popular books about psychopathy have primarily concentrated on murderers. However – though not overtly named as such – psychopathic cultures do feature prominently in films and novels. The corporate giant or police department that is rotten to the core, the oppressive dystopian community, the abusive school or children's home or the malicious secret society. In films and novels these themes may be caricatures of psychopathic cultures – but like all caricatures they are based on reality.

It is no coincidence that in recent decades we have seen a progression from films about cruel cattle ranchers to crooked cops to sinister politicians to dodgy financiers and lawyers. It is not just a case that vocations have changed over time but also that those with power have consolidated it as societies transform. The powerful psychopath, like most of us, has become more sophisticated.

This, however, does not mean that people should feel despondent that ruthless elite groups will continue to strengthen their positions. Education is a key way in which this can be challenged – and is being challenged every day. Furthermore, we all have a greater capacity now to not only identify pathological cultures but also challenge and expose them.

Most people would find it legally problematic to accuse powerful people of being psychopaths. If libel action is taken against them they would have to prove their assertion in court. If they could not they might well be destroyed financially. However, we do have more scope to publicly criticise organisations and governments that appear to be acting maliciously. From the perspective of defamation law, it is much safer to criticise a large organisation than question the integrity of an individual within it. Social media is also making this much easier.

Anticipating the rise of a psychopathic culture – but looking in the wrong direction

In an interesting but quite flawed 1972 book entitled *Psychopaths*, Alan Harrington suggested that psychopaths would become increasingly prominent and influential. He predicted that the public sphere would be dominated by alluring psychopaths who would transform our social and political worlds. We are all obviously now living in Harrington's future and can therefore evaluate the success of his predictions.

Given that, by definition, successful psychopaths evade being identified as such, we do not know if there are a greater number of them today than there were when Alan Harrington was writing. However, I would suggest that more significant than the quantity of psychopaths in societies is the prevalence of psychopathic cultures. Once psychopathic cultures form it does not take a large number of psychopathic individuals to sustain it. In fact, it may not require the direct leadership of any.

Having lived through 1960's America, Harrington was preoccupied with the counter-culture, psychedelic drugs and radical figures – including the psychologist Timothy Leary. Harvard lecturer Leary was transformed by experiments with LSD and other drugs and became an enthusiastic advocate of psychedelics. Leary famously encouraged people to "drop out" of conventional lifestyles. Characterising his friend Leary – and many other prominent figures – as psychopathic, Harrington viewed them as blueprints for a new society.

Harrington believed that the radicals then seeking to transform society would ultimately undermine the forces of conservatism and create an extremely individualistic society. This may be a society many contemporary readers recognise but, caught up in the excitement of rapid societal change, Harrington was looking in the wrong direction.

It actually turned out that conservatives – rather than psychedelic advocates – ultimately pushed selfish individualism to the extreme and spawned psychopathic cultures. It seems to me that powerful right-wingers – like Richard Nixon, Ronald Reagan and Margaret Thatcher – were much more significant in creating amoral, calculating, antisocial cultures than were any psychedelic-taking radicals of the 1960s or 70s.

It is impossible to measure how much influence Timothy Leary had on America – and indeed other societies – as he gained prominence at a time of considerable upheaval. Many revolutions were already in motion before LSD and other visionary drugs became widely available. The civil rights movement, feminism, anti-war protests, socialist movements and protests against dictatorships and colonisation all came to a head in the 1960s. Prominent figures were certainly influential but revolutions require that many people participate – and many did.

Psychedelics helped shake-up societies and added potency to the transformational messages of prominent figures. However, the upheaval of the era was not merely caused by chemically-altered states. People were becoming better educated than ever before, and this in itself altered the consciousness of individuals and transformed societies. Youth culture of the late 1950s and early 60s had evolved into adult political radicalism. Minds were becoming more receptive – with or without drugs – and those who were good at articulating progressive views were in a powerful position.

As Harrington states, Leary was indeed one of those people. Unfortunately he became grandiose as a result of his 'guru' status and his immoderate drug consumption. Substance use is fairly commonplace now and we live in a fast-moving, complex and rather hallucinogenic world. It is therefore hard for many of us to imagine how intense and transformative the psychedelic experiences would have been to early pioneers like Tim Leary and Ken Kesey. There is good evidence that Leary became domineering, dogmatic and ruthless but it may be unfair to characterise him as a psychopath.

There is no evidence that, when he finished his PhD in 1950, Leary was a particularly radical thinker. He was certainly subsequently inspired by substances but, perhaps more importantly, the stark realities he observed made him antagonistic towards conservative society and abuses of power. He was changed by a chaotic era more than he himself created a chaotic era.

As a youth, Leary attended West Point military academy and was victimised there, which no doubt undermined his faith in authority. It is not surprising, therefore, that when observing so many young people being sent off to kill and be killed in Vietnam, Leary would speak out against it. He may well have done this even if he had never tried psychedelics. Like other liberal figures, Leary noticed something monstrous about certain policymakers and social institutions – and sought to tackle it. He did this by lecturing and writing, as well as by promoting substances that would encourage people to look at the world more critically.

Harrington envisaged waves of Leary-eque 'psychopathic' gurus teaching hoards of people how to live in the moment and be more individualistic. There are elements of Harrington's vision that have come to pass – drug use, hedonism and free expression have increased in many societies. However, if he had paid more attention to Leary's concerns about authority, he might have focused on the fact that psychopathic cultures had already been established – by the Establishment.

Since the 1960s there has been a mushrooming of festivals, raves and other hedonistic events that might seem to correspond to Harrington's vision. However, a significant difference is that, while people obviously attend events to enjoy themselves, the collective dimension of cultural events is much more significant than individualistic aspects. In fact, for many people such events represent an effort to get away – albeit temporarily – from an exploitative, unfeeling capitalist system and be immersed within a supportive creative community.

In reality, of course, festivals are now big business and have become another aspect of the capitalist system. They have been subsumed into what Horkheimer and Adorno called "the culture industry". However, such events have become big business *because* of the strong desire people have to feel part of a community and have shared experiences with their fellow citizens. Such events are social occasions and not about antisocial selfishness. They are breeding grounds of the arts, activism and environmentalism, not the spawning grounds of psychopathy.

Despite Harrington's vision of 'psychopathic' liberal radicals undermining the forces of conservatism, the reality is many societies have actually become much more conservative. In America – 'the land of the free' – expressive individualism has largely been subverted by economic individualism. If people are willing to sacrifice considerable potentialities of their lives for money, they are free to consume. If they disregard money in favour of free expression, they may well end up on the streets or in institutions. Relentless money-grabbing has been rewarded in the West, relentless questioning often has not.

I would contend that psychopathic cultures within key areas of society – including politics and business – have strengthened since the 1960s. However, the radical subcultures that Harrington predicted would promote psychopathy have instead been concerned with inequalities, education, environmentalism and alternative spiritualities. They pursued those directions while being mocked and undermined by conservative culture – a culture which spawned and supported prime-time television presenters who turned out to be child abusers and rapists.

There may have been the odd predator lurking in new religious movements to prey on the vulnerable but we have not seen an army of 'psychopathic' Leary clones encouraging aggressive individualism. However, we have seen selfishness and greed in politicians, bankers, weapons traders, media groups and energy companies. These groups had considerable power when Leary and Harrington wrote and, in many countries, their power has only increased.

Dark figures in light entertainment

The apparently benign world of mainstream 'light entertainment' has been implicated in the support of people with psychopathic characteristics and psychopathic cultures in two ways. On the one hand, mainstream entertainment acts as a glittering distraction from the realities of life. On the other hand, broadcasters employed and supported a number of people who have been revealed to be child abusers and rapists.

It is no coincidence that the television of the late 1960s and 1970s, two of the most conflict-ridden and revolutionary decades the world has known, was dominated largely by mundane, apolitical fodder. With a few exceptions – which prove the rule – the comedy was obvious and the 'dramas' were soothing in their formulaic predictability rather than unsettling.

Neither the mainstream television or middle-of-the-road music of the era before the explosion of punk and 'alternative' comedy reflected realities of the era. It is hard to see much of it as anything but a distraction from a turbulent time of social conflict. This in a way seems reasonable enough as, after a hard time at work or dealing with other struggles, many people do not want to be confronted by harsh unsettling realities when they try to relax at home. However, state broadcasters like the BBC have an obligation to reflect and inform society and not merely produce numbing complacent distractions.

It is extremely troubling to consider that at a time when the public was being fed a monotonous diet of predictable comedies, game shows and soap operas bearing little resemblance to the regions where they were set, there were rapists and child abusers working for major broadcasters. There are many cases that have not come to court as I write but in the UK we have seen the recent conviction of Stuart Hall and Rolf Harris, both of which resulted from posthumous investigations of Savile's paedophilia.

Like Savile, Stuart Hall was a peculiar and larger-than-life figure. He started out as a journalist but in the 1960s, 70s and 80s he was best known in Britain for presenting the popular television show *It's a Knockout*. He was also a prominent sports presenter on BBC radio.

Few people would have found much sinister about *It's a Knockout* – which featured teams dressed in silly, restrictive costumes lumbering about over slippery surfaces trying to undertake tasks. It was slapstick comedy and Stuart Hall commentated while apparently being overwhelmed by laughter. There was even an edition involving members of the British royal family in 1987.

Many years after *It's a Knockout* was axed but while Hall was still working as a BBC radio broadcaster, allegations about him sexually assaulting girls and young women began to surface. In May 2012 *The Independent* newspaper received an anonymous letter from a woman who said Hall sexually abused her in the 1970s when she was still a schoolgirl.

The author of the letter said that allegations against Jimmy Savile encouraged her to disclose what Hall had done to her. She also stated that she was angry to see her abuser receive an OBE in the Queen's New Year honours, for services to broadcasting and charity work. The newspaper gave the letter to the police who undertook an investigation into that and other allegations against Hall, some of which came to light after he was first arrested.

On Hall's initial arrest, in December 2012, he was charged with three counts of indecent assault, involving a 16-year-old girl in 1974, a 9-year-old girl in 1983, and a 13-year-old girl in 1984. Hall, who was 82 when arrested, denied the charges and was released on bail. He made a statement through his solicitor claiming to be innocent of all charges.

His solicitor, Louise Straw, told the press: "Stuart Hall is innocent of these charges. He is unable to comment further at this stage." However, she went on to say: "It is a matter of concern that in the week following the publication of the Leveson report, there appears to have been systematic, measured leaks to the media, which have given a misleading impression of what this case it about." She also said: "Stuart Hall was not afforded the opportunity to attend voluntarily at the police station. In due course, the decision that he should be arrested will be the subject of some scrutiny."

Despite Straw's forthright statement and her strange suggestion that an accused child abuser should be able to pop down to the police station at his convenience, the decision to arrest him ultimately proved the right one.

Hall appeared before Preston Magistrates Court on January 7 2013, where he pleaded not guilty to all three charges. Publicity surrounding the case led to more victims coming forward and later that month further charges were brought against him. The additional charges consisted of indecently assaulting 10 more girls, then aged between nine to 17-years-old, between 1967 and 1986, and the rape of a 22-year-old woman in 1976.

Speaking to journalists outside Preston Magistrates Court on February 7 2013, where he pleaded not guilty of the new charges, Hall described the allegations as "pernicious, callous, cruel and, above all, spurious." However, at Preston Crown Court on April 16 2013 he pleaded guilty to 14 charges of indecent assault involving 13 girls aged between 9 and 17. Two of the offences related to penetration. Most of the attacks took place between 1972 and 1982, when he was one of the most popular television presenters in Britain.

After admitting to the above offences, Hall issued an "unreserved apology" to his victims via his barrister. The BBC also issued a statement which read: "The BBC is appalled by the disgraceful actions of Stuart Hall and we would like to express our sympathy to his victims."

A number of the sexual assaults by Hall took place on BBC property and consequently some of his victims are in the process of suing the organisation, as well as Hall himself. It emerged after Hall's conviction that, in February 2013 – weeks after he was first charged – he transferred ownership of his £1.2m house to his wife. Lawyers acting for his victims claim that he made his wife the sole owner of the property to avoid compensation claims.

In June 2013 at Preston Crown Court, Hall was sentenced to 15 months in jail. However, the attorney general insisted that the sentence was reviewed, in response to public complaints that it was lenient. The fact that he initially denied the allegations and called his victims liars was an aggravating factor that ultimately led to the court of appeal doubling the sentence the following month.

Hall was convicted of two further charges, in May 2014, of indecently assaulting a child. One of the attacks took place after Hall crept into the 13-year-old girl's bedroom while attending a dinner party. Two and a half years was added to his jail sentence as a result of those convictions.

After Hall's first convictions, but prior to sentencing, outspoken barrister Barbara Hewson caused outrage when she suggested in a *Spiked* magazine article that some of his offences were "low-level misdemeanours" and he should not have been charged so long after they happened. She called the Savile investigation "the Savile Inquisition", compared the English legal system to that of the former Soviet Union and also argued for the age of consent to be lowered to 13.

Appearing to hold children responsible for being abused, by "drifting into compromising situations", Ms Hewson stated: "It's time to end this prurient charade, which has nothing to do with justice or the public interest. Adults and law-enforcement agencies must stop fetishising victimhood. Instead, we should focus on arming today's youngsters with the savoir-faire and social skills to avoid drifting into compromising situations." Savoir-faire means to know what to do in any situation. The notion that children should be ready to deal with any predatory abusers suddenly invading their bedrooms as they sleep is clearly ludicrous.

Australian born Rolf Harris was at least as prominent an entertainer as Savile over a career of more than 60 years. He enjoyed great affection from the public and he did not have the creepy image of Savile. His curious mixture of often slapdash visual art and quirky songs made him popular among generations of children. He presented a broad range of programmes and was on television until his arrest in 2013.

As an adolescent in Australia, Harris was a champion swimmer and he achieved a teaching qualification before moving to England, in 1952. Within a year of arriving in London, Harris was working at the BBC. He delivered an art segment for children with a puppet. He continued making children's TV shows in both the UK and Australia, while also developing as a singer. Over the years he managed to retain his appeal among children while also attracting adult crowds at festivals.

Harris' TV work spanned *Animal Hospital*, in which he famously appeared to cry, numerous programmes about art and animation shows. His status as 'national treasure' in the UK was underlined in 2006 when he was commissioned to paint an official portrait of the Queen to mark her 80th birthday.

Harris was one of the first people questioned by Operation Yewtree officers and the tenth to be arrested. He was first questioned in November 2012 and his house was searched, although police did not identify Harris as a suspect at that point. He was arrested the following March, and charged with 13 offences in August 2013.

These included nine counts of indecent assault involving one girl aged between 13 and 15 at the time of the offences and another who was aged 16. He was also charged with four counts of producing indecent images of children, but these were later dropped. Harris was charged, in December 2013, with three further counts of sexual assault, involving a girl aged seven or eight at the time of the offence, 14 at the time and 19 at the time.

During his trial, which began in May 2014, Harris was accused of grooming a friend of his daughter's from when she was 13. Harris denied sexual contact with her until she was 18. The court was shown an apology letter written by Harris to the father of the victim, after she told her family about him having sexual contact with her. The letter alludes to her confronting him in Norfolk about abusing her from the age of 13, on one occasion while his daughter slept close by. The following extracts are from the letter, which was written in 1997.

> You said in your letter to me that you never wanted to see me or hear from me again, but now [the victim] says it's all right to write to you. Since that trip up to Norfolk, I have been in a state of abject self-loathing. How we delude ourselves.

I fondly imagined that everything that had taken place had progressed from a feeling of love and friendship – there was no rape, no physical forcing, brutality or beating that took place.

When I came to Norfolk, [the victim] told me that she had always been terrified of me and went along with everything that I did out of fear of me.

I said 'Why did you never just say no?'. And [the victim] said how could she say no to the great television star Rolf Harris. Until she told me that, I had no idea that she was scared of me. She laughs in a bitter way and says I must have known that she has always been scared of me. I honestly didn't know.

[The victim] keeps saying that this has all been going on since she was 13. She's told you that and you were justly horrified, and she keeps reiterating that to me, no matter what I said to the contrary.

She says admiring her and telling her she looked lovely in her bathing suit was just the same as physically molesting her. I didn't know. Nothing took place in a physical way until we had moved to Highlands. I think about 1983 or 84 was the first time.

When I see the misery I have caused [the victim] I am sickened by myself. You can't go back and change things that you have done in this life – I wish to God I could.

When I came to Norfolk, spent that time with [the victim] and realised the enormity of what I had done to [the victim], and how I had affected her whole life, I begged her for forgiveness and she said 'I forgive you'. Whether she really meant it or not, I don't know. I hope she did, but I fear she can never forgive me.

If there is any way that I could atone for what I have done I would willingly do it. If there is a way I can start to help [the victim] to heal herself, I would willingly do it.

I would like to talk to you to apologise for betraying your trust and for unwittingly so harming your darling [the victim]. I know that what I did was wrong but we are, all of us, fallible and oh how I deluded myself.

Despite protestations of his innocence and attempts to ingratiate jurors by singing one of his songs and describing how he plays the didgeridoo, Harris was found guilty of all charges. He was jailed for five years and nine months, in July 2014.

Handing down the sentence, Mr Justice Sweeney said: "For well over 50 years you have been a popular entertainer and television personality of international standing – with a speciality in children's entertainment. You are also an artist of renown. You have been the recipient of a number of honours and awards over the years. You have done many good and charitable works and numerous people have attested to your positive good character. But the verdicts of the jury show that in the period from 1969 to 1986 you were also a sex offender – committing 12 offences of indecent assault on four victims who were variously aged between 8 and 19 at the time."

"You clearly got a thrill from committing the offences whilst others were present or nearby. Whilst such others did not realise what you were doing, their presence added to the ordeal of your victims. It is clear from the evidence that what you did has had a significant adverse effect on each victim, and particularly so in relation to 'C' [the friend of his daughter] who suffered severe psychological injury in consequence."

The judge also said: "You have shown no remorse for your crimes at all. Your reputation now lies in ruins, you have been stripped of your honours but you have no one to blame but yourself."

The criminal cases against Hall and Harris were not only was influenced by the Savile scandal but there are similarities in how each used their fame to target and attempt to silence victims. There have been several hundred allegations of sexual assault against Savile and there is a general acknowledgement now that he preyed on some of the most vulnerable people in society. These included children in care homes and psychiatric wards and immobile people in hospitals.

In addition to abusing children himself, there have been allegations that Savile procured children for other paedophiles. Given that Savile was a relentless networker and spent time with numerous elite figures, many people – bloggers more than corporate journalists – have suggested he was a key figure in an elite paedophile ring.

There is good evidence that Savile had links with paedophile networks and spent time in places where it is now known that paedophile rings operated. One such place is the Haut De La Garenne children's home on the Channel Island of Jersey. A 2008 police investigation of the home has led to convictions in relation to the abuse of a large number of children over decades.

In 2008 Savile commenced legal proceedings against *The Sun* newspaper after it linked him to child abuse at Haut de la Garenne and stated that he had visited the home many times. He initially denied ever visiting the home but then a photograph emerged showing him surrounded by residents.

Jersey Police, in 2008, said that an allegation of indecent assault against Savile, made by a child who had been a resident in the 1970s had been investigated. However, they claimed that there had not been enough evidence to proceed with charges. Some of those who have come forward with allegations about Savile since his death are former Haut de la Garenne residents.

The Jersey political Establishment has been extremely defensive in relation to the case and banned at least one journalist from the island, curtailing their investigations. I am not suggesting that Jersey politicians were involved with the paedophile network linked to the home. However, in pathological cultures innocent people may unwittingly be roped in to protect predatory or toxic individuals. This could well have happened in this case. In their attempt to protect the reputation of the island, politicians may have unwittingly protected child abusers.

Despite concerns about the tourist trade and Savile's legal wrangling to distance himself from Haut De La Garenne, the reality is that more than 100 former residents have made allegations of rape, other violent assaults and false imprisonment at the home. There have also been allegations of murder at the home, although this has been dismissed by the police.

Former residents of the home have stated that Savile visited on numerous occasions. Some have also alleged that children from the home were 'rented' out to wealthy yachtsmen who abused them. The suggestion is that the home made it look as though children were getting a treat by having a day out when actually they were being passed around a paedophile ring. There have been claims that the then prime minister Ted Heath, who was a keen yachtsman, visited to island for the same purposes as his friend Savile.

Many people will resist the idea that Savile procured children for elite paedophile rings, let alone a British prime minister. The notion that such a garishly dressed, loud and instantly-recognisable man could covertly round-up children to be abused by powerful figures *does* sound strange. It sounds so bizarre that many people would instinctively dismiss the notion. However, it is worth considering that Savile and his allies recognised this. It comes back to the notion that he could hide in plain sight.

Before rejecting the idea completely, it is important to remember that doors were open to Savile. We know that he visited prime minister's residences on many occasions and was close to both Margaret Thatcher and Ted Heath. He got on well with the Queen and he reportedly 'counselled' Prince Charles and Princess Diana when they were experiencing marital problems. As strange as it now seems that Savile offered advice to the royal couple, it illustrates the trust he enjoyed at the upper echelons of British society.

The level of contact Savile had with aristocrats and political figures has alarmed many. However, it is just as concerning that Savile had the freedom to wander at will into incredibly sensitive specialist mental health units, children's homes and had access to vulnerable people in hospitals across Britain. He is alleged have abused people in at least 28 British hospitals, over decades.

As well as allegations of abusing living people, ranging from the age of five to 75, there have been claims that Savile was a necrophiliac. He is alleged to have performed sex acts on deceased patients in a hospital mortuary and boasted about stealing glass eyes from corpses and having them set into rings.

To date, 10 individuals have made allegations of sexual assault by Savile at Broadmoor high security mental hospital and he is also alleged to have indecently exposed himself to a child, who found himself alone with Savile on a minibus. The boy escaped from his predicament but subsequently underwent counselling. Six of the alleged sexual assault victims were patients, two were staff and two were children at the time. Reports have emerged recently that Savile took his celebrity friend – and fellow sex offender – Rolf Harris to the secure hospital and the pair watched female patients undress.

There are different levels of security of mental health units in the UK. Most adults requiring assessment or treatment are placed on acute admissions wards. These are termed 'open' wards as many patients may come and go, although some will have restrictions imposed as a result of their risk to themselves or others. Psychiatric Intensive Care Units (PICUs), low secure forensic services, challenging behaviour units, and secure rehabilitation wards are the first level of secure wards. They are deemed low secure units. Patients may be placed on such units if they are a risk to themselves or others or an abscondsion risk.

The next level is medium secure units. Some patients on medium secure units would have been admitted by court orders, some will have been transferred from prison and some patients will have been moved from less secure psychiatric wards. Some patients on medium secure units will have killed or raped people.

Places on high secure units are reserved for people who pose a grave and immediate danger to others. In Britain there are four high secure hospitals for such patients – Broadmoor, Rampton, Ashworth and Carstairs.

Some of the most prominent killers have been housed in such facilities, including Peter Sutcliffe, Ian Brady and Ronnie Kray.

Given the risk posed by this patient group – to one another, staff and themselves – it is vital that care and treatment is consistent, well-planned and takes into account the complexities of any personality disorder traits combined with mental illness symptoms. Such units are among the most challenging to work within, in part due to risk and complexity, but also because patients often try to get personal information from staff. This can be used to manipulate or intimidate. As a result, it is absolutely vital that staff maintain firm personal boundaries.

Considering all of the above, it is astonishing that Savile was not only allowed to visit Broadmoor whenever he liked but was reportedly also provided with keys to wards and even granted managerial power over staff. On secure units, ward doors should not be unlocked from the outside but instead controlled from inside by nurses, who are aware of the location and mental state of patients. It is not uncommon on locked wards for patients to hang around near doors, in the hope pushing past people when the door opens. It says something about Savile's pathological fearlessness and the management of Broadmoor at that time if the untrained celebrity wandered onto wards without staff supervision.

Savile's influence on Broadmoor began in the early 1970s when he began 'volunteering' at the hospital. This in itself seems strange, as to work in such a challenging environment takes considerable insight and many people would be afraid to set foot on the grounds. Savile reportedly got his own room in staff quarters and took young girls he had picked up elsewhere there to stay.

It might be that Savile felt some kind of affinity with some patients – he reportedly became friends with the 'Yorkshire Ripper' Peter Sutcliffe. However, it should be remembered that as well as being considered to be dangerous inmates, Broadmoor patients are also vulnerable people. Many patients will have been abused as children and, in the time Savile was involved with the hospital, young people were placed there.

Savile was a regular visitor to Broadmoor throughout the 1970s and 80s and raised money for the hospital. In what now seems an exceptionally foolish move, junior health minister Edwina Currie appointed Savile to chair a task force overseeing the management of the hospital in 1988. To put this in context, there was discontent among staff at that point and the union representing the nurses had recently voted for an overtime ban. The task force was put in place after the hospital board was suspended. Savile regarded himself as the ultimate manager of the hospital, bragging to an interviewer: "If you want to win any popularity awards you don't take the job of the boss here."

In a BBC *Panorama* programme screened in June 2014, Currie admitted that Savile was brought in to break the industrial action. She also admitted in the programme that, once appointed, Savile's methods of undermining the overtime ban amounted to "blackmail". However, rather than challenge Savile about this, Mrs Currie said she "made a note of it at the time, because I was so surprised." She also said: "If this meant we broke the strike and could help the patients then we had an issue of the ends justifying the means." However, it should be noted that the nurses were not striking, they were merely choosing to not do overtime.

In 1989 Savile instructed his lawyers to sue the *News of the World* in relation to an article the paper published in 1988 suggesting he had been granted the power to discharge dangerous patients from Broadmoor. This action seems strange as it is hard to see how Savile could have been defamed by such an assertion. The government and senior clinicians would have had more cause to feel defamed by such an article as it could have suggested negligence on their part. Nevertheless Savile was successful and he secured an apology from the then editor Kelvin MacKenzie.

Despite the apparent belief by policymakers that Savile was an appropriate person to have influence at one of the most challenging psychiatric institutions in the world, professionals had grave concerns. A nurse in charge of one ward regarded him as a psychopath and recently claimed that both staff and patients viewed him as a paedophile. However, as chair of the task force Savile had the power to override decisions of ward managers.

Speaking to *Channel 4 News* in October 2012, senior psychiatric nurse and former ward manager Richard Harrison was clear about how he and other psychiatric professionals saw Savile. He said: "I had long considered him, as many of my colleagues did, as a man with a severe personality disorder, with a liking for children. He was regarded as a paedophile by the staff and the paedophile patients."

Speaking on the same programme, another senior nurse Bob Allen said: "I'd say he was a psychopath, without a doubt. It was just the way his attitude was – his blasé attitude to everything. He didn't seem to care or worry about anything. A lot of the staff always said he should be behind the bars. " In the broadcast, *Channel 4* quoted a Department of Health statement issued to the press in 1989 after Savile was made chair of the task force. The statement reads: "He has a reputation for getting things done and he is the man in charge."

More needs to be discovered about Savile's relationship with Broadmoor and the political administration that appointed him. The hospital has an international reputation and there is nothing to suggest that the staff who were forced to work with Savile were incompetent.

Speaking generally, there *may* be a tendency, when dealing with extremely dangerous people, for some staff to develop a tolerance for personality disorder traits. Nevertheless, we would hope that, in the main, professionals working with patients with personality disorders become more adept at spotting psychopathy rather than desensitised to it. Broadmoor staff accounts suggest professionals were aware of Savile's antisocial personality disorder but had their hands tied by political powers.

For clinicians, the Savile case should be a lesson in how pathological cultures can take hold even in settings specifically designed to curtail the activities of psychopaths. For politicians it should be a lesson to not interfere with the complex work of health professionals and to not pollute sensitive clinical environments with shallow political agendas or celebrity cultures.

Savile appears to have had unrestricted movement at Stoke Mandeville Hospital in Aylesbury, Buckinghamshire, where he also was given accommodation. To date police have received 22 allegations of sexual assaults by Savile at the hospital, dating from 1965 to 1988.

Allegations have been made by 60 people in relation to Savile's activities at Leeds General Infirmary. Sexual assaults are reported to have taken place over a considerable time span – from 1962 and 2009. Some 19 of the alleged victims were children at the time and 33 of the 60 were patients.

A 2014 report into Savile's behaviour at the Leeds hospital states that investigators found little evidence of Savile's movements being controlled. He was allowed to work at a volunteer porter, attend ward rounds and even gave bed baths to patients.

The report states that Savile regularly visited the mortuary and it cites a 1982 *Sunday Express* interview, in which he mentions as interest in corpses. The article states: "The morticians are now my friends, so I help them on occasions to do their job, which I consider a tremendous life honour, being able to handle people who have just gone to heaven… When I lay those bodies away, I look at good muscles, good organs, good brains, beautiful eyes, liver and kidneys, and I think 'What a waste'" It is from the Leeds General Infirmary mortuary that Savile claimed to have taken glass eyes from deceased patients and performed sex acts on them.

A media statement from the hospital, issued with the report, admits that several managerial failures "provided a background for someone as manipulative as Savile to thrive, and to continue his abusive behaviour unchecked for years."

Of the cases of British based celebrities accused of sexual abuse that have not yet passed through the legal system, some of these have been defined by police as having links to Savile. Others have no links to him aside from the possibility that publicity about his actions prompted reflection by complainants and statements to the police. Given that some of the accused are now rather old and many alleged incidents were decades ago some commentators have suggested that cases should be dropped.

On the other hand, there are those – including a number of bloggers – who believe the focus since Savile's death on celebrity abusers has functioned as a distraction from paedophile rings involving politicians and other Establishment figures. A key area of focus in this respect is Elm Guest House in London, where it is alleged politicians and other powerful figures systematically abused children.

Elm Guest House and Dolphin Square

The guest house was located in Barnes, an affluent and quiet area in the west London borough of Richmond Upon Thames. Allegations of abuse at the house date back to the 1970s and 80s and reports suggest that procurerers took boys from children's homes to have sex with mature men. Some might describe the alleged victims as 'rent boys' but, given their age and powerlessness – and the systematic way in which it reportedly happened – a better way of describing them would be 'child sex slaves'.

The guest house was advertised in specialist publications, as 'gay friendly' accommodation. The newsletter of the Conservative Group for Homosexual Equality – which campaigned for the age of consent for males to be lowered – ran a positive feature about it in 1982.

A 'party' on the premises was raided by the police in 1982 and 12 boys subsequently gave evidence that they had been sexually abused there by various men. At that point the manager of the guest house, Carole Kasir, was convicted of running a disorderly house. In English law the term disorderly house alludes to any place where activities take place which pose a threat to public health, morals, convenience, or safety, and may create a public nuisance. The term is typically applied to brothels, illegal casinos or premises where illicit drugs are sold and consumed.

To apply the term to a place where children were allegedly sold and systemically raped seems euphemistic, to say the least. Nevertheless, in the case of Elm Guest House, allegations of child sexual abuse were not pursued at the time. Carole Kasir died in 1990, reportedly as the result of an insulin overdose.

Despite paedophiles linked to the guest house being convicted in the succeeding years for sex crimes taking place elsewhere, it took many years – until 2003 – before the case was re-examined. However, the 2003 investigation came to a dead end. It is not entirely clear why at this stage.

With the Savile scandal breaking in 2012, the year turned into something of an apocalypse for abusers and abuse victims alike. While abusers worried about dawn arrests by police, abuse victims were dragged back into awful experiences by the media coverage of prominent cases. By the end of 2012 the public was quick to believe horrendous allegations against public figures, as though they had been viewed with suspicion all along. Therefore what had once seemed like outrageous allegations about Elm visitors seemed increasingly plausible.

A preliminary scoping investigation, Operation Fairbank, was initiated after MP Tom Watson alluded in Parliament to a paedophile network linked to someone in Margaret Thatcher's administration. As discussed in Chapter 7, in October 2012 Mr Watson suggested that the Peter Righton police file contains information pertaining to a widespread paedophile ring linked to powerful people.

Operation Fairbank, which was led by the Metropolitan Police, was carried out covertly for several weeks before its existence was acknowledged by the authorities. Preliminary evidence examined within Fairbank, concerning the grooming and abuse of children by parties of men, led to Operation Fernbridge, which started in February 2013.

At the beginning of Operation Fernbridge two men were questioned about allegations of sexual offences and then bailed. The police also at that point investigated claims that a former Liberal Party politician had sexually abused boys at the guest house. The politician was not named at the time but it was reported that he is deceased. As Cyril Smith was known to frequent the house, it seemed likely that he was the unnamed Liberal politician.

Press coverage in early 2013 began to allude to a VIP paedophile ring operating at Elm Guest House in the early 1980s abusing boys from Grafton Close Children's Home. Newspapers referred to a guest list, seized by police in a raid in London in January 2013. According to the list guests include MPs, figures from the National Front and Sinn Féin, performers, a senior army official, an MI5 officer, a high-ranking policeman and a bishop. Obviously we cannot assume that people abused children just because their name exists on a list of Elm Guest House residents.

Part of the ongoing police investigation into Elm Guest House relates to photographic and video evidence. At least one witness has claimed Carole Kasir took photos of Establishment figures with boys at the house. One photograph allegedly shows a former cabinet minister with a naked boy in a sauna.

The inclusion of an MI5 officer on the list is concerning as there have been allegations of intelligence agents filming politicians and other influential people abusing children in other settings. If true, a motive for this could be to gain leverage over powerful people to manipulate their actions. Or it could simply be that MI5 monitored activities at the guest house.

The Kincora Boys' Home in Belfast is one such place where abuse has been proved to have taken place and MI5 connections have been alleged – but not proved. Speaking on a radio show in November 2012, the former MP Ken Livingstone claimed he told Parliament during the Thatcher administration that MI5 officers had filmed child abuse at Kincora in the hope of "catching" politicians of Northern Ireland in order to "blackmail" them.

Whether or not the intelligence service was party to the abuse at Elm Guest House, we know that the abuse was not simply a localised problem. As well as Grafton Close Children's Home, Elm Guest House allegations also link to the Islington children's homes abuse scandal (as mentioned in Chapter 7). Despite laudable efforts by *London Evening Standard* to expose the web of paedophiles who had abused care home children from London and beyond, most escaped justice then. Most still have.

However, a great deal of progress has been made in recent years due to the efforts of victims, campaigners and former care workers from children's homes. A major reason why Operation Fernbridge was initiated is the fact that people have had the courage to put allegations on the internet about prominent people abusing children at Elm Guest House. Once consistency in stories becomes apparent and more people become aware of scandals, it becomes increasingly difficult for authorities to disregard them.

Paedophile rings, like other psychopathic cultures, survive and thrive because of fear and division. Victims can be isolated or played off against one another. When one or two people try to shed light on these twisted cultures they can often be discredited, undermined or destroyed.

Witnesses are intimidated and it is not uncommon for victims to commit suicide, become addicts or die in suspicious circumstances.

In the case of elite paedophile rings, there is a particular problem that systems which are meant to serve the public can be manipulated. We only become aware of members who are caught and therefore must recognise that larger networks continue invisibly. Members may be involved with politics, criminal justice and other influential professions, as well as the underworld. As a result, in the event of an arrest of a member, mechanisms can be rapidly employed to either get that individual out of trouble or make it appear as though they are a lone predator.

Perhaps procurers are the most likely to be caught and, as they are likely to be of lower social standing than those they serve, the inclination will be to sacrifice them to protect the network. Some believe this is exactly what happened in the case of Belgian Marc Dutroux, who was convicted in 2004 of kidnapping, torturing and sexually assaulting six young girls and teenagers. Four were killed and Dutroux also admitted to murdering an alleged accomplice by burying him alive. Dutroux had seven houses, four of which were used in kidnappings and burials. Torture and rape, which was filmed, took place in a concealed dungeon.

Prior to these crimes, for which he was charged in 1996, Dutroux served just three years of a 13-year sentence for abducting and raping five girls. He was released for 'good behaviour' in 1992, despite the prison director being sent a letter from Dutroux's own mother expressing concern that he kept young girls captive.

Blunders in the murder investigation caused considerable public anger and such were the failures that many people believe that politicians and police were complicit. The original judge was taken off the case after attending a fundraising event for victims' parents. That judge, Jean-Marc Connerotte, was of the view that Dutroux was part of a powerful paedophile ring, which conspired against the investigation and threatened those involved. Failures in the investigation included ignoring leads, disregarding evidence and investigators being sacked. Some witnesses died in suspicious circumstances.

During the eventual trial, Connerotte broke down in tears while giving evidence as a witness. He talked about "shadowy figures determined to stop the full truth coming out" undermining the judicial process and threatening him and magistrates. Connerotte being taken off the case in 1996 led to Belgian workers striking and a 300,000 person-strong protest march in Brussels.

Dutroux insisted during the trial that he was part of a Europe-wide paedophile ring, which he claimed included politicians, police and bankers. In a media interview he said: "People want to believe that I am at the centre of everything. They are mistaken...I did things of which I was not the driving force. I was used as an instrument by others, who were themselves used as instruments by others." He received a life sentence in 2004. A parliamentary commission concluded that Dutroux did not have accomplices in powerful positions but benefited from investigative incompetence.

Whether paedophile rings are large powerful networks or small groups of depraved individuals, a code of silence means many perpetrators have evaded justice. Nevertheless, the re-opening of historic abuse cases as a result of fresh allegations and public pressure demonstrates that the stench of toxic cultures can actually intensify over time rather than abate. With enough tenacious people exerting pressure, even the most powerful abusers can be exposed and crimes that seemed easy to bury before the internet existed can suddenly come to light.

In July 2014, as a result of enquiries about a missing dossier alleging that British MPs abused children, it emerged that 114 files apparently relating to elite paedophiles had gone missing from Westminster. The dossier that led to the shocking revelation had been passed to the then Home Secretary Leon Brittan in 1983 by MP Geoffrey Dickens. When asked by a journalist about the dossier, in February 2013, Brittan said he could not remember it. By July 2014 he remembered it well enough to say that he had passed it onto Home Office officials to look over and report back to him if further action was required. In a statement Brittan said he does not "recall being contacted further about these matters".

When the media reported that the dossier was missing, some MPs played down the importance of the material and the loss, with former Home Office minister David Mellor stating that he did not see the dossier but did "remember some sort of chat around the department that this wasn't a very substantive thing at all." Keith Vaz, chair of the Home Affairs Select Committee, said: "I don't think ministers can be expected to know about every single piece of paper." This caused public outrage, because most people would regard a dossier containing allegations about VIP paedophile rings as important and memorable.

David Cameron at that point ordered an investigation of the missing dossier, which led to the knowledge that some 114 files were missing. This prompted former Conservative Party chairman Lord Tebbit to suggest that a cover-up of powerful paedophiles had taken place to protect the Establishment. He told the BBC: "At that time I think most people would have thought the Establishment, the system, was to be protected and if a few things had gone wrong here and there that it was more important to protect the system than to delve too far into them. That view, I think, was wrong then and it has spectacularly been shown to have been wrong, because the abuses have grown."

We cannot assume that every politician involved with covering up child abuse is part of a paedophile ring, although many people would regard them complicit. As Tim Fortescue, a whip in Ted Heath's government between 1970 and 1973, explained, covering up for an MP puts them in debt to the party. This means their voting behaviour can be controlled, which is obviously completely undemocratic.

Speaking to the BBC in 1995, Mr Fortescue said: "Anyone with any sense, who was in trouble, would come to the whips and tell them the truth, and say 'now listen, I'm in a jam, can you help?' It might be debt, it might be a scandal involving small boys, or any kind of scandal in which a member seemed likely to be mixed up in. They'd come and ask if we could help and if we could, we did.

"And we would do everything we can because we would store up brownie points…it does sound a pretty, pretty nasty reason, but it's one of the reasons because if we could get a chap out of trouble then, he will do as we ask forever more."

It is difficult to know if incidents of abuse, as Lord Tebbit suggests, have "grown", or if the reporting of incidents has increased and public awareness has grown. The internet has been a major tool for exposing pathological cultures of all sorts. It amplifies previously muted voices and allows people to speak out from relative safety. This in turn encourages politicians and other powerful supporters to get behind causes. Once politicians are made aware of injustices and crimes, in a way that is publicly visible – such as on social media – they can look complicit if they ignore claims. It appears to me that the tide is turning and, rather than help sweep cases under the carpet, politicians have an interest in getting behind campaigns early on.

For campaigners, researchers and journalists who had been following allegations about powerful paedophile rings linked to Westminster for some time, the role of Brittan in the missing dossier saga was everything from unsurprising, intriguing and infuriating. The reason for this is stories of Brittan being a child abuser had been around for some years. Despite knowledge of this among journalists, coverage related to the missing dossier and Brittan's role in it studiously avoided mentioning abuse allegations against Brittan – even when articles were published about powerful rings he had been linked to being responsible for child murders.

There had been some separate media reports in the summer of 2014 about Brittan being questioned about a rape of a 19-year-old woman, which allegedly happened in 1967. Police interviewed him under caution in June 2014 but he was not arrested. Brittan was a barrister when the alleged incident took place, having failed to become an MP in 1966. Following the police interview, Brittan described the rape allegation as "wholly without foundation."

The focus on Brittan intensified in October 2014 when it was mentioned in the House of Commons that the then Lord was directly linked to child abuse. During a debate on the 1984 miners' strike, Labour MP Jim Hood said: "The current exposé of Sir Leon Brittan, the then home secretary, with accusations of improper conduct with children will not come as a surprise to striking miners of 1984."

Mr Hood mentioning this in the House of Commons protected him from any defamation action that might otherwise have been brought by Brittan. This is because parliamentary privilege allows politicians to speak freely without risk of being sued for defamation. Conservative MP Conor Burns was quick to suggest Mr Hood had abused parliamentary privilege, stating "He has just made very profound, serious accusations against a noble lord. Is that in order?" Journalists reporting on Parliament have similar protection from defamation action and, consequently, Mr Hood's words in the chamber allowed journalists to report on something they had avoid previously. Even conservative press, such as *The Telegraph*, covered it. Although *The Telegraph's* piece focused on the parliamentary privilege issue, ultimately abuse allegations about Brittan were being circulated in the mainstream media.

More specific allegations about Brittan continued to circulate on social media throughout 2014. When he died, in January 2015, it became possible for politicians and newspapers to discuss openly what many had been talking about for years. Writing in *The Mirror*, Tom Watson said he had, like many, been aware of allegations for some time. He wrote: "Many have urged me over the past two years to reveal allegations against Brittan using parliamentary privilege. This allows MPs to say things that are not subject to libel laws. Some will ask why I've waited until his death to speak out. The reason is simple. I didn't want to prejudice any jury trial he might one day face. Newspapers and broadcasters were aware of the serious allegations made against him. However, they chose not to publish or air them."

Mr Watson also wrote: "I've spoken to a woman who said he raped her in 1967. And I've spoken to a man who was a child when he says Brittan raped him. And I know of two others who have made similar claims of abuse. To these people, the Establishment has closed rank and slammed down the shutters. They talk of their devastation. Today, one survivor said to me that Brittan 'showed me no kindness or warmth.' That Brittan was 'as close to evil as a human being could get in my view'."

A number Conservatives and right-wing journalists defended Brittan after his death, speaking and writing of a 'smear campaign' against him. At the same time quite a number of people on social media expressed the suspicion that Brittan had been bumped off by the Establishment in order to protect powerful paedophiles from facing justice. However, it was widely reported that Brittan had been battling cancer for some time and this was the cause of his death.

When he died, aged 75, Brittan was under investigation in relation to the abuse of several boys. Some of the cases relate to Elm Guest House and other alleged attacks took place at Dolphin Square, a block of luxurious flats in Pimlico, London. The proximity of the building to the Houses of Parliament, MI5 and MI6 premises have made it a popular residence among politicians, intelligence staff and civil servants.

Dolphin Square has been linked to what has sometimes been reported as 'orgies' involving 'VIPs' and children. I would take issue with the term orgy in that context - a better description of what has been alleged is systematic violent abuse of trafficked children by powerful people. One witness known as Nick, who gave information to the police following interviews by *Exaro News* and *The Sunday People*, reports seeing a Conservative MP kill a 12-year-old boy by strangling him at Dolphin Square in the 1980s. Nick has also spoken of another victim of the ring, aged 10 or 11, being deliberately run over and killed. A third murder claim being investigated by police is that a boy was beaten to death in front of Leon Brittan by two men.

When Nick was interviewed by detectives he gave them a list of 12 'VIPs', who he alleges abused him. He claims that Leon Brittan raped him numerous times from the age of 11 at Dolphin Square and other locations. In relation to the evidence given by Nick, lead investigator Detective Superintendent Kenny McDonald has said: "Nick has been spoken to by experienced officers from child abuse teams and experienced officers from murder investigations. They and I believe what Nick is saying is credible and true."

Two other witnesses have given evidence to the police about abuse by Brittan and others at Dolphin Square. One of these, known as Darren, says he was trafficked to Dolphin Square by Peter Righton. He believes a girl was murdered after being seen in the company of another, as yet unnamed, senior Conservative politician.

Chapter 11 – Managing psychopaths

The shifting sands of psychiatry

Developments within psychiatry are influenced by changes within society. Therefore, rather than simply being an applied science, psychiatry is a dynamic cultural mechanism with many external influences and internal tensions. Although diagnostic criteria and the dissemination of ideas about best practice help create a degree of consistency, the reality is that the field is full of competing perspectives. Consequently it works differently in different places and at different times.

Probably more than any other medical specialty, the philosophies and practices within psychiatry are influenced by non-clinicians. This is a good thing, in my opinion, as mental health is something that affects and is influenced by the entire society. Therefore members of the community – whether relatives, campaigners, academics or any other interested parties – should be able to raise questions about how it functions. In some mental health services, patients themselves are encouraged to give their views on how units function. Advocacy groups also have an important role to play.

Change within psychiatry occurs as a result of new insights into the brain and pharmacology but also because of changes within other disciplines and the wider society. Political ideologies and philosophies falling out of fashion and being supplanted by new perspectives has a significant impact on how psychiatry operates and how mental health patients are viewed. Research and trends within psychology and sociology also influence how mental health care is delivered.

Changes in the economic fortunes of countries and prosperity of citizens within them have an impact on mental health care. For example, psychoanalysis is popular in America not because the country is obsessed by Sigmund Freud but because many prosperous, individualistic Americans can afford what some would regard as a self-indulgence.

Similarly, the policy of care in the community in Britain, though supported by ideologies about equality, was driven by economic and political conditions and ambitions. The old asylums were on extensive and valuable estates which could be sold with little opposition from vulnerable patients. Some patients might have believed that the change would be positive but many others would have felt they had no power to resist the policy.

After the 1990 Care in the Community Act became law, many mental hospitals were sold to developers. Several have since become luxury apartments and office complexes. Sadly, it was not uncommon in the 1990s for bewildered former patients to turn up at their former homes. The land use had changed but their social needs had not.

Those psychiatric wards that did survive were often moved to buildings with no gardens in general hospitals. This was a sharp contrast to the large Victorian asylums, which often had their own farms and other occupational facilities where patients could undertake activities. To push the care in the community policy, politicians argued that psychiatric patients would be less stigmatised if either living in the community or housed on the grounds of general hospitals. In reality such stigma still exists.

Another factor that influences how psychiatry operates is public and media responses to dramatic incidents involving disturbed people. Flurries of extensively reported cases of former 'mental patients' killing members of the public puts pressure on politicians to question how psychiatry functions. Such cases have very often involved people tormented by schizophrenia living in the community or on leave from hospitals. After incidents there are sometimes calls in the media for greater supervision of mentally ill people but few commentators would expect a government to invest in sizeable asylums again.

However, homicides in Britain by people defined as having a dangerous severe personality disorder (DSPD) caused enough of an outcry for new specialist units to be opened. As has been stated, people with antisocial personality disorders have historically been less than welcome in mainstream psychiatric wards. There were few specialist services to manage such people and consequently most have tended to roam free unless convicted of a serious crime and imprisoned.

The conviction of Michael Stone, in 1998, for the brutal murders of Lin Russell and her six-year-old daughter Megan, shocked Britain. The pair, along with Megan's sister Josie and the family dog, were tied up and hit repeatedly with a hammer. Josie sustained extensive head injuries but mercifully survived and has gone onto to become a successful textile artist.

The Russell family were strangers to Stone, who had served three prison sentences in the previous decade for robbery, grievous bodily harm and assault. The Russells were enjoying a walk along a quiet rural Kent lane when they were accosted by the killer. Robbery appears to be a motive but the sustained nature of the attacks suggests an intention to kill.

Apart from the brutality of the attack, the British public were shocked by the fact that – despite being diagnosed with an antisocial personality disorder – mental health legislation did not contain the power to detain Stone. This is because psychopaths had long been regarded as untreatable. The 1983 Mental Health Act includes a treatability test, which meant that only people with mental conditions deemed treatable could be held against their will.

The Russell murders led the then Labour government to review the legislation and ultimately develop new units where people with dangerous and severe personality disorders could be detained. In order to ensure that people regarded as having a tendency towards violence could be detained without first being convicted of a crime, the Mental Health Act had to be updated. Consequently, within the 2007 Mental Health Act the treatability test had been replaced with an "appropriate medical treatment test".

The change meant that people could be detained against their will if there was a treatment available that could *potentially* alleviate or prevent the worsening of their symptoms. It did not have to be shown to cure the disorder. Therefore, the change meant that a non-convicted psychopath could be put into a secure unit if deemed to be dangerous, despite the likely permanence of their disorder.

The above legislative change is controversial. Proving that a cunning manipulator has committed a particular crime is often hard enough. To suggest that a non-convicted person has an intransigent condition of the mind, that makes them a grave danger to the public, is even more problematic. Many people would instinctively regard such an approach as unscientific and unjust. However, the reality is that there *are* people who lack normal feelings and are extremely dangerous. They have historically only been incarnated after being convicted of crimes but the above changes meant they could be detained more easily.

However, a 2011 joint review by the Department of Health and Ministry of Justice has resulted in DSPD units being decommissioned. The review concluded that resources invested in the national DSPD programme would be better spent within prison-based treatment programmes. Patients on such units have since been transferred to prisons or other secure psychiatric wards.

The above is an excellent illustration of how psychiatry is often driven at least as much by political agendas as medical science. The DSPD units were not created because there was a breakthrough in treatment but due to extensive media coverage of heinous crimes. The significant thing that happened between 2007 and 2011 is not that DSPD units were found lacking, merely that a different government was elected.

Acknowledging the reality of psychopathy and other personality disorders

It is understandable that many people argue against attempts to label people based on perceptions – by clinicians or others – of abnormalities of the mind. Even if we accept that mental illnesses like schizophrenia and bipolar affective disorder are valid classifications, it is critical to recognise that sufferers are first and foremost individual people, deserving of our understanding and compassion.

The same goes for people diagnosed with personality disorders. There are many different categories of these, some are closely related and others are extremely different. Such is the dynamism of the human mind and behaviour – and such is the subjective nature of observation – that patients might be labelled with one personality disorder before receiving another diagnosis.

Some patients and prisoners will have enough knowledge of different personality disorders and mental illnesses to choose which symptoms to express. Reasons for doing so include attempts to reduce time in prison or hospital or get particular medications. If someone with a personality disorder can convince clinicians that he has a treatable psychotic illness, he could subsequently convince them that he has stabilised. The strategy may backfire, however, as people placed in secure mental hospitals are sometimes incarcerated longer than killers are in prison.

The currently established personality disorder categories include paranoid personality disorder, which speaks for itself and schizoid personality disorder – which is characterised by a persistent lack of interest in social relationships and limited emotional expression. The similar sounding schizotypal personality disorder is also characterised by social unease but is frequently combined with distorted thinking and eccentricity. These are all distinguishable from schizophrenia, which is a form of psychosis rather than a personality disorder.

The borderline personality disorder category is one which many patients are placed into, often after lengthy treatment for depression. It is characterised by a pattern of instability in relationships, impulsivity and significant issues related to self-image. Instability in the individual's relationship with themselves is projected outwards, hindering their ability to form trusting relationships. Consequently they are managed more successfully in environments with continuity of care, where they can begin to trust staff. Self-harm is a common symptom of the disorder. Observers may note a level of hysteria, which is a defining feature of the closely related histrionic personality disorder.

Avoidant personality disorder is characterised by social inhibition. Individuals report feeling inadequate and assume that others also have negative perceptions of them. Their negative self-perceptions may rub off on others, reinforcing the problem. As the name suggests, dependent personality disorder is characterised by a desire to have one's needs met by others. In long-term psychiatric patients it may be difficult to distinguish between symptoms of the disorder and consequences of institutionalisation.

The narcissistic personality disorder presentation is characterised by an obsession with the self and an inflated sense of self-importance. The grandiosity in the condition is distinguishable from that within psychotic illnesses like schizophrenia, where it forms part of a complex delusional system. For those with a narcissistic personality disorder, the relentless focus on the self occurs at the expense of a genuine interest in and empathy for others.

Readers will have noted overlaps between the symptoms listed above and features of psychopathy. The co-morbidity between different conditions is one of the things that makes psychiatry so interesting and challenging. People with an antisocial personality disorder are not simply like robots. They are complex and often bright, extremely engaging individuals. They may lack respect for the feelings of other people but they are not immune from depression or drug and alcohol problems. They may also have histrionic traits and some share a tendency towards self-harm with those with a borderline personality disorder.

Given that various difficult to manage symptoms may exist together, some being more prevalent than others at various times, we can appreciate the limitations of diagnostic categories. However, given the threat some people with personality disorders pose to themselves and others, we can also appreciate efforts to understand and define the conditions. Until mental health professionals and families know what they are dealing with, it is extremely difficult to effectively manage problems.

Even after being presented with clinical notes and police records of people defined by experts as psychopaths, some people might insist that it is a made up concept. They might argue that the label 'psychopath' is a way of stigmatising or demonising those who live beyond our understanding or who challenge our social rules. These sort of individualistic discourses, whether forwarded innocently or maliciously, can have the effect of supporting psychopaths and psychopathic cultures.

The critic of psychiatry might evoke *One Flew Over the Cuckoo's Nest* and other popular novels and films in order to talk about individuals having their freedom curtailed. This is a reasonable way to start an interesting debate, but it should be noted that *One Flew Over the Cuckoo's Nest* is a satire of how power operates throughout society. Rather than being exclusively *about* psychiatry, the author Ken Kesey uses psychiatry as a metaphor to discuss how power operates across the 'military industrial complex'.

Kesey's anti-hero character Randle McMurphy is described – rightly or wrongly – as a psychopath. However, the pathological culture of the military industrial complex is much more concerning than any one psychiatric patient, fictional or otherwise. Kesey did not use the term psychopathic cultures but he was certainly at least as concerned with power operating outside of psychiatry as he was with oppression within mental hospitals.

There are extremely interesting debates to be had in relation to psychiatry, power, labelling theory, social inequalities and crime. Within such debates it is crucial to acknowledge the reality that poorer people are more likely than wealthy people to be placed in prisons or mental hospitals and regarded as psychopaths. This does not, however, prove that more psychopaths come from disadvantaged backgrounds than prosperous ones.

Given what we now know about psychopaths in corporate environments and politics, we must conclude that the most powerful psychopaths have eluded diagnosis. Conversely, we must consider the possibility that some poorer people labelled psychopaths may have been misdiagnosed and unfairly treated. When desperate, frustrated aggression is seen as a greater threat to society than sophisticated Machiavellian manipulation, angry people will be incarcerated while exploiters prosper. Often anger is justifiable and does not make one a psychopath.

It is troubling to consider that the quintessential angry young man lashing against what they experience as an oppressive or unjust society is no more likely to be a psychopath than the policeman who bludgeons him or the politician who sanctions it. This does not mean that we should not, as a society, seek to identify and curtail psychopaths. It just means we need to look in a broader range of places for them and find new ways to tackle them.

This is already happening – many people are increasingly concerned about the callousness and deviousness of elite groups and large companies. Many are also concerned about illegitimate violence, corruption and cover-ups by police forces and militaries.

Ironically, those who choose to insist that there is no such thing as psychopathy show a lack of empathy and compassion for those with the disorder. Only by acknowledging the condition can we consider what psychopaths experience, how they perceive others, their strategies, what interests them and what roles in life they are drawn to.

By sharpening our awareness of these things we can better protect members of society and social institutions from psychopathic individuals and cultures. If we ignore the reality of psychopaths, they will continue to exploit and infiltrate key institutions. While we disregard the reality of psychopathy we allow psychopathic cultures to thrive, which normalises social toxicity and makes it harder to diagnose and treat.

Understanding psychopaths

In the recent decades there have been some interesting developments in the study of psychopathy. Neurobiological research has been supported by developments in imaging, such as MRI scanning. This in turn has strengthened evidence that psychopaths have brain abnormalities. Medical research into hormones and neurotransmitters have also focused on biological factors that support psychopathic traits.

Over the decades, research psychologists and psychiatrists have refined questions they ask psychopaths to gain insight into their cognitive processes. One interesting approach, which is often used, involves asking subjects to suggest what emotions people in photographs might be feeling.

In normal volunteers there will be some variation, especially in young people, but psychopaths tend to give particularly intriguing responses. Such tests can help demonstrate a marked lack of empathy. A person who seemed perfectly ordinary prior to a test can quickly reveal themselves to be notably abnormal, by showing little insight into others' feelings.

Researchers are also refining their own perceptions by making distinctions between different 'types' of psychopaths. This may not offer immediate comfort to people who are currently locked into disturbing relationships with psychopaths but it does have long-term ramifications. For example, it may help refine assessment tools to identify pathologies and help prisons and hospitals place different people more appropriately.

As has been stated in previous chapters, studies of psychopathy have spread out of the mental hospitals and prisons to the corporate world. The last few years – with so much abysmal practice found in banks and other corporations, political bodies and churches – suggests that this work has further to go. The barriers to do so, however, are significant.

Persuading incarcerated people to have brain scans and other tests is easier than persuading disgraced politicians, chief executives, brokers, bankers and priests to be undergo testing for personality disorders. Then, of course, there are the large number of powerful people who have not yet been disgraced but who exhibit psychopathic tendencies. It would seem unlikely that they would volunteer to be assessed and they may very well threaten legal action at the merest suggestion that they have abnormal brains.

Often the pathology is staring us in the face but, for a variety of reasons, powerful psychopaths remain unchallenged. The most successful psychopaths will not only choose to work within environments where they can maximise their power but they also often select organisations where they will be shielded.

However, given that we now know much more about psychopaths and we have a greater awareness of the sort of roles they are attracted to, avenues of tackling powerful psychopaths are opening up. For example, organisations that would like to present themselves as ethical might be persuaded to allow external experts in to examine their organisational processes and executive teams.

As well as identifying people in organisations who exhibit symptoms of psychopathy, such studies could investigate how psychopathic cultures operate. It might often be the case that psychopathic cultures exist long after those who helped create them have gone. The investigation of such cultures could bring together psychiatrists, business experts, psychologists and other social scientists.

Given that most experts agree that psychopaths will always be psychopaths, and that those in the most powerful positions in societies will avoid revealing themselves as such, some readers may think that little can be done to tackle them. I would respectfully disagree.

Over the last century a great deal has been learned about psychopaths and the approaches used to deal with them. It is only recently that we gained the ability to examine the functioning of living brains. This historical absence of concrete proof of brain abnormalities did not stop psychiatric professionals – as well as prison staff – from managing psychopaths and attempting to understand them. When you work closely with psychopaths you *have* to continuously attempt to understand them and respond appropriately to and manage their pathology.

Having to respond to extremely difficult behaviours and strategies from psychopaths has helped different services and professionals develop a range of approaches. Various psychotherapies have been tried over the decades, as have behavioural approaches of rewarding acceptable behaviour and taking privileges from those who exhibit malicious behaviour.

Some nations simply execute such people but this does not help us understand their behaviours and minds. In fact, it may be that leaders of states where execution is commonplace have a vested interest in psychopathy not being understood. Insights into the minds of those who are now executed would have the potential to shed light on the pathology of tyrannical and ruthless leaders. The insight could ultimately undermine the powerful.

Individuals in the community and workplaces who have had prolonged encounters with psychopaths will also have used various approaches in dealing with them. Whatever the outcome of their interactions, they will have developed valuable insights and are therefore potentially excellent reservoirs of knowledge. Rather than regarding such people as simply victims of psychopaths and assuming that psychiatrists and other professionals have all the answers, it would be better to draw on their experiences.

A key characteristic of psychopaths is they manipulate others by being different things to different people. Another way of phrasing this is they respond differently to different approaches. Yet another way of putting it is different communication strategies towards a psychopath can alter their behaviour. This is a critical insight, as it makes the difference between being at the mercy of psychopaths and retaining some power.

Influencing the actions of ruthless, skilled manipulators is challenging, but any shred of control that stops a target from being dragged down is valuable. It may seem at the time that the psychopath is so relentless, callous and cunning that they will always get their own way. However, the experience of people who deal with them professionally proves that this can be avoided.

When psychopaths are housed on specialist psychiatric wards, their ability to manipulate is reduced. Attempts to play people off against one another, manipulate staff and bully other patients will be quickly noted and discussed. The strategies of staff will then be adapted to take into account the newly-observed behaviours. The psychopath may have many unpleasant tricks up his or her sleeve but, faced with an informed and united team of professionals, they will have limited scope to exploit the situation.

Individuals in the community or workplace dealing with psychopathic behaviour will not have a team of expert observers to help them do the above and adapt their strategies. However, books and online resources can help them grasp what they are dealing with and explore different approaches. Although their condition and inclinations will not vanish when faced with different approaches from those around them, even subtle changes can alter a psychopath's behaviour.

Psychopaths are not all the same and some are much more sophisticated than others. Police, courts, prisons and clinicians often struggle to manage some of them. There is, unfortunately, no sure-fire way of removing them from your life if they have targeted you. However, support from those with experience in dealing with them can be pivotal in reducing the damage they cause.

For every callous psychopath there will be many decent people who have had negative experiences with them. If potential targets can make contact with those who have successfully navigated thorny relationships with psychopaths then they can have a better chance of doing the same.

Attempted treatments and management

Many different treatments have been tried on psychiatric patients over the last century, with mixed success. Some, such as psychosurgery and electro-convulsive therapy (ECT), have sometimes had a permanent effect on individuals while others have simply dampened down some symptoms in the short-term.

Although 'treatments' involving cutting part of the brain have had a permanent effect on many patients, this has not always been a positive one for the person concerned or their families. One reason for this is the patient often has very different views to those of psychiatrists about their needs. Behaviours regarded by psychiatrists as symptoms to be controlled may be valued by patients themselves. For example an aggressive person may value their ability to intimidate people, whereas psychiatric staff obviously find them easier to manage when more amiable.

Psychosurgery has killed quite a few mental health patients and caused more problems than it solved for many more. Furthermore, having surgery – or other treatments – against one's will tends to reinforce perceptions that psychiatry (and the state itself) is intrusive, oppressive and callous. Patients who are already suspicious about psychiatry may be no better disposed to it after having part of their brain forcibly cut.

Psychosurgery on psychiatric patients became quite common in Europe and the USA from the late 1930s. In the UK, the bulk of the operations happened in the period from 1940 until the mid-50s. There were around 1,500 psychosurgery operations annually in the UK alone in that period and there were several resultant deaths each year. Brain damage, epilepsy and strokes were common adverse effects resulting from surgery. By the late 1970s the number of annual operations in the UK had declined to around 150 and declined further in the 1980s.

The 1983 Mental Health Act stipulated that psychosurgery on psychiatric patients could only be carried out with consent. Since then there have only been a handful of cases each year in the UK. However, it is still used more extensively in some countries, notably China, India and Venezuela. The USA, where there were around 5,000 psychosurgery procedures a year in the 1940s, still uses the operation but on a much smaller scale. Refinements in techniques have led to fewer negative outcomes.

In Europe and the USA psychosurgery is now primarily used on patients with treatment-resistant depression, obsessive–compulsive disorder and extreme cases of anxiety. However, in the past attempts were made to use it to treat schizophrenia and a broad range of other conditions, including personality disorders, with extremely limited success.

Psychosurgery has not turned born psychopaths into non-psychopaths, and few modern psychiatrists would expect a condition that defines the entire character to be cured by surgery. Therefore any focus has been on particular problems, such as aggression. Though there has been some evidence of some patients exhibiting less aggression following psychosurgery, studies have been limited.

Pharmacology is the most common treatment of all mental health patients. Despite the consensus that psychopaths are untreatable, they – and other personality disordered patients – are frequently given medication. The argument that drugs only treat *symptoms* of those with personality disorders can, unfortunately, be extended to other patients. For example, those receiving pharmacological treatment for schizophrenia, other psychoses and bipolar affective disorder will often rapidly relapse if their medication is stopped.

Such patients will typically stabilise in hospital, feel better, get discharged, stop taking their medications, relapse and end up being admitted again. This is the tragic revolving door of modern psychiatry. The inability of any drug to cure serious mental health problems or personality disorders emphasises the importance of good psychological and emotional support, whether the vulnerable person is in hospital or the community.

In the UK community psychiatric nurses play a key role in encouraging drug compliance and in psychological and emotional support. They also pick up on warning signs that a person is relapsing and will arrange re-admission. However, with personality disordered patients it may not be desirable to admit them whenever they are having problems but to try to instead to manage them in the community. This may involve attending outpatient clinics to see doctors, mental health nurses or other psychiatric professionals.

Neuroleptics (also known as antipsychotics) are commonly prescribed to a range of psychiatric patients, particularly those with a psychotic illness. For those people, neuroleptics can reduce distressing symptoms like hallucinations and paranoia. They are also quite often administered to people with personality disorders in the absence of psychotic symptoms. The reason for this is the tranquillising effect of neuroleptics helps reduce tension, frustration, anger and the incidence of both aggression and self-harm.

In the last 50 years or so there have been considerable developments in neuroleptic drug production, with some of the unpleasant side-effects (such as movement problems and weight gain) reduced. Nevertheless, antipsychotics are powerful mind-altering drugs and there are risks associated with both taking and suddenly stopping them. Outpatients prescribed them generally require careful monitoring. This is something that many psychopaths would find or create problems with. Therefore, as with many other mental health patients, maintaining them on neuroleptics in the community can pose challenges.

As with antipsychotic medications, there have been many new antidepressants developed in recent decades. The primary groups of antidepressants are selective serotonin reuptake inhibitors (SSRIs), serotonin–norepinephrine reuptake inhibitors (SNRIs), tricyclics and monoamine oxidase inhibitors (MAOIs). A drug from one of these groups may be prescribed to psychopaths or sociopaths to treat depressive episodes. However, they may also be used to reduce symptoms and behaviours related to their personality disorder, such anger and impulsivity.

The mood-stabilising drug lithium is most commonly prescribed to people suffering from bipolar affective disorder. However, it has also been used in the management of other conditions. It has been found to reduce impulsivity and aggressive outbursts in psychopath patients.

When psychopaths are patients on psychiatric wards their behaviour and mood is closely monitored and their medication is reviewed as required. When they are living in the community it is more difficult to ensure that their prescription is effective for them, that they adhere to their medication regime and any side-effects are managed. Tremors, coordination problems and excessive thirst are some of the side-effects of lithium. For an already antagonistic psychopath, these side-effects may well impact onto their relationship with those around them.

Benzodiazepines, of which the branded product Valium (diazepine) is a prominent example, are used to control anxiety. However, benozos are highly addictive and frequently abused – both in the community and on psychiatric wards. Therefore caution is exercised in prescribing them, particularly to those who would sell them without regard for the safety of purchasers. While it is desirable that psychopaths are calm, there is always a risk that they will request tablets with the aim of selling them. This emphasises the importance of observing them effectively when receiving medication on wards or in prison.

Medicines used for epilepsy are sometimes prescribed to people with psychopathic disorders, as well as those with bipolar affective disorder and other mental illnesses. Such products have been found to be effective in reducing volatility, aggression and the incidence of self-harm.

As well as being useful in themselves at reducing symptoms, the medications discussed above also can make psychopaths more amiable to talking therapies and to the environment of psychiatric units.

Talking therapies

It has been received wisdom for many years, within the psychiatric establishment, that psychotherapy makes psychopathic individuals worse rather than better (D'Silva et al 2004). However, not all practitioners would agree and it should be acknowledged that psychotherapy evolves over time. The fact that units have been developed in the UK and elsewhere offering treatment to people with antisocial personality disorders demonstrates that received wisdom is sometimes questionable.

The Dangerous Severe Personality Disorder units discussed above were obviously designed to offer interventions for psychopaths. Furthermore, those on acute, low secure and medium secure units also should – ideally – have access to groups and one-to-one sessions with their key workers. Although many clinicians would not expect a psychopath to be any less of a psychopath as a result of psychotherapy, counselling or any other talking therapy, these do have value.

Within a psychiatric ward, group work and individual sessions with staff give patients opportunities to talk about their current or historic problems. This can help patients manage their symptoms and interactions while also offering staff useful opportunities to assess patients.

It should be acknowledged that often patients with personality disorders will be less than honest. However, regardless of the reliability of the content, the way in which patients communicate – whether to staff or other patients – helps teams develop a better picture of the person. Subtle – or indeed vivid – changes within different situations are extremely interesting and can be important to document.

Sometimes psychiatric staff will encounter people with personality disorders who are not patients themselves but relatives of patients. This is particularly an issue in specialist child, adolescent and eating disorder units. In these services the model of family work – whether presented as structured family therapy or more informally – is integral to the treatment of the patient. Rather than be viewed as the sole disturbed person, patients can be seen as 'symptom bearers' of a dysfunctional system.

To be able to tackle the child's problems, staff must engage with parents – and sometimes other siblings – in an open manner which appears non-judgemental. This is particularly difficult when a parent is highly belligerent, cold, abusive or neglectful. It is not uncommon for psychiatric staff meeting with parents to develop the view that it is the parent rather than the child who should be placed in an institution.

Even when faced with a parent who has the hallmarks of a psychopath, it is not always possible or even desirable to attempt to have the child taken into care. Being taken away and put into children's homes or foster care is not always preferable to being parented by people with personality disorders. It is possible for mental health services to take parents to court and win the power to keep the child in hospital against the will of parents. However, it is much more common for teams to engage as best they can with families in order to encourage different ways of responding to the children and familial disharmony.

When it is the psychopath themselves in hospital, a range of approaches will be used. Multidisciplinary teams of psychiatrists, psychologists, nurses, health care assistants, occupational therapists and psychotherapists have a breadth of experience, knowledge and skills. This should encourage an eclectic approach to care. It is rare nowadays that a single therapeutic model is used dogmatically on psychiatric wards, as has sometimes happened in the past.

Overall, a pharmacological approach has gained primacy within psychiatry. Nevertheless, when dealing with psychopaths – as well as any other patients – staff cannot rely on medication and they therefore require sophisticated interpersonal skills. These will have been developed within training, therapeutic groups, clinical supervision and day-to-day experience.

Patients differ enormously and people with the same diagnosis respond in different ways at different times to different approaches. Some patients struggle to tolerate the briefest of conversations, while others will engage with hours of different group sessions. In units where there are a range of patients with different problems, it may be of concern when psychopaths seek out groups where others are likely to expose their vulnerabilities.

A core model underpinning group therapy has historically been psychodynamic psychotherapy. The model, which is based on the theories of Sigmund Freud and his successors, assumes that there are different drives within each person that are sometimes at odds with one another and the external world. Stemming from this assumption is the belief that the relationship between these drives can be altered and the person enjoy a more adaptive life.

Within the psychodynamic approach life history is key, because how one responds to people in the present is influenced by their life experiences. Contemporary interpersonal conflicts may be traced back by therapists or group members to early childhood issues, such as abuse or neglect.

Perhaps due to television and film representations, many psychiatric patients assume that psychoanalytical exploration will be part of their stay in hospital. However, many psychiatric wards lack a group programme, let alone regular psychoanalysis sessions. Nevertheless, even in services lacking such resources, and where a pharmacological model reigns, staff should have knowledge of psychodynamic principles and this helps inform how they interact with patients.

There are some mental health units based on a therapeutic community model, in which there are many groups in which patients are encouraged to talk through their problems. Units that take many personality disordered patients often have extremely well thought out and well-managed therapeutic groups.

The psychodynamic approach in relation to antisocial personality disorder patients is interesting as it considers the ways in which the personality develops and recognises that current maladaptive behaviour is an expression of underlying personality structures. That is not to say that the biological basis of temperament is ignored but that that person's relationship with the world, sense of self and defence mechanisms will be of considerable interest to therapists.

In group sessions, individuals will often recognise a behaviour, self-deceit or dynamic in another more readily than within themselves. Even a patient who lacks empathy may be able to recognise conflicts and contradictions in another and learn from observing that. Furthermore, conflict between personality disorder patients can be reduced if they have the shared experience of going through intense and challenging groups together.

As many personality disorder patients find it difficult to speak about their feelings, experiences and problems, drama therapy can be a useful approach. This model can enable them to explore emotional and interpersonal conflicts from an abstracted perspective rather than head on. As with Gestalt therapy, drama therapy can enable patients to move between different and conflicting roles. This has the potential to encourage empathy and insight into behaviours, though may be more effective for other personality disorders than for psychopathy.

It should be emphasised that therapy in psychiatric hospitals does not just take place in formal groups and one-to-one sessions with staff. Significant interactions with staff or fellow patients can take place at any point of the day or night. Many patients, especially those who are particularly guarded, will say more while unwinding before bed or at a meal time than in a formal therapy group.

Some of the surviving and former large psychiatric hospitals in Britain and elsewhere have histories of being therapeutic communities. A small number still exist. The concept of therapeutic communities was developed in the UK after World War Two. By the 1960s, in the context of criticisms about how power operated within psychiatry, the model was extensively used in the UK and USA. The focus was to move away from an authoritarian system in which doctors and nurses have ultimate control over patients' lives to one where 'residents' were encouraged to take responsibility for themselves and the hospital environment.

This meant that ward doors in some old asylums were opened to allow patients freedom to walk around the site and community meetings were introduced to give a sense of democratic control. Rather than being passive recipients of medical and behavioural treatment, patients were given a stronger voice and greater choice. This, it was hoped, would help counter the consequences of institutionalisation and groups would encourage patients to become more open about their needs and feelings. This in turn would encourage them to make progress in their interpersonal relationships and with their internal conflicts.

To critics there was sense that 'the lunatics have taken over the asylum'. However, given the conditions experienced by patients prior to the new approach, allowing patients a voice and giving them responsibility seemed a rational and humane thing to do. It should be stressed, however, that one of the factors that allowed many patients to be afforded greater freedom was the development of new medication. The neuroleptic chlorpromozine particularly, which was first synthesised in 1950, greatly reduced the symptoms of patients with psychosis and other conditions.

The psychiatrist David Clark discusses the rise and decline of the therapeutic community model in his fascinating 1996 book *The Story of a Mental Hospital: Fulbourn 1858-1983*. Under Dr Clark's leadership from the 1950s, Fulbourn Hospital – located just outside Cambridge – became a pioneering therapeutic community. The therapeutic community ethos was at its strongest in the 1960s, after which there was a gradual shift towards a more top-down medical model approach.

Nevertheless, most of the remaining wards at Fulbourn maintain a group programme. This contrasts sharply with many mental health services in the UK, where therapeutic groups are scarce – or entirely absent – and patients have little to do but watch television or lay around in bed. Such inactivity can exacerbate symptoms of psychosis and other disorders.

When medication is regarded as the primary method of improving mental health, there is a tendency for talking approaches to be disregarded by some clinicians. This is regrettable for a number of reasons. Firstly, patients are part of society and if psychiatric wards fail to help people improve how they negotiate interpersonal relationships then all they are doing is tinkering with brain chemistry. Secondly, conflicts on wards – which are common – can be reduced and dealt with more easily when there are groups to encourage patients to communicate. Furthermore, many patients – and not just those with personality disorders – do not show much improvement with drug therapy. It is important, therefore, to explore different ways of managing symptoms.

Interestingly, the adult mental health units that still adhere most closely to the therapeutic community approach tend to be those who care for large numbers of people with personality disorders. The term 'milieu therapy' is often used interchangeably with 'therapeutic community' but there are differences to consider, especially in relation to forensic patients.

The 1960s therapeutic community ethos of patients making decisions about the running of hospitals has largely been abandoned. However, some services use a milieu approach. Child and adolescent units often have a milieu therapy approach and clearly such patient groups are not given the level of responsibility residents were in 1960s therapeutic communities. Nevertheless, in milieu-based units, the group of patients is regarded as instrumental in the progress of individuals.

Groups may be led by staff, but positive peer pressure is used to challenge maladaptive behaviours, including self-harm. Expectations of group members is made clear and the patients themselves then reinforce those standards as a group. Some patients will be further along with their progress than others and this presence of positive role models in the patient and staff groups encourages behaviours that are safer and more socially acceptable.

Settings where a milieu approach is employed tend to use a combination of different psychotherapies as well as drug therapy. Patients may experience community meetings, intensive group psychotherapy, individual psychodynamic psychotherapy and cognitive therapy approaches. However, milieu therapy is about creating an entire environment in which the individual can make changes in their relationship with the world. Therefore, it extends beyond formal therapeutic meetings to all aspects of the hospital experience.

Cognitive approaches in relation to personality disorder patients – and many other people – have become popular in recent decades. There are different systems – including cognitive behaviour therapy, rational emotive therapy and dialectical behaviour therapy. The general focus of cognitive approaches is to encourage patients to reflect on their thoughts and feelings and ways in which these influence behaviour – and therefore their lives.

The assumption is that behaviours are controlled by the way people think and their emotional responses to the world around them. By altering how patients perceive things, there is the potential to change their responses. Because dangerous and threatening behaviour is common in incarcerated or hospitalised psychopaths, cognitive approaches can be an effective way of keeping them and those around them safer. The techniques can help individuals gain more control over their anger by identifying trigger points and alternative ways of dealing with potentially explosive situations.

Behaviour therapy

Behaviour therapy is sometimes perceived as a dated and rather simplistic approach to get people to respond differently to the world. Techniques can be traced to before the word psychiatry had ever been used and to a variety of religious and philosophical traditions, including stoicism.

Within the history of psychiatry and the prison system, behaviour therapy has often focused on rewarding desirable behaviour. Rewards include stars (for star charts), cigarettes, treats, privileges and access to phone calls and electronic equipment. Conversely, undesirable behaviour results in sanctions, in the hope of eradicating – or at least diminishing – maladaptive behaviour.

However, the field is broader than reward-based approaches and relates to a variety of techniques of encouraging children, adult psychiatric patients and prisoners to learn from mistakes and develop more socially acceptable behaviours. Principles of the behavioural model have also been incorporated into different cognitive approaches, such as cognitive behaviour therapy.

The assumption of the behavioural approach is that maladaptive behaviour is acquired through poor conditioning rather than something intrinsic to the person. As behaviour – and personality itself – is acquired through learning, it can therefore be modified by new experiences. In relation to psychopaths, this rather conflicts with the view that the condition is inherent. However, it seems likely that a born tendency towards aggressive, manipulative and deceitful behaviour can be reinforced if society allows that person to be rewarded and go unpunished. This may be particularly relevant to 'successful psychopaths'. It may also help explain why some environments seem to produce more psychopaths than others.

Some institutions are more likely than others to use reward-based systems to change behaviour. Prisons, children's homes and psychiatric units for young children are more likely to have such an approach than adult acute admission wards and adolescent units. In contexts where conditions are considered to be illnesses rather than poor behaviour, the use of such approaches seems punitive.

In practice, behavioural approaches in psychiatric services are a long way from the extreme reprogramming seen in *A Clockwork Orange,* in which a young offender is reprogrammed by a variety of dramatic images, drugs and aversion therapy. Groups dedicated to anger management, assertiveness and social skills are all rooted in the behavioural model.

If we take it as a given that psychopath patients – as well as those with chronic mental illnesses – have a condition that effects their entire mind, then the point can be made that behaviour therapy only deals with symptoms. Another weakness of the behavioural approach, with psychopaths, children and other patients, is they present a reality that does not exist. We do not live in fair meritocracies, where good conduct is always rewarded and unpleasant behaviour is necessarily punished.

The inequalities between the haves and the have-nots have got bigger and bigger in many countries over the past century and most people would be well aware of the general unfairness of the world. Therefore to suggest that a behavioural approach will teach people to adapt to the 'normal' world can seem something of a nonsense. To tell people that they would get on better in the outside world if they learn to be less aggressive and less devious only makes sense when the economic, educational, political and vocational worlds are not rigged against the poor.

While the less successful psychopaths are being encouraged to undertake anger management in hospitals and prisons, the highly successful psychopaths are out in the community lying, manipulating, cheating and eroding society for their own benefit. They are also building pathological cultures which help reinforce their own dominance. If it makes sense to *try* to encourage more moderate behaviour in detained psychopaths, it makes even more sense to tackle pathological cultures that harm many more people.

Chapter 12 – Treating pathological cultures and toxic systems

Some readers may be wondering at this stage how psychopathic or pathological cultures can be treated if it is so difficult to have any leverage to change the behaviour of individual psychopaths. To this I would say it *should*, theoretically, be rather more easy. This is because culture is fluid and is created by us all. Once we identify pathological structures, we have the power to weaken them and ultimately create healthier systems that support communities.

If we consider the history of humanity we can recognise that we have been tackling psychopathic cultures for a considerable time. Battles all around the world are happening in relation to those who dominate communities of all sizes – from families, to institutions to corporations to governments. Those involved in such fights may not have described it as treating psychopathic cultures. Nevertheless, attempts to remove power from malicious, domineering, callous individuals, who just exploit others for their own gains do just that.

Given how much influence powerful psychopaths have in societies – from politics, banking, the media, religion and corporate management – it can seem like an incredibly daunting task to tackle the problems we face. However, given the power of such people – and of the pathological systems they drive – any success in undermining these cultures and individuals has a considerable impact on a large number of people.

For people in societies where the powerful psychopaths do not need to hide behind business suits and lawyers, but can be transparent in their brutality, the task is even more frightening. Nevertheless, many people are confronting them and forcing change in even the most oppressive states.

The rewards in tackling powerful psychopaths and psychopathic cultures are to stop a rot that had eaten into not only organisations but the minds of those ensnared in pathological systems. This is a culture that makes the most grotesque injustices seem acceptable. It is a culture where the eradication, starvation and incarceration of communities for the benefit of more powerful nations or groups is made to seem acceptable.

Although these injustices are real and happen on a daily basis, they will never be acceptable to right thinking people. When a psychopath dominates a family and abuses and neglects them it is vividly real and becomes lived reality for those people. Victims may be resigned to their fate but they are more likely than not to recognise that it is wrong. It may be the case that many people experience such oppression at some point in their lives but this does not mean it is acceptable. It was never acceptable and never will be. It is malicious and inhumane.

Similarly, psychopathic cultures, dominated by small groups of oppressive people may seem too powerful to do anything about. But they are not as culture can shift. Furthermore – and importantly – more people benefit from them being challenged and undermined than benefit from them existing. Therefore despite risks and fear, there will always been a propulsion for communities to challenge oppressors. The shift in power in the media, to the situation where citizens have stronger voices, makes this easier and easier.

Just as the psychopathic individual dominating a family may make their victims feel that they need him or her, elite psychopaths make out that society needs them. The banking crisis in the UK, USA and other nations has been a good example of this. The point was often made by politicians – on behalf of their banker donors – and by bankers themselves, that if they were not bailed out by taxpayers the banks would go elsewhere and society itself would suffer. Having thus taken hard-earned money from the public, the bankers promptly gave themselves bonuses worth many times more than most peoples' homes. This proved too much for the public, which has since subjected bankers to more scrutiny than they have ever experienced.

In my mind the above is akin to an abusive, exploitative, oppressive bully in a family knocking everyone around, dominating everyone with fear, emptying his partner's purse and the children's' piggy banks and then having to audacity to claim that if he leaves they would all be in danger.

Citizens are victims to this sort of mentality from aggressive powerful psychopaths who will exploit society, lie, cheat, manipulate to maintain power and get whatever they want. Whether they are bankers, politicians, owners of toxic corporations or corrupt and abusive churchmen, they will not stop unless we recognise the problem and stop them. Furthermore, psychopathic cultures will flourish unless we stop assuming that pathological, unjust systems are necessary for the survival of our societies.

Doomed to be victims?

Writing in 1994, Robert Hare said: "The implications of being able to identify psychopaths are as much practical as academic. To put it simply, if we can't spot them, we are doomed to be their victims, both as individuals and as a society." I would add that unless we, as communities, recognise the existence of psychopathic cultures, we will remain subject to their oppression.

Of course many people will feel that oppressive people in their lives – whether partners, bosses, teachers, children or neighbours – *must* be psychopaths. Some will be but others will have other problems or simply be non-pathological unpleasant people. Unless their diagnoses will ensure that they are locked up, it may in practice make little difference to those around them if a person is clinically defined as a psychopath or not. However, knowledge that someone we find extremely difficult to get along with has a personality disorder may make us feel better about struggling to deal with them.

In this internet era, people frequently do online tests to 'find out' if they have a mental illness or personality disorder. Self-diagnosis for complex conditions of the mind – especially with the aid of questionable online tests – is unwise and unscientific. A mentally sound but sensitive person can be devastated to 'discover' when surfing the internet that they have a serious mental illness or personality disorder. They may not dare to go to a doctor and share their concerns and the 'diagnosis' can have an impact on their long-term self-image, mood and behaviour.

Therefore it is critical that clinical diagnosis is left to specialists. As has been said, there are a variety of other disorders that closely resemble psychopathy and any of these may appear more dominant than others at any given time. Diagnosing particular personality disorders and mental illness is a complex and problematic endeavour, not least because peoples' presentation changes over time. To have a solid diagnosis of a specific personality disorder requires good evidence gained over a period of time, not a snapshot from one interview.

Although few people have the training required to make fine distinctions between different personality disorders and mental illnesses, the reality is that the public is much more aware of and interested in the mind than ever before. This is partly because the stigma of mental illness has reduced and people are more confident talking about their experiences.

It is also because the last 100 years has seen a huge increase in interest in the fields of psychology and criminology.

A relentless stream of shocking events unfolding over the last century has helped prompt questions about the stability – or otherwise – of the human mind. Genocides, wars, bloody revolutions, riots, mass murders and systematic abuse of children and others have helped focus attention on our shortcomings as a species as well as human potentials.

As a species we are better educated than ever before, more suspicious about inherited 'wisdom' and more likely to question authority figures. Religious explanations of reality have, for many, given way to more rationalistic, social scientific and philosophical explanations. People today are much more likely to consider that a dream, for example, is the product of their experiences, thoughts and feelings than a direct message from a god. Terms used by a small number of psychiatrists and therapists 100 years ago are now popular expressions.

With the above in mind, it seems likely that some of those people who members of the public believe to be psychopaths are indeed so. They may be successful psychopaths who have eluded diagnosis or less successful psychopaths who have been observed causing pain, distress and fear for decades. To a large extent, psychopaths are defined by their impact on others. It would therefore be an arrogant and irrational psychiatrist who disregards the perceptions of people in close proximity to such a person simply because they are laymen.

In reality, however, members of the community rarely get to share their views with a psychiatrist about another's psychopathy unless they are a relative or close friend. Consequently, most people have no way to safely challenge such a person unless they are accusing them of a crime or something like workplace bullying. Many would take the view that – regardless of how strong our suspicions are that an individual is a psychopath – it is wise to not confront them with this accusation. It is safer to disentangle from the individual and gain an emotional and physical distance from them before making allegations about their activities to the police, employers, social workers or other agencies who could help.

Many of us will have met low-performing psychopaths and sociopaths (and non-pathological petty criminals) who like to be characterised as 'psychos'. They might think it gives the status and power but this may not stop them from feigning outrage and reacting badly when defined as one by a neighbour or colleague. Those who fit the description of wealthy successful psychopath may find it easy to smear and destroy those who accuse them of wrongdoing or being psychopathic.

If it is true – as Martha Stout suggests – that as many as four percent of the population in the western world has an antisocial personality disorder, we may not have enough psychiatrists to ensure that a sizeable proportion of psychopaths are ever diagnosed. Moreover, we certainly do not have psychiatrists in the right places in society to diagnose powerful psychopaths. The psychopaths most likely to get diagnosed are less prosperous ones who find themselves in mental hospitals or prison. By definition, the most successful psychopaths are not being curtailed and these are the ones with the power to cause the greatest harm to society and cultures.

Most psychiatric professionals I have known are concerned about psychopaths in powerful positions in life. If you get a psychiatrist or psychologist drunk she or he may tell you which politicians, celebrities and other people in the public eye fit particular personality disorder categories. Few, however, would go public with their impressions.

Psychiatrists and forensic psychologists tend to be too busy attempting to assess, treat and manage patients to do anything about powerful and famous people who they believe to have damaging personality disorders. Furthermore, there is a considerable danger of undermining their own career if they make public proclamations about the psychopathy of prominent people.

To make a claim about someone's mental instability or pathological personality can lead to an expensive libel suit unless it can be backed up with evidence. One cannot demand that those initiating a defamation action undertake a psychiatric assessment. The onus is on the defamer to prove the validity of their assertion but gaining enough evidence to back it up is extremely difficult. Furthermore, wealthy litigants can easily hire other psychiatrists to dispute any claims about their pathology.

There have been exceptions, however, where psychiatrists have stuck their necks out and gone public with their concerns about prominent people. Over the years, a number of experts publicly expressed their opinions about George Bush junior's mental condition. While in power Mr Bush was described by clinicians as having a narcissistic personality disorder. Some also speculated on the damage that may have been done to his brain by alcohol and cocaine misuse.

In the case of a man as unpredictable, arrogant, dogmatic, powerful and therefore dangerous as Bush, it seems reasonable that psychiatrists took professional and personal risks to share their views. The dissemination of concerns about potentially dangerous powerful people has the potential to save lives, whether in the country they live or abroad. The job of doctors is to protect life, and therefore clinicians who publicly express concern about people with the power to harm citizens can be seen to be doing just that.

Despite articles appearing about his apparent pathology, George Bush junior won a second term as president. That does not, however, mean that the communications were valueless. Raising concerns about one powerful figure can help people identify similar characteristics in others and also help inspire public debate about standards in public life.

Mitt Romney's bid for the presidency in 2012 was dogged with as many online attacks on his integrity, compassion and ability to empathise with the public as questions about his competency. Once it became apparent that Romney would be the Republican candidate, some commentators focused on personality flaws. They also presented episodes from his life where he allegedly showed callous disregard for others and extreme deviousness.

I, of course, am not claiming that Mitt Romney is a psychopath, merely pointing out that some of the attacks he faced as a candidate involved psychopathologising. The unfortunate reality is that callous disregard for others and deviousness are not unusual characteristics among politicians. In fact, these 'qualities' are so common among political candidates that we must question selection processes.

It is critical to consider which sections of society and interest groups particular candidates represent. Given the huge financial cost of getting elected in America, it can seem as though Bush senior and junior, Romney, Nixon and indeed Obama, Kennedy and Clinton have represented wealthy and powerful groups rather than the electorate.

It is often said that the American president is just a figurehead and there are wealthy, shadowy people above them pulling the strings. As my last book, *Beyond the End of the World* (2010) demonstrates, I have the inclination to be wary of conspiracy theories. However, when it comes to politics and economics, I am of the opinion that some powerful unelected people have an inordinate influence on the decisions of politicians.

Over the last couple of decades, interest has grown in New World Order beliefs. These centre on the notion that a cabal of powerful people are attempting to bring about a single world government through nefarious means. For those who subscribe to the belief, terrorist attacks are often perceived as false flag attacks designed to cause conflict. The rationale for this would be to have the excuse for oppression by systems of surveillance, military invasions and neocolonial governance of 'unstable' states.

The New World Order is often linked to the Illuminati, which was a real organisation at one point, but there is no evidence that it survived and expanded as some people believe. The Bavarian Illuminati was established in 1776 with the goal of promoting rationalism by challenging superstitions and curtailing the influence of religion on public life. It also had the agenda of opposing abuses of state power and encouraging greater gender equality through educational opportunities for females.

The Illuminati met the wrath of the Catholic Church and, by 1785, the group of intellectuals was outlawed by the Bavarian government and disbanded. However, myths about the group continued, with some people believing that the Illuminati had survived and were behind the French Revolution. Since then, without any good evidence that it exists in any form related to the original society, various people have claimed that it has become so powerful it orchestrates global political events. It is also often linked to Zionism and much of the 'information' about it is spread on websites and via films found on YouTube. Recently it was held responsible, by some, for the disappearance of Malaysia Airlines flight MH370.

Given that there *are* networks of powerful people trying to maximise their impact on world events, it is hard to completely dispel Illuminati myths or beliefs about a New World Order plot. There are certainly megalomaniacal rich people who believe they should or even *do* control the world. There is a strong element of narcissism in such a view. Just as some thugs like to be described as psychopaths because it adds to their power, some power-obsessed people no doubt enjoy letting people believe that they are part of some mysterious elite secret society.

My view is, despite the appetite for control and collusion between powerful figures, life on earth is far too complex and dynamic for groups of rich people to have anything like the influence that some imagine. There are too many variables. Technology and ideas evolve in an unpredictable manner, and nations and industries that had vast wealth in the past often lose ground rapidly. Wealth can help historically powerful families retain influence, but innovation and a visionary approach to business and technology seems more valuable in this era.

Nevertheless, there is a modern group of powerful people that fuels beliefs in a New World Order plot. Whether they feel connected to the Illuminati or not and whether or not they conduct any esoteric rituals, the shadowy Bilderberg Group is a cause of concern for many. Anti-capitalists, New World Order conspiracy theorists and campaigners for transparent democracy all have reason to be concerned by the Bilderberg Group and its annual private conference.

The conference, which press are not allowed to attend, generally involves just over 100 invited guests from the corporate world, politics, academia and other influential sectors. Monarchs also have been known to attend. Guests are primarily from North America and Europe.

The inaugural Bilderberg conference took place in 1954 in a Netherlands hotel, after which the group took its name. The focus of that event was the relationship between Europe and America. Conference organisers were concerned about popular sentiments of anti-Americanism in Europe. The event was intended to encourage improved trade relations and greater political harmony.

Perhaps because of the belief some people have that the Bilderberg group is antidemocratic and focused on world domination, there have been communications aimed at reassuring the public. In 2008, when the conference took place in Virginia, a press release from the American Friends of Bilderberg stated: "Bilderberg's only activity is its annual conference. At the meetings, no resolutions are proposed, no votes taken, and no policy statements issued." Items on the agenda that year included Afghanistan, Pakistan, Islam, Iran, Africa and cyber-terrorism.

One of the attractions of the format for attendees might be that they can debate issues without been subjected to press and public scrutiny. It is this very thing, however, which outrages critics. Given that many of the people there are *our* politicians, it goes against the principal that our elected officials should work on our behalf in a transparent manner.

The covert nature of the discussions and power of those involved is enticing fodder for those who look for sinister conspiracies. This has not been helped by at least one regular group attendee discussing the desirability of a one-world government. In 2001, Denis Healey, the former deputy leader of the Labour Party and a Bilderberg founder, said: "To say we were striving for a one-world government is exaggerated, but not wholly unfair. Those of us in Bilderberg felt we couldn't go on forever fighting one another for nothing and killing people and rendering millions homeless. So we felt that a single community throughout the world would be a good thing."

While critics on the right imagine Bilderberg to be working towards global communism, those on the left are concerned that the concentration of owners of large corporations means the group is working towards capitalist domination of the world.

The reason for taking a small detour into different beliefs about Bilderberg is that it sheds light on some of the problems of 'diagnosing' psychopathic cultures. I am not saying I believe that Bilderberg is a psychopathic culture, or even speculating about its motives. I genuinely do not know exactly what goes on within it – and this is the point. If a culture is closed off and there are only snippets of information available about it, what tends to happen is people will project their fantasies and fears onto it.

In the case of Bilderberg, some look for 'evidence' that it is working to create a New World Order. Others view it as powerful capitalists dividing up the resources of the world, while some believe they are the fabled Illuminati and perform strange rituals. Some, while also believing the above, believe members are shape-shifting world-dominating reptilians.

Just as the lack of transparency of Bilderberg encourages people to imagine sinister conspiracies, corporations, governments, religions, media groups, police forces and other powerful organisations are often regarded with suspicion and hostility for the same reason. To have great power without appearing compelled to be honest and open with citizens is something the public finds exasperating and is increasingly antagonistic about.

Even in democratic countries, politicians, bankers, church leaders, media bosses and the security services are sometimes – and perhaps increasingly – viewed as devious, manipulative, callous, deceitful, malicious, self-serving and insincere. They are also viewed as exploitative and lacking in concern for feelings, needs, or suffering of others and lacking in remorse about their impact on citizens.

Large corporations often demonstrate a marked lack of social responsibility, whether in relation to the damage they cause to the environment, their exploitation of relatively powerless people or their aversion to paying fair tax contributions.

There are also sectors of the corporate world where risk taking – despite the potential impacts on society – have become acceptable and greatly rewarded. Investment bankers, brokers and hedge fund managers may not like to be regarded as impulsive gamblers but the evidence is that these qualities – combined with greed and arrogance – helped create the most recent widespread recession.

However, the greatest risk was not to themselves. Bankers and brokers syphoned off massive salaries and bonuses as huge numbers of homes were repossessed and the poorest people were hit harder than anyone by swingeing government cuts. In many countries, bank loans became unavailable to large numbers of individuals and businesses. Already struggling people resorted to borrowing at exorbitant rates from 'pay day loan' firms, some of which have strong links with politicians.

The financial crisis – a test case in assessing and treating psychopathic cultures?

If there was a deliberate strategy to bring down economies in order to push government spending cuts and shrink the state, then the global financial crisis was malicious, manipulative and self-serving. If it was not deliberate, but those involved were just greedy and indifferent to the needs of citizens, many people would still see hallmarks of psychopathy.

Speaking on Channel 4's 2013 *Psychopath Night* the prominent psychologist Oliver James described the credit crunch as a "mass outbreak of corporate psychopathy which resulted in something that very nearly crashed the whole world economy." The lack of remorse senior figures expressed after causing great hardship to members of society and risk to economies is something the public and some politicians found shocking.

Even when presented with strong evidence that elements of the market had been rigged, bankers sat in front of politicians and television cameras as though there had been no wrongdoing. However, their glib responses, cold detached demeanour and apparent lack of remorse outraged the public, for good reason.

I believe that in the aftermath of the crisis many citizens recognised a psychopathic culture in action. They might not have used the term 'psychopathic culture' but more and more people came to regard powerful bankers and brokers as crooked, rotten, malicious, detached and cold. An antagonism, which had previously been found primarily among critical activists rapidly spread.

Many people no doubt felt completely powerless, even as bankers and brokers appeared on their television screens justifying a rigged system. However there have been some efforts since to alter the way that the banking system and the financial markets work. Some would describe this as an attempt to prevent excesses and risk. Given the nature of those involved and the pathology of the systems, I personally regard it as an attempt to treat a psychopathic culture.

If it proves possible to challenge and reconfigure an industry worth trillions, run by some of the slickest manipulators who have ever walked the earth, then it is possible to deal successfully with other psychopathic cultures. Not least because few other groups have society and politicians over a barrel in the way that bankers and investment corporations do.

If, however, the financial sector resists external control in the coming years – perhaps by blackmailing governments via threats of relocating – then it will prove to even more people that the system is rotten. Future efforts to resist change will be harder as more of the public become antagonistic towards banker bail-outs, tax breaks and colossal bonuses for people who actually destabilise societies.

The global financial crisis that began in 2007 was avoidable, according to the US Financial Crisis Inquiry Commission. Its 2011 *Financial Crisis Inquiry Report* states: "The crisis was the result of human action and inaction, not of Mother Nature or models gone haywire. The captains of finance and the public stewards of our financial system ignored warnings and failed to question, understand and manage evolving risks within a system essential to the well-being of the American public. Theirs was a big miss, not a stumble."

The report went on to state: "Despite the expressed view of many on Wall Street and in Washington that the crisis could not have been foreseen or avoided, there were warning signs. The tragedy was that they were ignored or discounted."

In relation to transparency – or rather a lack of transparency, the report also states: "Within the financial system, the dangers of this debt were magnified because transparency was not required or desired. Massive, short-term borrowing, combined with obligations unseen by others in the market, heightened the chances the system could rapidly unravel.

"In the early part of the 20th century, we erected a series of protections – the Federal Reserve as a lender of last resort, federal deposit insurance, ample regulations – to provide a bulwark against the panics that had regularly plagued America's banking system in the 20th century. Yet, over the past 30-plus years, we

permitted the growth of a shadow banking system – opaque and laden with short-term debt – that rivalled the size of the traditional banking system. Key components of the market…were hidden from view, without the protections we had constructed to prevent financial meltdowns. We had a 21st Century financial system with 20th Century safeguards."

Of course the report does not use the term 'psychopathic culture', but it does refer to "a systemic breakdown in accountability and ethics" and states: "The integrity of our financial markets and the public's trust in those markets are essential to the economic well-being of our nation. The soundness and the sustained prosperity of the financial system and our economy rely on the notions of fair dealing, responsibility, and transparency. In our economy, we expect businesses and individuals to pursue profits, at the same time that they produce products and services of quality and conduct themselves well.

"Unfortunately – as has been the case in past speculative booms and busts – we witnessed an erosion of standards of responsibility and ethics that exacerbated the financial crisis. This was not universal, but these breaches stretched from the ground level to the corporate suites. They resulted not only in significant financial consequences but also in damage to the trust of investors, businesses, and the public in the financial system."

In relation to culture within the offending organisations, the regulatory system and society itself, the report concludes: "We place special responsibility with the public leaders charged with protecting our financial system, those entrusted to run our regulatory agencies, and the chief executives of companies whose failures drove us to crisis. These individuals sought and accepted positions of significant responsibility and obligation. Tone at the top does matter and, in this instance, we were let down. No one said "no." But as a nation, we must also accept responsibility for what we permitted to occur…we acquiesced to or embraced a system, a set of policies and actions, that gave rise to our present predicament."

For me, the financial crisis is a perfect illustration of how the public as a whole can be led into tolerating, participating in and then ultimately bailing out a pathological culture. As Michel Foucault observed, we all play our part in systems of power and oppression, therefore we have to acknowledge that as consumers we play a role in the exploitation and inequalities inherent our economic systems. Nevertheless, some people are more implicated in creating pathological cultures than others.

One of the factors that led to the crisis was the indiscriminate sale of sub-prime mortgages in the USA, Britain and elsewhere. To wish to own the roof over one's head is a reasonable ambition to have. In the context of rapidly increasing house prices, the pressure to get on the housing ladder was great and the assumption that prices would keep rising – thus mitigating the problem of being over-exposed to debt – was common.

For mortgage brokers selling such products, it was logical to turn a blind eye to suspicions about individual buyer's ability to cover the mortgage in the long-term. However, the reality is that city traders, bankers and many wealthy investors were well aware of the risks associated with sub-prime mortgage overselling. This drove the market of credit default swaps, designed to mitigate investment risk – in this case in relation to mortgage-backed securities (clusters of mortgages sold to investors). From one perspective credit default swaps are simply insurance policies against risky investments or loans but in practice they worked like bets on market failure.

In the eyes of some investors it became preferable to bet on market failure rather than on success. Very wealthy, extremely well-advised people cynically gambled on much poorer people being unable to keep up their mortgage payments. Given that they knew many would default, it was not much of a gamble. In fact, some of those who were selling credit default swaps were also involved with selling risky investments that would contribute to the crisis. They were selling investments designed to make money out of the failure of other investments they were selling.

The complexity of the financial system makes it hard for authorities, let alone laymen, to understand enough to prove wrongdoing. However, what is clear is that hedge fund managers and their clients made fortunes while struggling families went into default, homes were repossessed, mortgage-backed securities and other investments became toxic, credit crunched, banks collapsed, taxpayers were made to prop-up banks and governments slashed spending on critical public services.

Therefore, as is often the case, those people who were already impoverished and burdened with debts ended up suffering the most while those in the know – those controlling the casinos – increased their fortunes.

Furthermore, the banking crisis gave right-wingers the excuse to cut public services and benefit payments as well as push for economic restructuring of other nations. It is not far-fetched to think that elite beneficiaries of the crisis further exploited it by pushing for policies that took more resources from the pockets of ordinary citizens and put them in banks. This then enabled even more money to be plundered from the public – money which ultimately went to those who cultivated market instability.

The deceitful might push the narrative that the financial crisis was a 'perfect storm' of unfortunate accidents, and the naïve might believe the story. However, I suspect fewer people believe this now than they did in 2008, when the story was covering newspapers and filling television news bulletins.

Key players in financial corporations have close relationships with regulators and politicians. In fact, many regulators have been senior figures in suspect organisations. Consequently any investigations are mistrusted by the public and 'evidence' is often 'he said, she said' competing narratives rather than smoking guns. However, there have been exceptions – such as the Libor (London Inter-bank Offered Rate) fixing scandal.

In 2012 the UK government published its *Review of HM Treasury's management response to the financial crisis*. This is a curious document as it focuses much more on how well the government "managed" the crisis than what more should have been done and which alarm bells were ignored.

The report begins by stating: "The financial crisis of 2007 to 2009 was arguably the most difficult set of economic circumstances that the Treasury has faced in its history. The crisis has had huge ramifications for the economy, the public finances and people's living standards. Its impacts are still being felt. In its response, the Department proved itself flexible and adaptable, ramping up resources right through the crisis. The commitment and dedication of staff working directly on the crisis – or covering for those who were – was highly impressive."

It does at least acknowledge that "there are lessons to be learnt", stating: "The Treasury, like many other institutions, did not see the crisis coming and was consequently under-resourced when it began. The Treasury responded nimbly – with a strong 'esprit de corps'. It drew in outside expertise where it did not have the skills in-house. Resources could have been brought in more quickly and greater investment should have been made in staff and project management."

For me an extremely troubling part of the report is a section where the authors seem to suggest broad complacency about the realities of markets and of the economic cycle. Perhaps alluding to innovations like credit default swaps, the report states: "Crises by their nature are complex, largely unexpected, out-of-the-ordinary events that demand immediate actions. Before the 2007-09 financial crisis, regulators across the international financial system championed the economic benefits of rational, self-correcting markets and the merits of financial innovation. A global consensus emerged that new modes of finance had reduced systemic risks."

This seems like shocking naivety, arrogance or disingenuity to me, particularly since the 2011 American report cited above acknowledges that many people had been flagging up concerns for years. Furthermore, when it talks about "a global consensus" one has to question who this includes. If the Treasury is referring to financial experts around the world then the statement is erroneous since as, has been said, many experts were predicting the crisis for some time.

Given the frequency in which politicians suggest that unless bankers and brokers can get huge bonuses – sometimes from taxpayers' money – they may move abroad, some aspects of the report are really shocking. In a section about financial services and financial stability, the report states: "Financial services were not a high profile area of the Treasury's business. The area did not receive significant attention from Ministers or from top management. Indeed, one of the attractions continued to be the relative autonomy that it afforded to more junior officials."

The report continues: "After the 9/11 terrorist attacks in the US, there was a shift towards financial crime related issues. Financial stability was not a significant area of Treasury business. After 2003, when the Bank [of England] began to reduce its own staffing on financial stability, the Treasury chose not to increase its capability.

"In the immediate run-up to the crisis, in summer 2007, there was, intentionally, limited capacity on financial stability issues – a team of three people. The strong global consensus at the time, of which the Treasury was part, believed that the regulatory approach and new methods of securitising debt had substantially reduced systemic risk in the financial sector."

Given the discussed changes in the banking, investment and mortgage sectors – as well as a general overheating of influential economies, it seems breathtakingly complacent and negligent to not concentrate a large number of experienced staff on this area. Readers of a suspicious nature might suggest that running down Treasury resources in this area allowed the ruthless and self-interested free rein across the financial sector. Gamekeepers were absent, asleep or indifferent as heavily armed ruthless poachers ran amok.

One reason the UK Treasury felt it could shift attention away from financial services is that, in 1997, the government established a tripartite regulatory framework, within which the Financial Services Authority (FSA) became responsible for the regulation of all financial services including banks and building societies. At the same time, the Bank of England gained powers to set interest rates, independent of government. The Bank of England also was freed of responsibility for the FSA.

Under the tripartite framework, the Treasury was left with responsibility for the institutional structure of financial regulation and legislation and – in the event of a crisis – for authorising financial interventions. So essentially the UK government farmed out responsibility for regulating banking but ultimately would take taxpayers money to bail out banks which they had failed to monitor. The Chancellor of the Exchequer, George Osborne, eventually abolished the FSA in 2013 – amid accusations that the organisation had failed in its function.

For taxpayers who ended up bailing out banks – and ultimately paying massive bonuses to executives of failing banks – the chain of events can seem crazy. To campaigners and critical experts who expressed concern about the banking system and markets for years before the crisis, it looks much worse. It looks as though self-interested, greedy people, lacking in both morals and compassion for citizens, were given power to plunder the wealth of nations.

Furthermore, it is not just a problem for society at large because we tightened our belts to bail out banks. It is also because banks should exist for the public good. Their function is not simply to make money – it is also to oil the wheels of industry, help people buy homes and support new and growing businesses. Instead of that, many banks were allowed to become under-regulated supercasinos and it was brokers, executives and powerful investors who benefited rather than society.

Many people will look back with hindsight and recognise that selfish psychopathic cultures thrived in the financial sector. Given what we know about some of the people at the top of such organisations, what happened perhaps should not have been surprising. Their position in relation to society is comparable to birds of prey looking down and ready to swoop on vulnerable smaller creatures.

It is troubling to me that politicians should have been well aware of the characteristics of leading financiers – many were educated together after all – yet they permitted them colossal power. Perhaps, in some cases, personality flaws of politicians made them blind to characteristics of bankers, brokers and key investors who exploited the system. A more worrying possibility is that personality disorders of certain politicians gave them a camaraderie with personality disordered financiers – and limited empathy for the public they were supposed to serve.

The FSA's own report into the global financial crisis was published in March 2009. The Turner Review, on which the report is based, was named after Baron Jonathan Turner, then chairman of the FSA. The report has been criticised widely. Some of the most damning criticisms are that the FSA, within the report, fail to take any responsibility for the crisis and that it uses the publication to justify its own existence.

The report focuses in a rather esoteric manner on individual nuts and bolts within the system rather than the responsibility of the engineers charged with maintaining the machine i.e. the FSA. If there is justification for a 120 page report outlining what went wrong , it seems ingenuous to claim that *the* regulator had no inkling that anything was going wrong.

There is one particular passage in the report that I find extremely troubling as it appears to suggest that regulators assumed that markets behave like computer programmes, rather than are driven by the actions of human beings, with all our variability and irrationality.

It states: "The predominant assumption behind financial market regulation – in the US, the UK and increasingly across the world – has been that financial markets are capable of being both efficient and rational and that a key goal of financial market regulation is to remove the impediments which might produce inefficient and illiquid markets.

"A large body of theoretical and empirical work has been devoted to proving that share prices in well-regulated liquid markets, follow 'random walks', and that it is therefore impossible to make money on the basis of the knowledge of past patterns of price movement, with prices instead changing as new information becomes available and is assessed by a wide range of independently acting market participants. And the assumption has been that these independently acting market participants are in general rational in their assessments and that the overall level of prices as a result has a strong tendency towards a rational equilibrium."

However, the report goes on to state: "These assumptions have always been subject to some challenge. Many market participants accept on the basis of pragmatic observation that significant temporary bubbles in market prices are possible. And scepticism about the rationality of markets and the benefits of liquidity has a long intellectual lineage."

This final section makes one wonder why the FSA – and perhaps other national regulators – maintained any conviction in the assumption that the market would ultimately work in a logical and therefore predictable manner.

I found the following paragraph both amusing and shocking: "Individual behaviour is not entirely rational. There are moreover insights from behavioural economics, cognitive psychology and neuroscience, which reveal that people often do not make decisions in the rational front of brain way assumed in neoclassical economics, but make decisions which are rooted in the instinctive part of the brain, and which at the collective level are bound to produce herd effects and thus irrational momentum swings."

The above section is reminiscent of Mr Spock from *Star Trek* or Sheldon Cooper from television's *Big Bang Theory* saying – in an aloof and convoluted way – that human beings are not robots. Nevertheless, it is welcome that the reality of instability is acknowledged. I would add, however, that if we are to consider the mental condition of brokers, bankers and investors, we should also consider the use of cocaine, which encourages arrogance and risk-taking behaviour. This is not something the FSA report mentions but eminent psychiatrist and neuropsychopharmacologist David Nutt has suggested a link between cocaine use within the sector and the financial crisis.

Among those criticising the Turner Review report when it was published was then Liberal Democrat shadow chancellor of the exchequer Vince Cable, who described it as "little more than a watered down summary of policy changes". Alluding to a recommendation in the report that a proportion of bonuses of some city high-flyers should be paid in a deferred way, to discourage risk-taking for short-term benefits, Dr Cable also said: "If the proposals on pay and bonuses had been followed five years ago, Britain would not be facing such a huge financial crisis now."

He adds: "This report completely fails to call for the separation of low-risk high street banking from high-risk banking. Banks should be safe places for people's savings, not huge roulette wheels. Banks that act like gamblers in a casino, taking massive risks for big returns, cannot be allowed to come begging to the taxpayer when things go wrong in the future."

What the above information about the banking, regulators and their relationship with politics suggests to me is that, what might be presented and perceived by some as sophisticated, respectable and trustworthy pillars of society are often far from it. Rather than functioning to support industry and economies, the finance sector exploited vulnerabilities in society (such as our compulsion to get onto the housing ladder during house price inflation) and then manipulated taxpayers into bailing it out and funding excessive remuneration.

That is not to say that everyone working in the sector deliberately undermined society and exploited taxpayers. However, this is what the callous amoral machine of finance ultimately did. There were certainly people working high up in the system who were committing crime, but there were many more people participating in a system that they knew in their hearts was rotten. This is how seductive pathological systems or psychopathic cultures work.

People working within such cultures may realise they are unhealthy and unsustainable but they continue to do so for a variety of reasons. One does not want to rock the boat or – perhaps more accurately – jump off the gravy train. Another reason is fear of dominant people within the cultures. Yet another reason is other powerful pathological systems support them, such as politicians supporting disreputable corporations, shadowy lobbyists supporting all manner of questionable enterprises and the mass media doing PR for all of them.

Nevertheless, the above example helps illustrate that pathological systems are inherently unstable and unsustainable. From hunter and gatherers to large democracies, most human beings have a sense of fairness and recognise corruption and cultural pathology. Some people are cautious about sticking their heads above the parapet and questioning distorted power relations – which are essentially community problems. However, as more voices are heard, the walls of pathological organisations and networks begin to crack.

Powerful corporations, including political parties, project a sense of importance and permanence. They do this by using symbols of power – including imposing buildings, brand logos, coverage in the media and even the voices and clothing of representatives. They also do it by spreading influence into other areas of the Establishment.

The reality is, however, that organisations are transient cultural creations – they are not the buildings they are located within. Culture is always in flux and being contested, therefore no single corporate body is permanent or indispensable. If they do not satisfy society, they will vanish. And if an increasingly vocal and media savvy public decides that particular organisations are toxic and damaging, it is more likely than ever before that they will ultimately change or vanish – and those behind them will be shamed. This happens within political administrations all the time. It also happened – to a degree – within the banking sector and the media.

Stopping the rot within the news media

The problems within the Murdoch empire are not unique to that organisation. At the point that the *News of the World* was paying private investigators to get information about prominent people, other news organisations were doing the same. News Corp is significant, however, because it was one of the most powerful media groups in the world and it was weakened by the hacking scandal. That is not to say it has been mortally wounded, but news of the hacking scandal did stymie its takeover of BskyB. The thwarted takeover meant years of planning by the Murdoch empire was wasted and its broader global satellite broadcasting strategy was derailed.

The News Corp hacking scandal in the UK led to mistrust of the group in the USA, with politicians asking difficult questions about the organisation and the FBI launching an investigation into the hacking of American citizens. Investigators in Rupert Murdoch's native Australia also began to examine hacking claims there. Since the scandal, the Murdoch clan has been widely criticised and ridiculed and suffered a loss of respect among investors, the public and politicians.

In June 2012, as a result of the hacking scandal, Rupert Murdoch – under pressure from other News Corp shareholders – was compelled to split the organisation into two companies, one oriented primarily towards visual media and the other towards publishing. This seems to me to be an acknowledgement of toxicity or rot within the newspaper side of the business and an attempt to protect the more lucrative entertainment business from contamination from print side.

However, as the television media side of the business also includes news stations, the split may not ultimately prevent contamination. Many shareholders and members of the public would naturally regard Rupert Murdoch and those he put in positions of power as sources of contamination. It is therefore questionable that shifting furniture around will rid the Murdoch empire of the toxic stench that emanates from it.

The public has a long memory and is extremely unforgiving of deceit, betrayal and attempts to manipulate it. Once a powerful individual is regarded with disdain and once an organisational culture is regarded as toxic, no amount of sugary PR will completely restore them. Unfavourable stories about people and organisations are no longer 'yesterday's fish and chip paper' because coverage and comments stay on the internet and get repeated endlessly.

When things were going well, Rupert Murdoch and his former editors Rebekah Brooks and Andy Coulson did little to dispel perceptions them being arrogant, ruthless and devious. As a result, meekly claiming to be overwhelmed and hurt by allegations about the company – as Rupert Murdoch did – is of questionable value. It might actually reinforce public perceptions of him being an ingeniously cunning master manipulator.

During the 2012 House of Commons Culture, Media and Sport Committee Inquiry and the 2012 Leveson Inquiry, Rupert Murdoch came across as a slightly bewildered kindly old man, as shocked as anyone at the very idea of criminality within his empire. Speaking with a timid voice, he croakily expressed regret for the distress caused to hacking victims. However, neither he nor his son James admitted to being in any way complicit. Rupert Murdoch was unwittingly helped in his bid to appear bumbling when he was accosted in the Culture, Media and Sport Committee by comedian Jonathan May-Bowles brandishing a shaving cream pie. Bowles was jailed for six weeks as a result.

Rupert Murdoch's apparent sorrow about crimes committed within his organisation began to seem like a flimsy mask in March 2013, however, after he was recorded at a meeting at *The Sun*. Given the centrality of the hacking scandal in the culling of the *News of the World* and fall from grace of News Corp, it is ironic that Murdoch's true feelings were shared with the outside world as a result of covert recording by his own staff. The digital sound files from the meeting were passed to the investigative news site ExaroNews.

The reason Rupert Murdoch's staff turned on him is because they were angry that he had passed information to the police that led to arrests of journalists. Murdoch did this through a management and standards committee, which he established in the wake of hacking allegations and claims of payments to public officials.

Staff making the recordings felt they had been scapegoated in order to protect people at the top. The fact that numerous staff at various levels within the organisation felt they had been scapegoated seemed to support the allegation of extensive criminality at the *News of the World*. According to Murdoch's candid speech in the meeting, bad practice was not only extensive at the *News of the World*, but widespread across the newspaper industry.

At the start of the meeting a senior employee said: "One thing that everybody in this room shares – everybody in this room shares – whether we are 20-something, 30-something, 40-something, 50-something or 60-something, is that we were arrested, thrown into police cells, treated as common criminals in front of our children, our families, and our neighbours, and our friends and our colleagues, for doing nothing more than the company expected of us – nothing."

In response, Rupert Murdoch said: "I'm just as annoyed as you are at the police, and you're directing it at me instead, but never mind. And if you want to accuse me of a certain amount of panic, there's some truth in that. But it was very, very – I don't know – it's hard for you to remember it, it was such – but it was – I was under personal siege – not that that mattered – but it was – the whole place was – all the press were scream- ing and yelling, and we might have gone too far in protecting ourselves. And you were the victims of it. It's not enough for me to say you've got my sympathy. But you do have my total support."

Then Murdoch was asked what assurances he could offer about the future of individuals within the company if they go to court and are convicted. To which he replied: "What you're asking is, what happens if some of you are proven guilty? What afterwards? I'm not allowed to promise you – I will promise you continued health support – but your jobs – I've got to be careful what comes out – but frankly, I won't say it, but just trust me. Okay?"

With an extraordinary acknowledgement of a culture of wrongdoing in his organisation and across the newspaper industry, Murdoch then said: "I will do everything in my power to give you total support, even if you're convicted and get six months or whatever. I think it's just outrageous, but – and I don't know of anybody, or anything, that did anything that wasn't being done across Fleet Street and wasn't the culture... we got caught with dirty hands, I guess, with the *News of the World.*"

Talking specifically about payments to police officers for information, he went on to say: "Payments for news tips from cops – that's been going on a hundred years, absolutely." Then making light of the scandal and criticising the investigation, Murdoch added: "But why are the police behaving in this way? It's the biggest inquiry ever, over next to nothing."

Given how much his titles sensationalise trivial news, it is ironic that Rupert Murdoch appeared to describe voicemail hacking and bribing police for stories as "next to nothing." It is not next to nothing for police officers or other public officials if caught. Misconduct in public office is a serious offence and can lead to jail sentences.

However, I have no reason to believe that Murdoch lied when he said the practice is common and he certainly knows the business better than I do. Newspapers have historically been full of stories with quotes attributed to "an insider" or "a source". Nevertheless, it is worth reiterating that in the 2014 'hacking trial' verdict, Rebekah Brooks was not found guilty of making payments to public officials and the jurors failed to agree on a verdict for Andy Coulson and Clive Goodman.

Weaknesses in regulation and vulnerabilities within toxic cultures

In relation to banking, media and other scandals, many people will be left feeling that the wrongdoing has been allowed to happen and has often gone unpunished due to weak regulators and inept (and perhaps even corrupt) politicians and police.

However, it is important to note that these toxic cultures were exposed and tackled despite the inadequacy of regulators and disturbingly close relationships between offending companies and politicians. A growing number of citizens are committed to exposing rot in powerful organisations. Whistle-blowing from within organisations helps this process considerably and modern technology, such as email, memory sticks, camera phones and digital voice recorders, make it easier to expose wrongdoing to the external world.

In the case of the press, in Britain print journalism has been overseen by the Press Complaints Commission (PCC). I say overseen rather than regulated as, in my view, the PCC is made up of powerful media figures and has shown little desire or ability to deal with abuses of editorial and corporate power. It lacks legal power and is too close to those it is meant to exert control over. Therefore the notion that it has been truly a regulator is highly questionable. The organisation has adjudicated on individual complaints about newspapers but it has failed to ensure high ethical standards within the newspaper industry.

The PCC has a Code of Practice and members of public can bring a complaint if a newspaper or magazine breaches the code. However, after adjudication the PCC can only make suggestions of remedy, such as printing a correction or an apology. It cannot impose financial penalties on publications. The PCC had been criticised for many years and, after the *News of the World* scandal, more people than ever were calling for its abolition in favour of an independent regulator.

The House of Commons Culture, Media and Sport Select Committee in 2010 described the PCC as "toothless". In a parliamentary debate in 2011 it was said to be as much use as "a chocolate teapot" and the same year David Cameron described the PCC as "inadequate". It is curious that Mr Cameron commented on the inadequacy of the PCC as failings related to the *News of the World*, which had been edited by one of his best friends, Rebekah Brooks, and a man who he employed as his head of communications, Andy Coulson.

The examples of the FSA and the PCC are extremely interesting because both organisations have been heavily criticised – for failing to deal with incompetence and criminal acts in finance and newspapers respectively. While I agree that each of those bodies is deserving of criticism, I also believe that one or both of them were *designed* to be weak and ineffective. Furthermore, the reality is that politicians put them in place and therefore have to take responsibility for the failure of effective regulation.

Whether politicians and administrations rested on their laurels or consciously turned a blind eye to shortcomings of the FSA and PCC – and consequently turned a blind eye to wrongdoing in both sectors – may never be fully clear. It is probably different for different politicians. However, in relation to MPs who had studied economics or worked previously in the media or communications, it is hard to believe they were oblivious to the existence of the poor practice that has now been exposed.

Just as different politicians will have different perceptions and therefore different levels of complicity, different members of the public will have different views. Some will believe that the banking crisis was a perfect storm of unpredictable events. Others may view it as a controlled demolition for political and financial reasons, which was callously exploited. For those people with suspicious minds, reports of poor regulation fuels the fire of Establishment conspiracies.

Despite the treatment of whistle-blowers, the tide seems to have turned internationally and organisations of all sorts are exposed for abysmal practice on an alarmingly regular basis. Bradley Manning and Edward Snowden respectively exposed war crimes and mass governmental spying on ordinary citizens. These are notable cases because the pathological cultures they exposed were within the American military and the American and British intelligence services. However, there are many thousands of brave people in organisations of all sizes and sectors sticking their necks out to expose crime, corruption and deceit.

Attempts are often made to discredit whistle-blowers by casting doubt on their integrity, sanity, honesty and motives. However, this in itself will be yet more evidence for critical observers that the organisation concerned is pathological – just as the whistle-blower claimed. The more an organisation does to silence and discredit people who express concerns about wrongdoing, the worse it will look. Also, the more the mainstream media does to support the Establishment's efforts to smear whistle-blowers, the more complicit and out-of-touch with public values it looks.

The tide has turned so much in recent years that it is getting to the stage where people working within pathological cultures often have more to lose by not exposing it than by doing so. A curious vulnerability of capitalist individualism is that some people will happily bring an organisation down in order to save themselves and their loved ones. Rather than remain immersed in the rot – and risk being regarded as complicit – they will go public with their concerns. Fortunately most people would rather be viewed as a supporter of justice than an agent of corruption, deceit, and malice.

People are very aware now of their own psychological and emotional health, as well as the impact of their distress on loved ones. To stay within an organisation doing things that you find objectionable – and staying silent – takes its toll on personal health and family life. An obvious resolution to that distress is to expose the pathology within the organisation. If the individual feels safe, this should be preferable to allowing the toxicity to keep infecting one's life.

It is important to acknowledge that there are organisations and regimes in the world where people would be killed for exposing pathological cultures. And there are many places where an independent media – which is valuable when going public with concerns – does not exist. However, in the age of social media there are more ways than ever of getting stories out to the world while protecting one's identity.

Examples given in this chapter relate to toxic cultures in extremely powerful organisations, such as international media groups, finance, the military, intelligence agencies and governments themselves. I have chosen these examples to not only demonstrate how widespread pathological cultures are but also to show that even the most powerful organisations have vulnerabilities. Whatever the size and type of organisation, dysfunction and toxicity can be exposed as such. It is rather like dealing with psychopathic individuals in that challenging them is daunting but once more people are aware of the situation their influence can be curtailed.

Individuals attempting to tackle pathological cultures have to use whatever allies, authorities and media are available to them. As more cases come to light this will get easier, as the public becomes more sensitised and those who have successfully tackled other toxic cultures will be able to offer support.

As has been seen with paedophile rings, banking and other examples given above, dominant individuals within pathological cultures may escape justice even when the systems they control are exposed as corrupt or toxic. They will often find equally powerful positions elsewhere, frequently moving from the corporate world to politics and back again during their lives. However, once pathological cultures have been exposed and either culled or treated, powerful people linked to them will be watched more closely by the public, press and colleagues.

Conclusion

Psychopaths have a much broader repertoire of behaviour than the two-dimensional killers of films we often associate with the disorder. They can be hard to recognise for what they are, let alone deal with effectively. They can be incredibly alluring but ultimately they are frequently destructive to those around them and to society itself. They are often different things to different people – and very different things to the same people over time. However, it is often the case that their manipulations, deceit and malice are not apparent until it is too late for those they exploited.

According to the American Psychiatric Association, psychopaths derive their self esteem from personal gain, power, or pleasure. They have a tendency to set goals based on personal gratification, lack socially adaptive internal standards and fail to conform to lawful or culturally normative ethical behaviour.

They also lack concern for the feelings, needs and suffering of others and lack remorse after hurting or mistreating people. They struggle with long-term intimate relationships and exploitation is often their primary means of relating to others. Psychopaths are deceitful, domineering and sometimes sadistic and may use intimidation and aggression to get their own way. They also often use charm to manipulate people yet lack remorse about their negative impact on them.

Psychopaths also are notable for their irresponsibility and failure to honour financial and other obligations, commitments and promises. They are easily bored and – as they lack internal controls – they are impulsive and frequently indulge in activities that are both dangerous to themselves and others. They may fear losing control more than they fear pain, injury or hurting other people.

The above makes them not only really tricky, upsetting, scary and bewildering people but they are also fascinating not only to mental health experts but also to the wider public. To a large degree, the history of film has been an exercise in describing psychopaths. From ruthless dictators to manipulative media magnates, to bloodthirsty cowboys and malicious cattle ranchers – to cunning gangsters, sophisticated murderers, callous spies, tyrannical space emperors and corrupt financiers.

What is interesting to me about this list of film representations of psychopathic characters is they are so varied. Just as in real life, the psychopath does not have just one costume and mask. Their nature and a key source of their power is to be – or rather appear to be – however or *whoever* gains them most advantage.

When psychopaths operate in a desperate and violent environment it will make sense to them to capitalise on their ability to be aggressive and sadistic. If functioning within a corporate or political setting, using charm, playing people off against one another and manipulating them with money or other resources will be more effective than physical brutality.

There is further to go in understanding specific behaviours and inclinations of psychopaths at different levels of society – and how these are amplified or muted as circumstances change. For example, to ascertain if psychopaths in more deprived environments are more likely to be violent because of an inherent proclivity or because it is simply more effective in that setting than, for example, subtle Machiavellian game playing.

However, it is difficult to conduct studies comparing petty criminal psychopaths with powerful successful psychopaths because, by definition, successful psychopaths avoid detection. Therefore research generally makes use of jailed subjects or those detained under mental health legislation. This perhaps adds to a skewed public perception of psychopaths. Like many recent commentators, I would suggest that the majority of psychopaths manage to avoid incarceration and are drawn to positions offering power, status, wealth and protection from criticism.

Despite the fact that research subjects are often detained violent criminals, there has been interesting recent evidence suggesting that, rather than being consistently callous and brutal, even psychopathic killers can experience and show empathy. Evidence from brain scans has demonstrated that psychopaths can switch empathy on and off. This allows their repertoire to include apparent sensitivity and compassion as well as predatory ruthlessness and aggression.

This ability does not ultimately make them easier to relate and respond to but a great deal harder. If they *never* expressed compassion for other people they would be easy to spot and have a limited ability to charm. Being able to switch empathy on makes it easier to navigate relationships and also careers. The combination of cold ruthlessness, desire for power and selective sensitivity to feelings may provide psychopaths with ideal set of tools to rise to the top of all sorts of fields.

Therefore it may transpire that the Dutch study, described in Chapter 1, has at least as much significance for our understanding of powerful psychopaths as for those convicted of violent crimes. The study opens up a great many new avenues of research. Rather than showing that psychopaths characters are rigid, it provides scientific insight into their chameleon tendencies.

There is a growing recognition that psychopaths seek out and thrive within occupations where they have considerable authority. This power may be over colleagues or it may be over vulnerable groups in society, such as children in care or elderly people. Some individuals are able to exert power over society at large – whether through politics, the media, terrorism or economic manipulation.

Malicious, callous people being able to exert power over organisations or societies enables them to create and shape pathological cultures. It is likely that this is helped by a widespread tendency for people to be swayed by the demands of those who claim and exert power – even when these demands are ultimately damaging.

When callous individuals manage to dominate organisations or societies enough to get formerly decent people to become oppressive, cruel, deceitful and callous, I would suggest that a psychopathic culture exists. This may be a controversial concept but I suspect it is something many people would intuitively recognise – even if they have not previously used that phrase to describe it.

The dangers of conformity

Experiments devised by social psychologists Stanley Milgram and Philip Zimbardo demonstrated that mentally normal people can be encouraged to become oppressive, needlessly cruel and even torturous, if instructed to by 'authority' figures. These studies, beginning in the 1960s and 1970s, have huge implications for human societies everywhere. They show how easily perfectly normal, intelligent people can be manipulated into doing deeply unpleasant things to others.

In our rapidly changing societies, different people with claims to authority come to the fore all the time. These may be politicians, religious leaders, corporate bosses, academics, military figures or celebrities. We see the influence such people have every day and, thorough specific examples, we see how culture is contested and citizens are often used as the rope in a tug of war for power.

For me, one of the most troubling things about the apparent tendency for humans to become sadistic when authority figures 'press their buttons' is that it is hard to create societies where this vulnerability is ameliorated. Whether the state is large, or we live within unrestrained capitalism, we cannot be sure that those who amass power will wield it in a way that benefits society. In countries with a powerful state, processes of oppression may be obvious. In capitalistic systems, those with power are mainly unelected, they have no need to demonstrate personal ethics and the systems of oppression are often sugar-coated.

Milgram's experiments, showing that people could be made to give what they believed were potentially-fatal shocks to strangers, were devised to shed light on why Nazis followed such malicious orders during the Holocaust. These experiments have been repeated many times and in different places since first being performed in 1961 at Yale University.

One might hope that, over time, citizens become more independently-minded and less willing to harm others when instructed to do so by authority figures. However, the disturbing reality is that around two-thirds of various groups of volunteers have proved willing to give a series of ever-increasing electric shocks to audibly distressed strangers. The fact that the shocks were not real makes no difference, as the volunteers believed them to be so.

Not all pathological cultures are as obvious as Nazism. They may be as subtle as a popular newspaper or political party expertly twisting facts to play different parts of society off against another or 'nice' teachers grooming pupils. Pathological cultures exist in all sorts of organisations – from paedophile-infested children's homes to the institutionally racist police force. Or the faceless bank that bets on people losing their homes – while creating the conditions for them to do so.

Human nature, capitalism and psychopathy

Some might argue that the very notion of psychopathic organisations and other cultures is absurd. They might say, for example, that organisations are not the same as people and that commercial enterprises are *supposed* to be exploitative, devious, aggressive and ruthless. They might argue that corporations are more like vast machines than they are like people – and therefore do not have a prefrontal cortex encouraging behaviour based on empathy.

Another way of putting this would be to say that capitalism itself has psychopathic characteristics. If this is the case, since people have a tendency to conform to powerful cultures, we have to consider the disturbing possibility that the current prevalent system is psychopathogenic – capitalism encourages psychopathy.

However, rather than put blame on one mode of production for encouraging our unpleasant capacities, some might argue that human beings are inherently exploitative, devious, ruthless, selfish and aggressive. This analysis, however, fails to recognise the most important element in our species' evolutionary success – our capacity to live and cooperate within groups.

Our inclination to build communities and find ways of binding them together, resolve conflicts and a transcultural ideology of justice have been key to human survival and progress. Furthermore, many other creatures – from bees to bats, badgers to wolves and lions to non-human primates – benefit from community living. As well as being afforded greater protection and food security, species that live as groups develop a social intelligence that is lacking in solitary creatures.

The social organisations built through human history have been designed to bind individuals and communities together, rather than exploit, dominate and defeat one another. From marriages – which historically have often bound two distinct and sometimes feuding communities – to religions and collective irrigation systems, we have used social organisation as glue to hold communities together.

At the root of various binding social organisations is the recognition that we need stable communities in order to thrive. They might also indicate an ancient awareness of dangers associated with individualism. These include predatory, exploitative behaviour and conflicts fuelled by inequalities. Given how closely together people in tribal communities live, there is the likelihood that psychopathic inclinations were recognised a long time ago, and therefore a function of social structures and traditions was to curtail them.

People often assume that humans who lived in the distant past – particularly in hunter gatherer societies – were fundamentally brutal and callous. Anthropological studies of surviving hunter gatherers challenge this assumption. Those left occupy some of the most inhospitable regions – and consequently struggle with scarce resources – but they are known for having a strong sense of community. Sharing resources is expected and individuals show great interest in one another.

Conversely, in capitalism there is great inequality, the wealthiest essentially feed off the poor and people are often treated as mere commodities. Health and educational opportunities are not fairly distributed and poverty and debt effectively incarcerates people. These factors lead to inequalities being passed down and exacerbated through the generations, and efforts to redistribute resources and power are undermined by politicians on behalf of the wealthy. We therefore have to acknowledge that callous savagery is very much present in 'advanced' societies. The savages, however, wear expensive suits rather than loin cloths.

Despite the huge changes that human beings and societies have gone through, many people find it hard to imagine how life could be very different from how it is in their current era. However, anthropology and history demonstrate that no economic system or political structure is inevitable or permanent. The fact that various different systems have worked and do work globally is proof that change, rather than continuity, is inevitable.

Humans have existed for hundreds of thousands of years. Therefore capitalist systems – which produce wealth and power for small 'elites' while exploiting the many – are relatively new constructions. Furthermore, capitalism itself changes over time. For example, since the financial crisis that began in 2007, struggling members of the public have been forced to prop up mismanaged and sometimes corrupt banks. This is a very long way from the economic 'survival of the fittest' notion, which is a misreading of Charles Darwin misapplied to capitalism.

Weaknesses of capitalism being dramatically exposed, however, has not stopped politicians and others from attempting to turn public resources into capitalist ventures. Various arguments are used to push for this, from the ideological to promises of better services. Few proponents admit that they favour privatisation of public services because they, their families and associates will gain vast wealth from it. However, this is very often the reality.

The ethos of capitalism took hold quickly and has become so entrenched that even prosocial organisations, such as public hospitals and universities, have been forced to adhere to capitalist values. That is not to suggest that financial accountability is a bad thing, as public resources should be used effectively. However, when organisations established to care for the sick or educate society are forced to cut valuable clinical services and courses because they are not as profitable as others, it becomes apparent that systems have moved from their core values.

Despite the fact that organisations – especially commercial ventures – tend to be preoccupied with budgets, cost centres, market share and other numerical indicators of success, it should be remembered that they are *human* cultures. Organisations or all sorts – from Amazonian hunting groups to banks and newspaper empires – are composites of human brains, experiences and hearts.

Human cultures are living collective minds and, as such, should have a capacity to empathise with those affected by them. In fact, they should possess more empathy than any single person does. If that empathy is just switched on to work out how to exploit and dupe people and then switched off again, then organisations are doing something remarkably similar that what psychopaths do.

We live in a highly competitive world in which many resources have become scarce and expensive to access. On the one hand, this has made commercial organisations even more ruthless, devious, manipulative and exploitative. If the goal is profit maximisation and increasing market share, then companies have to continually improve their ability to exploit staff, cut costs, exploit markets and reduce their tax bills. On the other hand, there is increasing recognition among the public that resources – including human resources – are precious and should not be aggressively exploited to the detriment of the wider world.

There is therefore an inherent conflict between capitalist drives – which can be callous, cold and antisocial – and social justice, stable societies, equality and sustainability. Nevertheless, this book is not a Marxist polemic. As was mentioned in the discussion about Zimbardo and Milgram's work, since human beings seem to have a vulnerability to manipulation by authority figures, oppression and exploitation can happen in any political system. Powerful people in communist states have shown as much desire to dominate, exploit and abuse others as those within capitalist societies.

It is perhaps too much to expect politicians, owners of capital and those who dominate institutions to not abuse their power to exploit people or enlist others to do so for them. Therefore, perhaps our best hope is for us, as societies, to become increasingly educated about the dangers of manipulation and conformity.

Globally we are certainly becoming better educated in general. However, many educational programmes encourage students to unquestioningly memorise facts rather than question received 'wisdom' or learn to challenge the undeserving powerful. This problem is exacerbated when education is thought of as a way of gaining material wealth rather than mental wealth or wisdom.

In many countries, both teachers and students who become critical of powerful people and institutions are victimised and sometimes killed. Nevertheless, there are increasing numbers of people who are willing to speak out about oppression and brutality. When this becomes a critical mass, dramatic change becomes more likely. Modern technology helps oppressive regimes track and arrest people deemed to be subversive. However, it also enables critics of oppressive regimes to communicate with one another, gain supporters and publicise their concerns to the wider world.

The sickly smell of rot

Psychopathic individuals and pathological cultures can exist in organisations that are in other ways virtuous. For example, the BBC was a shelter for the predatory paedophile Jimmy Savile while it was also making some enlightening and entertaining programmes, including many for children.

The presence and power of Savile and other paedophiles at the BBC does not mean the entire culture was or is pathological. However, those who knew about Savile's perversions allowed rot to fester within the organisation and, by the time real attempts were made to cut it out, it had spread.

One key factor that enhanced the stench of rot at the BBC is that Savile appears to have been protected from scrutiny, despite allegations surrounding him. It could be that his ratings meant he was the golden goose that the corporation did not want to slay. However, an even more chilling suggestion some have made is that Savile was a procurer of child victims for powerful paedophiles and his influence within the Establishment extended well beyond the BBC.

If it is the case that he was protected by British intelligence services and politicians – as has been claimed – then the pathological culture revealed by Savile's depravity runs through numerous key organisations. It would suggest a conspiracy so extensive and malicious that most people would be sickened.

If it is ever proved that British spies stood by as members of the Establishment abused children, so that intelligence agencies could gain greater leverage over the abusers, the public's confidence in key institutions could be shattered. It is hard to imagine anything more sinister and damaging than vulnerable children being mistreated for the pleasure and the ambitions of powerful people.

Cultures that have been created by or touched by psychopaths can remain pathological long after they have gone. Zimbardo masterminded a culture in which previously pleasant people quickly adapted to and perpetuated an oppressive, cruel system. His research demonstrates that pathological cultures can be created by clever manipulators and then take on a life on their own.

Zimbardo's rationale for creating the culture of oppression was laudable – as it demonstrated what perfectly ordinary people are capable of. By contrast, psychopaths who create pathological cultures do what they do because they *can*, they gain from it and they enjoy the power. People follow them due to conformity, obliviousness, fear and sometimes self-interest. Charisma of leaders also plays a part.

Research of both Zimbardo and Milgram demonstrates that cultures of oppression and cruelty can be formed quite easily and then be perpetuated by apparently decent people. This should be a cause of great concern for all of us.

Even if we do not physically work within a pathological organisation, our taxes often support violent and oppressive systems. Furthermore, our elections give politicians power to do things on our behalf. Few of us, hopefully, would want to fire missiles towards civilians. However, we *are* complicit when we support politicians who ultimately order this to happen or act as cheerleaders for weapons traders.

Those of us who are fortunate enough to live in democracies have to take responsibility for pathological cultures that are allowed to form – and their impact anywhere in the world. This is obviously extremely difficult to contend with as one pathological culture often spawns another, and the average voter feels they have little power. However, they did have the power to set the ball rolling and therefore have the power to get rid of politicians who act maliciously. It often takes many years for pathological cultures to be treated or die out. Ignoring them or denying responsibility slows down the process.

The example of the impact of paedophiles in children's homes and approved schools is a good illustration of how pathological cultures survive after instigators have gone. Furthermore, the shadow cast over their victims' lives in many cases casts a shadow over their own family's lives. Therefore, not only does the pathological culture survive but it filters down from powerful institutions into the smaller cultures of families, from where it can also spread outwards.

That is not to suggest that all abuse victims become abusers, but simply to acknowledge that venom, shadows and imprints are left within cultures long after primary perpetrators have gone. Another way of describing this is a process of psychological and emotional rot that can spread from those with the greatest power to others within the system – and even to those outside of the system.

A tragedy of paedophilia becoming such a prominent issue is that children are often overprotected and consequently miss out on enriching experiences with their friends and other members of the community. The spectre of paedophilia has therefore made societies more suspicious and robbed children of enjoyable and memorable activities, such as exploring the outside world without adults.

This caution may have stopped some children being abused but it has also encouraged many to fear the outside world, play primarily on electronic devices, become unhealthy and miss out on experiences that would help them develop resilience and social skills. A lack of challenging social situations may also reduce their capacity to resist conformity when older, which ultimately makes societies more vulnerable to pathological cultures. Wrapping children up in cotton wool, therefore, may in the long-run be more detrimental than it is protective.

It seems as though some sexual abusers – as well as murderers – not only seek to mistreat and destroy individual victims, but also to abuse society itself by leaving it shocked and sickened by ruminations on depravity. I suspect that Savile and former Lostprophets singer Ian Watkins may fall into the category of narcissistic sadists who seek to make the world seem as rotten and dangerous as they are malignant and damaged.

Watkins for jailed in 2013 for a string of sexual offences, including the attempted rape of a baby. The trial judge said he had plumbed "new depths of depravity" – for which he may well be proud. He appears to have gained pleasure, as Ian Brady did, from deliberately deviating as far as possible from morality – and he showed no compassion for those he abused in this malicious endeavour. As with other narcissists, victims were only viewed in terms of what he could do to them. Watkins actually referred to 'owning' a devoted fan and, by extension, her baby. He has shown no remorse whatsoever and such is his narcissism that he told a fan, after being convicted, that he planned to issue a press statement saying what he had done was funny, or – as he put it – "mega lolz".

Given the efforts Savile made to undermine accusations when he was alive, it may seem strange to suggest that he deliberately sought to make society feel contaminated and sickened. However, it is worth remembering that much of Savile's life was spent in front of cameras and he was as media savvy as he was aware of allegations against him. When I see footage of Savile now, it seems as though he knew his abuse would be exposed after his death and he perhaps relished the idea of leaving a hideous scar on society. It is extremely disturbing to consider that, when posing for photographs for particular events, Savile knew he was also posing for photos that would be shown after his depravity was finally revealed.

The shadow cast over society by influential people with psychopathic traits means we can end up perceiving maliciousness and rot everywhere. It is perhaps analogous to the way in which toxic debt spliced up into financial instruments resulted in the whole market being viewed with mistrust. Just as investors were spooked because they could not be sure where the toxicity lay, the public can be forgiven – after so many betrayals from influential people – for perceiving rot at the heart of all institutions and elite networks. Citizens are highly suspicious of the motives of powerful people and more willing and able to criticise them than in previous centuries.

In this book I have included a broad range of examples to illustrate how pathological cultures have had a profound and detrimental impact on individuals and societies. There are, of course, many more that have not been mentioned, in some cases due to ongoing investigations and legal cases.

Although the paedophile rings mentioned are, tragically, a tiny proportion of those that are known about internationally, the examples given show how devious psychopathic cultures link to systems of power operating within societies. These broader systems of power – and arguably oppression – include churches, gangs, governments, police forces, the care sector and intelligence services.

Navigating the forest of distraction and deception to demolish the gingerbread house

There are many obstacles to tackling pathological cultures in our societies and wrongdoing by powerful people. One is fear – especially in situations where individuals feel unsupported and have little hope that others will believe them or help. Another key obstacle for all of us is actually identifying problems. One reason for this is that we are all subjected to so much distraction in our lives.

It is not pleasant to spend one's time looking for examples of cruelty, corruption, deception, maliciousness and exploitation. There are so many horrors in the world that many people feel powerless to do anything about them – and therefore avoid focusing on them.

For those who want to avoid considering problems in our world, there are many easy ways of distracting ourselves, beyond alcohol and other drugs. These distractions have become more transitory and insubstantial over time, from religions to art to novels to cinema to radio to television to video games and apps. The insubstantial nature of modern distractions does not make them any less addictive, in fact it means that addicts are always craving more, finding more and creating more.

In recent years we found ourselves in the strange situation where vast numbers of adults spent considerable time growing imaginary crops and raising make believe animals on virtual farms on Facebook and other platforms. This activity – like many others – creates a weak illusion of power and progress but feeds nobody. It does, however, use vast amounts of time and electricity.

In the 1940s the sociologists and philosophers Horkheimer and Adorno coined the term 'the culture industry' to describe an all-consuming system of mass deception, in which the public are stultified by glittering – but empty – distractions. Having witnessed the rise of Nazism and then been exiled from their native Germany to America, they recognised parallels between Nazi propaganda and the mass culture of 'liberal democracies'.

The pair found that the ultimate result of cultural productions for mass markets – such as films, radio and magazines – was a distraction from reality for large numbers of people. They noted that although mass media *appears* to offer exciting novelty, it actually discourages critical thinking and encourages uniformity of thought and blunted feelings.

Adorno and Horkheimer therefore believed that the drives of controllers of cultural industries are similar to those behind fascism – they actively promote a narrow consciousness in which citizens are blinded to the manipulations of the powerful. Furthermore, because the culture industry undermines our progress towards critical thinking and autonomy, we can end up with the illusion of democracy rather than true democracy.

The ramifications this has in relation to the ideas about psychopathic cultures are significant. Horkheimer and Adorno did not suggest that the culture industry is just random economic activity, which just happens to distract consumers from reality. They argued that it is an *orchestrated* deception specifically designed to stop people thinking clearly, feeling deeply or challenging authorities.

The culture industry therefore can be seen as part of a vast apparatus of systematic control, which gives the illusion of freedom rather than actual freedom. This is an incredibly damning indictment of modern living. It also has a parallel in the relationship between psychology, marketing and political focus groups.

Focus groups allow political parties to find out what concerns floating voters – and these concerns then have an inordinate influence on policy and campaigning. The broader electorate may be given the illusion of choice but differences between parties – and consequently progress – is ultimately limited. Elections can be won by appealing to the desires of floating voters, without having to satisfy large numbers of the electorate. Therefore apparent choice can mask a lack of genuine freedom.

In terms of cultural productions and other products, if you can feed society an endless array of gadgets and entertainments, it is possible to create the illusion of freedom, power and prosperity for people with very little. Integrity, independence and clarity are often harder to gain than a smart phone and harder to sustain than a Facebook account.

The culture industry in itself is lucrative and powerful – as we saw in the discussion of media empires in Chapter 9. However, as well as being able to make fortunes – often for extremely ruthless and unethical people – and shape political views, it also distracts us from other abuses of power.

It might be pushing it to claim that politicians and owners of corporations in all sectors are enmeshed in a conspiracy with the owners of culture industries. However, it does not need to happen in that way. Distracting entertainments have simply become part of the human habitat – and other sectors rely on them in the way that hunters might use trees for camouflage. For those who have the most power and wealth, anything that distracts the masses and stops us from making our societies fairer is of great value.

Much has changed since Horkheimer and Adorno wrote – although their ideas are certainly still valid and we can all think of examples of novel offerings from the culture industry which distract people from thinking, feeling and action. Despite the cacophony of distractions, we are more politically and socially aware than ever before, and people in many countries have access to news from a variety of different sources.

Furthermore, the spin churned out by mainstream media on behalf of politicians is rapidly unspun by independent commentators on social media. Therefore mediums like Twitter and Facebook – which on the surface can seem like mere distractions – undermine the ability of the powerful to shape public consciousness. Consequently, as the public gains greater ability to engage with and challenge information – rather than be passive recipients – the culture industry steadily changes hands. It is already shifting from being a weapon of the wealthy to being a citizen-controlled resource.

Amid the glittering distractions, there are aspects of the culture industry that challenge pathological cultures and elite psychopaths. Provocative documentaries and overt satire is particularly powerful in that regard, but novels, films, music and other arts also encourage a critical awareness. They can also inspire consumers to create their own cultural productions. This again pulls the culture industry from the hands of the historically powerful to the fingertips of the masses.

If the culture industry has historically been a weapon of mass distraction, used to dupe and exploit citizens, computers and mobile phones have become weapons of mass destruction of the old order. Citizens witnessing examples of state or corporate oppression in previous decades would have been lucky (and brave) to talk to a journalist. Then, having taken risks to pass on the story, it may not run as it would have been one person's word against that of a powerful organisation with sharp lawyers. Or because the media company had allegiances to the offending organisation and so spiked it to appease their ally.

Things are very different now. Any person who has a mobile phone with a camera can share what they witness with the world in seconds. Citizens are therefore not merely seeing through distractions and deception more clearly than in the time of Horkheimer and Adorno, but we also have an unprecedented ability to help others to do so.

This is something that political administrations and large corporations are poorly prepared to deal with, particularly those with closets full of skeletons. Illusions created by decades of carefully controlled marketing and PR can be shattered by one person with a mobile phone or digital voice recorder. Therefore pathological cultures of all sorts are perpetually vulnerable to being exposed. It has quickly become a David and Goliath situation and, as we know, it only takes one well-aimed stone to bring down a lumbering giant.

The mainstream media has been highly critical of citizen journalists and bloggers. One reason for this is they are a threat to the livelihoods of traditional journalists. Another reason is that media corporations are often owned and managed by ruthless, malicious, dogmatic control freaks who enjoy manipulating public consciousness. They certainly do not want their critics shaping public awareness.

The often repeated claim that citizen journalists are unprofessional is a red herring. It is not particularly difficult to become a journalist and the training is far from uniform. In fact, quite a few prominent journalists had no formal training. Furthermore, many people in newsrooms are unpaid, untrained interns who are able to be there because they have enough wealth behind them to live with no salary. This demographic bias has helped make news organisations extremely conservative. What citizen journalists lack in training they make up for in integrity and a desire to expose wrongdoing. Also, by being outside of the corporate machinery, they have editorial freedom that is denied to most mainstream hacks.

As we saw in the 'Arab spring' and subsequent uprisings, social media and citizen journalism is often key to real change happening in oppressive regimes. There are pathological cultures of all sizes that are being shaken by the ease in which unpalatable truths can be shared with the world. We have got to the stage where many people not only assume that states, corporations, religious organisations and politicians are up to no good, but also relentlessly look for ways of holding them to account.

If I had to choose a story to describe where I believe we are, as citizens, in relation to dangerously powerful individuals and organisations, I would say we are towards the end of Hansel and Gretel. That which was once enticing and perceived as nourishing is now recognised as a malicious trap. A place where the vulnerable are consumed – or at least subsumed – if they cannot escape the gingerbread house or defeat the devious architect. In reality, the architect is not just one cannibalistic 'witch' but a large number of predatory people and systems.

The gingerbread house we find ourselves in is made up of many interconnected pathological cultures. From the political establishments meshed with large corporations, to media empires that effectively do public relations for politicians who help them, to supporting cultures that bolster the whole sickly structure. The latter category includes unethical financiers and lawyers, as well as educational organisations that perpetuate gross inequality.

There is a parallel between the seductive, manipulative words of the charming psychopath and the alluring culture of pathological organisations. Just as the callousness, coldness and vindictiveness of the psychopath may not be apparent until we are in their grip, the ethical barrenness and oppressiveness of pathological cultures may only be revealed when we are caught within them. Or when we dare to challenge them.

As the gingerbread house of pathological culture is made up of a large number of institutions, corporations and systems, it can seem impossible to demolish. The fact that many of these cultures support one another makes the task more daunting as the oppression seems ubiquitous. However, this interconnectivity is actually a weakness of the system, because once any part of the structure is weakened other bits come apart. We have witnessed instances of this in recent years – the perilous connection between the news media and members of the political Establishment being a prominent example.

In order to tackle pathological cultures, it is critical that they are recognised for what they are – deceptive, dangerous, self-serving and oppressive. Pathological cultures will do all they can to survive, but defensive hostility can lead to more people becoming aware of their malignant nature. Machiavellian manoeuvres, such as undermining critics by spreading misinformation about them – which worked well in previous eras – can actually lead to more unfavourable public relations.

It is no coincidence that whistle-blowers have come into their own in this era of internet communication and revolutions in data storage. Prominent whistle-blowers have had their characters assassinated by politicians, intelligence agencies and media groups in cahoots with them. However, the amount and clarity of data that modern whistle-blowers can disseminate makes the wrongdoing by states and organisations abundantly clear. Consequently, much of the population will side with the whistle-blower. Attempts by the Establishment to tarnish their names only reinforces beliefs that offending organisations are pathological and the individual has therefore done the right thing.

This is not to suggest I believe that all whistle-blowers are pure of heart, unselfish paragons of virtue – or that security services and politicians should never be allowed to keep any information from the public. Nevertheless, the dynamics mentioned above are a reality and they have created fascinating situations in recent years that have made politicians, militaries and intelligence services look callous, sadistic, untrustworthy and also inept.

The long-term impact on whistle-blowers like David Shayler, Edward Snowden and Bradley Manning notwithstanding, powerful states and their institutions of control have come off extremely badly from recent leaks. The American and British governments particularly have lost trust of voters, especially after it was found in 2013 that their intelligence services – and commercial organisations contacted to work of their behalf – were illegally spying on citizens.

One interesting consequence of this loss of trust is that politicians have a diminished ability to use reports from intelligence services to push for military action. This was seen in August 2013 when David Cameron lost a vote to attack Syrian targets after gas attacks attributed to the Syrian government. Members of the public did not trust the intelligence being presented or those presenting it, and the defeat in the House of Commons reflected that.

This was extremely significant as it was the first time a British prime minister lost a vote pushing for a military attack since 1782. It was also the first time Britain had rejected a request from the USA to participate in an attack since the Vietnam war. Britain's reticence appears to have influenced Barrack Obama's decision to refer the matter to Congress rather than launch a hasty attack. As of the time of writing, both nations have refrained from direct military intervention in Syria.

It is fascinating that in the decade between the American and British invasion of Iraq – supposedly to eradicate weapons of mass destruction – and today, the public has become party to abuses by security services but also trusts the intelligence presented less. From Edward Snowden's leaks we know that intelligence agencies have been spying on citizens on an industrial scale. Therefore, as the data gathered is real, it is clear that what is not trusted is the organisations themselves or the politicians who attempt to use intelligence to manipulate.

As information is being gathered on an industrial scale, agencies and politicians are clearly being extremely selective about the data they share with the public. Therefore, it is clearer than ever that attempts are made to manipulate citizens via partial stories so that powerful people can do exactly what they like. Consequently, what might previously have seemed like compelling enough intelligence to launch an attack on another country, can be easily dismissed by the public as tainted.

Over recent decades we have become much more aware of co-dependent relationships between the weapons industry, other commercial organisations that benefit from war, callously ambitious politicians, a bloodthirsty sensationalist media and intelligence agencies.

It is therefore harder than before for intelligence services to get away with covertly undermining political stability in strategically useful states – perhaps by using 'false flag' attacks – and then installing puppet leaders. It is harder than in previous eras because more citizens now recognise that such underhand methods *are* used. Therefore, the cynical ways in which the public were manipulated by governments and security services in the past have made citizens themselves more cynical. This has helped diminish respect for politicians and other powerful groups.

Pathological cultures – from the largest to the smallest

Not all pathological cultures are as extensive or hold the same level of expertise at manipulation as exploitative conglomerates, political bodies or intelligence services. Many are located within relatively small organisations owned or dominated by unpleasant people who create oppressiveness in their little empires. Pathological cultures also exist in even smaller units, such as families.

The misery inflicted on people within small groups can be as distressing as that experienced in conflict zones or large unethical corporations. Workplace bullying, family conflict and crime in the neighbourhood alters how individuals think, feel and function.

These examples of oppressive small-scale cultures are ones in which psychiatry takes an active interest. When a patient is admitted onto a ward, some key things to find out about are their family background, current home life, work situation and social situation. It is surprising, therefore, that larger pathological cultures – which can have considerable impact on how people think, feel and function – have not historically been the concern of psychiatry.

To assume, however, that psychiatric professionals are uninterested in the impact of wider cultures on individuals is unfair. Psychiatrists, psychologists, psychotherapists, psychiatric nurses and social workers have a grounding in social science, tend to be politically aware and are therefore mindful of the impact of inequality and other injustices.

Nevertheless, the primary focus of psychiatric professionals is to exert leverage in areas that can immediately improve the lives of patients under their care and those around them. This might involve placing them in a safer environment, giving medication or working therapeutically with them and their families. Clinicians attempts at leverage are much less likely to extend to overtly criticising patients' employers, political bodies, religions or other cultures that have had a long-term detrimental impact on patients and the community at large.

It is interesting to contrast this with clinicians who deal with contagious diseases. There are many medical and veterinary scientists working at the highest levels with policymakers to minimise the risk of disease outbreaks. For governments and agencies to invest in this activity makes perfect sense as, beyond reducing illness, efforts to control contagious diseases supports economies, food safety and food security. This in turn promotes political stability and ecological sustainability.

Perhaps a key reason why pathogenic human cultures are not focused on in the same way that infectious disease risks are, is that the impact is less visible and therefore harder to monitor. However, this arguably makes them even more dangerous. It is akin to complex, debilitating and sometimes fatal – yet largely hidden – pathogens ravaging lives and communities. This, of course, often has been the case with infectious agents. Until a virus or bacterium is identified and examined by scientists, all we have to go on is the symptoms of a disease process.

In the case of pathological human cultures, however, it may be that medical science has known about the pathogen for many decades. It perhaps just underestimated the impact that successful psychopaths – and those who mirror their characteristics – have on societies. A multidisciplinary focus on this impact – using examples of prominent pathological cultures like post mortem case studies – could be extremely beneficial.

Bacteria and viruses caused disease in communities long before we had the ability to visualise them. Once they could be observed, we gained a greater ability to tackle the diseases they cause. Psychiatry has, over the decades, improved its ability to recognise psychopathy and predict the behaviours of psychopaths within clinical and custodial communities. Applying these insights into psychopathy to broader cultures in which psychopaths operate – especially where they have considerable power and impact – could be comparable to the use of microscopes to study pathology.

However, it seems unlikely that forensic psychiatrists will be entering corporations, political organisations, religious institutions or other powerful bodies en masse any time soon. Ironically, if this was to happen it could make psychiatry itself look like a pathological culture – it could seem like a hostile inquisition or witch-hunt.

Therefore, perhaps the most effective role experts could have in tackling the problem of pathological cultures is to help educate the public about the scope of psychopathic behaviour. While members of the public imagine that psychopaths are knife-wielding killers, there is a danger that they are blind to actions that have a devastating and far-reaching impact on our world.

References

American Psychiatric Association (1994) *Diagnostic and Statistical Manual of Mental Disorders* (4th ed). Washington

American Psychiatric Association (2012) *Rationale for the Proposed Changes to the Personality Disorders Classification in DSM-5*. Online document, link now removed.

American Psychiatric Association (2013) *Diagnostic and Statistical Manual of Mental Disorders* (5th ed). Arlington, VA

Babiak, Paul and Hare, Robert (2006) *Snakes in Suits: When psychopaths go to work*. New York: Harper Collins

Boddy, Clive (2010) 'Corporate Psychopaths and organizational type'. *Journal of Public Affairs.* 10: 300–312

Boddy, Clive with Richard Ladyshewsky and Peter Galvin (2010) 'The Influence of Corporate Psychopaths on Corporate Social Responsibility and Organizational Commitment to Employees'. *Journal of Business Ethics.* 97 (1):1-19

Chief Medical Officer (2006) *Good Doctors, Safer Patients*. London: Department of Health

Clark, David (1996) *The Story of a Mental Hospital: Fulbourn 1858-1983*. London: Process Press

Cleckley, Hervey (1941) 'The Mask of Sanity: An Attempt to Reinterpret the So-Called Psychopathic Personality'. *JAMA.* 117(6):493

D'Silva, Karen with Conor Duggan and Lucy McCarthy (2004) 'Does Treatment Really Make Psychopaths Worse? A Review of the Evidence'. *Journal of Personality Disorders.* 18 (2): 163-177

Dutton, Kevin (2012) *The Wisdom of Psychopaths: What Saints, Spies, and Serial Killers Can Teach Us About Success*. New York. Scientific American

Financial Crisis Inquiry Commission (2011) *Financial Crisis Inquiry Report: Final Report of the National Commission on the Causes of the Financial and Economic Crisis in the United States Washington*: US Government Printing Office

Financial Services Authority (2009) *The Turner Review: A regulatory response to the global banking crisis*. London: The Financial Services Authority

Foucault, Michel (2006) *Madness and Civilization. A History of Insanity in the Age of Reason*. New York: Pantheon Books

Gao, Yu and Raine, Adrian (2010) 'Successful and Unsuccessful Psychopaths: A Neurobiological Model'. *Behavioral Sciences and the Law.* 28: 194–210

Hare, Robert (1994). 'Predators: The disturbing world of the psychopaths among us'. *Psychology Today.* Jan/Feb

Harrington, Alan (1972) *Psychopaths.* New York: Simon and Schuster

Her Majesty's Treasury (2012) *Review of HM Treasury's Management Response to the Financial Crisis.* London: HM Treasury.

Hewson, Barbara (2013) 'Yewtree is destroying the rule of law'. *Spiked,* 8th May.

Kesey, Ken (1962) *One Flew Over the Cuckoo's Nest.* New York: Viking Press

Lundberg, Ferdinand (1936) *Imperial Hearst: A Social Biography.* New York: Equinox Cooperative Press

Masters, Alexander (2005) *Stuart: A Life Backwards.* London: Fourth Estate

Meffert, H with V. Gazzola, J. A. den Boer, A. A. J. Bartels and C. Keysers (2013) 'Reduced spontaneous but relatively normal deliberate vicarious representations in psychopathy.' *Brain.* 136 (8): 2550-2562

Nurcombe, Barry (2000) 'Child sexual abuse 1: psychopathology'. *Australian and New Zealand Journal of Psychiatry.* 34: 85-91

Plotnikoff, Joyce and Woolfson, Richard (2000). 'Where Are They Now? an evaluation of sex offender registration in England and Wales'. *Police Research Series Paper 126.* Home Office.

Righton, Peter (1981) 'The Adult', in Brian Taylor (ed), *Perspectives on Paedophilia.* London: Batsford Academic and Educational

Stout, Martha (2005) *The Sociopath Next Door.* New York: Broadway Books

Waterhouse, Ronald (2000) *Lost In Care - Report of the Tribunal of Inquiry into the Abuse of Children in Care in the Former County Council Areas of Gwynedd and Clwyd since 1974.* London: The Stationary Office